THE REGIMENTAL BADGES OF NEW ZEALAND

Pouch badge of the Forest Rangers formed 31 July 1863 with Major W. Jackson commanding No. 1 Company and Captain von Tempsky commanding No. 2 Company. This is presumed to be the first badge worn by volunteers in New Zealand.

The Regulations of 1889 specified that the pouch and badge be worn:

Cavalry and Mounted Rifles:

OFFICERS: Black patent or morocco leather with plated crown on leaf (flap).

TROOPERS: Black or brown leather.

Mounted Rifles: Black patent leather with white metal bugle on leaf.

Rifle Corps: Black leather with white metal bugle.

The Regimental Badges of New Zealand

An illustrated history of
the badges and insignia
worn by the New Zealand Army

D. A. Corbett AFRAeS

RAY RICHARDS
Publisher   Auckland

First published 1970
This revised and enlarged edition 1980

RAY RICHARDS PUBLISHER
49 Aberdeen Road
Castor Bay
Auckland, New Zealand

© D. A. Corbett

ISBN 0-908596-05-7

Typeset by Linotype Service
Palmerston North, New Zealand
Printed by Colorcraft Limited
Hong Kong

Dedicated to the memory of all the men and women who have contributed to the history and the renowned achievements of the New Zealand Army

ACKNOWLEDGEMENTS

THIS EDITION has been improved by the suggestions and assistance given by the New Zealand Military Historical Society, a society which was formed to foster the study of New Zealand military history and to encourage research into the traditions, uniforms, insignia and arms. Many members are experts in their own fields and are only too willing to advise those less experienced — be it in the collecting of some aspect of militaria or in the knowledge of source material for those interested in research.

Two members of the Society have made notable contributions, Bryant Haigh in the field of historical research and Allan Young in the study of badges and the format of this book. Their assistance has determined the quality of the publication.

Specialised knowledge and advice were received from:
    Staff Sergeant C. J. Andrews RNZEME
    S. Baldwin
    Tony Bayly
    Staff Sergeant P. W. LeGros
    G. P. Oldham
    Warrant Officer A. J. Polaschek
    Queen Elizabeth II Army Museum
    Dr J. M. Ross
    D. W. Sinclair
    Lieut-Colonel T. Wallace QSM, ED, JP
    Major R. P. Withers RNZIR

CONTENTS

	PAGE
PREFACE	7
Design of New Zealand Cap Badges	9
Regimental Mottoes	15
Royal Cypher and Crown	19
Dress Regulations for Volunteers	20
3 February 1866	20
1 September 1895	21
31 May 1905	22
Rank Badges pre 1927	25
Badges of rank for Warrant Officers and Non Commissioned Officers: 1927	26
Distinguishing badges	28
Efficiency and skill at arms badges	29
Badges of Rank as worn today	32
Badges of appointment and qualification	35
Corps and Regimental dress distinctions	40
Emblems	41
Coloured berets	41
Stable belts	42
Corps	42
Regimental	42
Officers gilt badges	43
Anodised aluminium badges	44
Corps and ceremonial shoulder titles	45
New Zealand puggarees	47
Service dress and felt hats	47
The New Zealand militia battalions	49
North Island militia companies	50
South Island militia companies	52
New Zealand Militia	53
Armed Constabulary	54
Volunteer Corps	57
Order of precedence 1866	66
Order of precedence 1903	68
New Zealand Military Forces	
Order of Precedence 1927	73
New Zealand Army — organisation 1903-1911	74
The Defence Act 1911	84
Military Districts	84-7

Brigades	85
Field Batteries	86
Garrison Artillery	87
Field Ambulances	87
Signal Companies	87
New Zealand Staff Corps	88
New Zealand Permanent Staff	90
Staff instructors and inspectors	93
Artillery	96
New Zealand Naval Artillery Volunteers	96
New Zealand Regiment of Volunteer Artillery	100
New Zealand Field Artillery	103
New Zealand Garrison Artillery	105
Regiment of New Zealand Artillery	108
Royal Regiment of New Zealand Artillery	109
Engineers	111
Corps of Royal New Zealand Engineers	111
New Zealand Engineer Volunteers	112
Submarine Mining Volunteers and Torpedo Corps	115
New Zealand Railway Corps	116
Corps of New Zealand Engineers	117
New Zealand Signal Corps (NZE)	119
New Zealand Post and Telegraph Corps (NZE)	120
Signals	121
New Zealand Corps of Signals	121
Royal New Zealand Corps of Signals	122
Cavalry and Mounted Rifles	123
New Zealand Mounted Rifles in South Africa	125
Queen's South Africa Medal	131
King Edward's Horse	132
Imperial Camel Brigade — Fourth Battalion	135
New Zealand Cyclist Corps	136
Mounted Rifles	138
1st Mounted Rifles (Canterbury Yeomanry Cavalry)	138
Queen Alexandra's 2nd (Wellington West Coast) Mounted Rifles	142
3rd (Auckland Mounted Rifles)	145
4th (Waikato) Mounted Rifles	147
5th Mounted Rifles (Otago Hussars)	150
6th (Manawatu) Mounted Rifles	153
7th (Southland) Mounted Rifles	155
8th (South Canterbury) Mounted Rifles	158
9th (Wellington East Coast) Mounted Rifles	160
10th (Nelson) Mounted Rifles	163
11th (North Auckland) Mounted Rifles	164
12th (Otago) Mounted Rifles	166
New Zealand Forces serving overseas	167
Samoan Expeditionary Relief Force	167

First New Zealand Expeditionary Force (NZEF)	168
Home Service Branch NZEF	171
Reinforcements to NZEF	172
Camp Military Police	191
Base Records	192
C1 Camp	193
British Section NZEF	194
Rifle Regiments	195
1st (Canterbury) Regiment	195
2nd (South Canterbury) Regiment	199
3rd (Auckland) Regiment — Countess of Ranfurly's Own	201
4th (Otago Rifles) Regiment	205
5th (Wellington Rifles) Regiment	208
6th (Hauraki) Regiment	210
7th (Wellington West Coast Rifles) Regiment	212
8th (Southland Rifles) Regiment	215
9th (Wellington East Coast Rifles) Regiment	217
10th (North Otago Rifles) Regiment	220
11th (Taranaki Rifles) Regiment	222
12th (Nelson) Regiment	224
13th (North Canterbury and Westland) Regiment	226
14th (South Otago) Regiment	228
15th (North Auckland) Regiment	229
16th (Waikato) Regiment	231
17th (Ruahine) Regiment	232
New Zealand Rifle Brigade	234
Maori Battalion	236
NZ Native Contingent	236
NZ Pioneer Battalion	237
NZ Maori Pioneer Battalion	237
NZ Cook Islands Company	238
Machine Gun Corps	239
The New Zealand Regiment	241
Royal New Zealand Infantry Regiment	243
2nd New Zealand Expeditionary Force (2 NZEF)	244
Long Range Desert Group	246
Royal New Zealand Armoured Corps	247
1st NZ Armoured Car Regiment (New Zealand Scottish)	249
New Zealand Scottish Volunteer Units	251
1st Ranger Squadron (NZ Special Air Service)	254
New Zealand Army Air Corps	255
Flying duties badges	256
Royal New Zealand Army Service Corps	258
Royal New Zealand Army Medical Corps	260
Otago University Medical Company	262
New Zealand Veterinary Corps	263
Royal New Zealand Army Ordnance Corps	264
Corps of Royal NZ Electrical and Mechanical Engineers	266

New Zealand Army Legal Service	267
Royal New Zealand Dental Corps	268
Royal New Zealand Chaplains Department	270
New Zealand Army Pay Corps	272
New Zealand War Contingent Association	273
New Zealand Army Postal Service	273
Royal New Zealand Provost Corps	274
Royal New Zealand Army Educational Corps	276
Royal New Zealand Nursing Corps	277
New Zealand Woman's Royal Army Corps	279
Woman's War Service Auxiliary	280
Woman's Land Service	281
Woman's National Service Corps	281
Officers Training Corps	282
Regular Force Cadets	283
Defence Cadet Corps	284
Coronation Contingents	288
Legion of Frontiersmen	289
King's Empire Veterans	291
The Home Guard	292
YMCA	293
Security Guards	294
Volunteer period buttons	295
Waist-belt claps	299
Bridle bosses	300
Army Service Associations	302
Home Services Association	304
National Reserve	305
APPENDIX I	
Battle honours of WWII	306
Royal NZ Infantry Regiment, battle honours	308
APPENDIX II	
Army, Corps and Saint's Days	311
APPENDIX III	
Regimental Alliances	313
INDEX	316

PREFACE

THIS BOOK is intended as a reference guide for the collector of badges relating to and worn by the various militia, volunteer, territorial and New Zealand army units since the Militia Act of 25 March 1845. Until that date, the defence of the Colony of New Zealand was the sole responsibility of British regiments and naval units. Attempts had been made to recruit a local force but without government approval. The British Government would have preferred to have had a local police force to maintain order within the colony since they felt that the colonists could be expected to assume the duties of internal order and security by the formation of local police forces and militia units. The presence of a British garrison was presumed to assure the safety of the colony from an attack by a foreign power. The first force raised in the colony was the Kororareka Association of 1838 but this was declared an unlawful assembly and the second, the Kororareka Volunteers which acted in conjunction with the British troops in 1840, was not a legally embodied force. None of the various volunteer corps in the Wellington district had any legal sanction until the introduction of the Militia Act of 1845. New Zealand unit badges date from 1863.

It is important that collectors of New Zealand badges realise that over the years there has been little attempt to standardise the wearing of badges. Members of a particular corps would decide for themselves as to what badge they would wear and this was done without seeking government approval. Prior to 1911 soldiers were required to purchase their own badges if they wished to wear them, thus permitting members of a unit to parade without badges if they so wished. A similar situation existed during World War I when the reinforcement troops were not issued with badges. As a result, these troops purchased their badges from the various jewellers in the vicinities of the training camps and this is the explanation for the multiplicity in the designs of these badges. Some attempt was made to control the wearing of these particular badges however, since, as soon as the troops arrived in England, they were issued with the badges of the unit to which they were posted. Many of the soldiers defied the authorities and wore their original New Zealand badges throughout the war. Late 1915 saw the appearance of the New Zealand 'Onward' badge, similar to that worn by the British Section, NZEF but with fern-leaf surrounds. This badge proved popular as it gave the wearer immediate recognition as a New Zealand soldier.

The majority of New Zealand badges were made by the firm of J. R. Gaunt of London; these badges are easily recognised as they have the maker's name on the back. In order to supplement the supply of badges, local firms produced badges following the design of the Gaunt badges but with enough differences to be apparent, resulting in distinct varieties. Bronze badges were produced for officers but apart from the different finish, their badges are essentially the same as the brass variety.

The Volunteer period saw the introduction of helmet-plates, pouch-belt plates, shoulder-belt plates, waist-belt plates and waist-belt clasps. A number of the Volunteer Corps had specifically designed buttons which now enhance any collection of militaria. After 1911, with the reorganisation of the New Zealand Forces into seventeen Line Regiments and twelve Mounted Rifle Regiments, there was a rapid decline in the variety of badges worn until the adoption of the standard badge of World War II and the general pattern badge used today. Corps badges have changed very little since 1911 other than the type of crown on the badge.

The supply of militaria is not equal to the demand by collectors and this, together with the speculation by investors in this field, has made the hobby increasingly more expensive. Volunteer badges are now priced beyond the means of the modest collector and it seems in these days of inflation that there will never be a return to normality. The answer lies in the approach to the collecting of badges. It is preferable to have a few badges of quality and devote one's time and energy to collating the history of the unit and the men who served in it, than to have a quantity of badges about which one knows very little. A specialist collection is the best basis for exchanging badges with other collectors, as distinct from only purchasing badges, which are often difficult to buy or are sold at inflated prices.

Collar badges were frequently worn as cap badges and it was a common practice to use the stocks of K/C badges before the issue of Q/C badges even though these latter badges were available. Such practices and peculiarities in uniforms add interest to the collection of badges and the background data that makes the study of this aspect of militaria so absorbing.

Reference sources for information on badges are few, but two societies exist which offer the collector useful research material, and periodicals plus access to other collectors. The serious collector would gain much by belonging to one or both of these:

The Military Historical Society – Hon. Secretary: J. W. F. Gaylor, 7 East Woodside, Leighlands, Bexley, Kent DA5 3PG England. Annual fee £5.00.

New Zealand Military Historical Society – Hon. Secretary, P.O. Box 5123, Wellesley Street, Auckland 1, New Zealand. Annual fee $14.00.

2 Spencer St., Remuera.   D. A. CORBETT

DESIGN OF NEW ZEALAND CAP BADGES

THE FERN-LEAF has always been synonymous with New Zealand and it is appropriate that this was chosen as the base upon which the majority of the cap badges were designed. The honour of featuring the Garter with motto, or incorporating a crown in the design of a badge, is not restricted to royal regiments so that the crown usually forms an important part in the ready identification of the period during which the badge was worn.

The use of the Victorian crown and the Royal Cypher (VR) ceased with the coronation of Edward VII and it was at this time that the crown was changed in pattern to the Tudor crown and the Royal Cypher (EVIIR). The Tudor crown (normally referred to as 'K/C') remained as the official crown during the reign of George V and George VI although the Royal Cypher was changed to (GVR) and (GVIR). Her Majesty Queen Elizabeth II introduced a new Royal Cypher and crown. The Royal Cypher (EIIR) embodies the Saint Edward's crown and this is the crown now used on regimental badges (the badge referred to as 'Q/C').

As an aid for identification of the badge and of the main feature shown, the following table should assist.

BIRDS

Crane (White Heron): 1st (Canterbury) Regiment
1st North Canterbury Battalion (helmet plate)
2nd North Canterbury Infantry (helmet plate)
4th Canterbury Cadet Battalion

Eagle: N.Z. Army Air Corps

Hawk: 3rd (Auckland) Mounted Rifles

Huia: 21st Reinforcements
Napier Rifle Volunteers

Huia Feathers: 13th (North Canterbury) Regiment
First Battalion Otago Rifle Volunteers
33rd Reinforcements

Kaka: 4th (Waikato) Mounted Rifles

Kea: 14th (South Otago Rifles) Regiment

Kiwi: Hastings Rifle Volunteers (helmet plate)
2nd (South Canterbury) Regiment
South Canterbury Battalion
New Zealand Dental Corps
1st Battalion Otago Rifle Volunteers (collar badges)
4th (Otago Rifles) Regiment
New Zealand Permanent Staff
17th Reinforcements (collar badges)
New Zealand Regiment
Royal New Zealand Infantry Regiment

Moa: 20th Reinforcements
22nd Reinforcements

Phoenix: The Wellington, West Coast, Taranaki Regiment

Sparrow Hawk: 7th (Southland) Mounted Rifles

Tui: Women's Auxiliary Army Corps
New Zealand Women's Royal Army Corps

MAORI MOTIFS

Canoe:	26th Reinforcements
Mask:	19th Reinforcements
Taiaha (held in hand):	16th (Waikato) Regiment
Taiaha (crossed):	New Zealand Native Contingent
	Maori Pioneer Battalion
	New Zealand Cadet Corps
Tiki:	23rd Reinforcements, (collar badges)
Warrior:	8th (Southland Rifles) Regiment
	23rd Reinforcements
	25th Reinforcements
	New Zealand Pioneer Battalion
	Cook Islands Company (Pioneers)
	Otago and Southland Regiment
Whare and Warrior:	30th Reinforcements

ANIMALS

Boar's Head:	3rd Auckland Mounted Rifles
	11th (North Auckland) Mounted Rifles
Bulldog:	24th Reinforcements
Camel:	New Zealand Camel Companies
Stag's Head:	10th (Nelson) Mounted Rifles
	12th (Otago) Mounted Rifles
	9th (Wellington East Coast Rifles) Regiment
Stag:	12th (Nelson) Regiment
	12th (Nelson and Marlborough) Regiment
	12th & XIII Nelson, Marlborough and West Coast Regiment
Horses:	9th (Wellington East Coast) Mounted Rifles
	23rd Mounted Rifle Reinforcements
	24th Mounted Rifle Reinforcements
	NZ Mounted Rifle Reinforcements
	Royal NZ Electrical and Mechanical Engineers
Horse (winged):	NZ Mounted Rifle Reinforcements (25th to 47th)
	These badges were die-pressed as the 25th but had a superimposed disc which varied the number of each Reinforcement.
Lion:	Wellington Rifle Battalion (helmet plate)
	2nd (Wellington) Regiment
	5th (Wellington Rifles) Regiment
	7th (Wellington West Coast Rifles) Regiment
	6th (Hauraki) Regiment
	New Zealand Rifle Brigade
	27th Reinforcements
	Dunedin Highland Rifle Volunteers
	College Rifles
	Te Awamutu 1st RNZVC (helmet plate)
	Auckland Scottish Volunteers
	2nd Wellington (West Coast) RV (helmet plate)
	Hauraki (helmet plate)
	2nd Regiment Otago Mounted Rifles (helmet plate)
Dragon's Head:	Canterbury Highland Rifles

Ram: 1st (Canterbury Yeomanry Cavalry) Mounted Rifles
2nd Regiment North Canterbury Mounted Rifles
Kaikoura Mounted Rifle Volunteers (helmet plate)
Cust Mounted Rifle Volunteers (helmet plate)
Amuri Mounted Rifle Volunteers (helmet plate)
North Canterbury Mounted Rifle Volunteers (helmet plate)
Camel: Imperial Camel Brigade

PERSONAL ARMS
Cowie Nichols: 1st Regiment Otago Mounted Rifles
5th Mounted Rifles (Otago Hussars)
Earl of Ranfurly: 8th (South Canterbury) Mounted Rifles
Ashburton Mounted Rifles (helmet plate)
Earl of Liverpool: New Zealand Rifle Brigade
Duke of Wellington: 5th (Wellinton Rifles) Regiment
Dickson Crest: Territorial Force Officers, unattached to units
Regular Force Cadets

STARS
Southern Cross: Orepuki Rifle Volunteers
28th Reinforcements
3rd Battalion Otago Rifle Volunteers
10th (North Otago Rifles) Regiment
New Zealand Staff Corps
New Zealand Volunteers (helmet plate)
Star, eight points: Company Quartermasters Store
New Zealand Cavalry Volunteers (helmet plate)
New Zealand Army Service Corps
6th (Hauraki) Regiment
Royal New Zealand Army Service Corps
Star, five points: Royal New Zealand Nursing Corps
17th (Ruahine) Regiment

ARMORIAL SHIELDS
Canterbury Province: South Canterbury Rifle Battalion
1st Canterbury Rifle Battalion
Board of Ordnance: New Zealand Army Ordnance Department
New Zealand Army Ordnance Corps
NZ Army Ordnance Corps
Royal New Zealand Army Ordnance Corps
Otago University: Officers Training Corps

LETTERING
NZE: New Zealand Engineers (Tunnellers) large badge
New Zealand Engineers
DC: New Zealand Dental Corps
CMP: Camp Military Police (Featherston)
Camp Military Police (Trentham)
HG: Home Guard

11

CCG: Christchurch City Guards (helmet plate)
CRV: Christchurch Rifle Volunteers (helmet plate)
NZ: British Section NZEF
34-47th Reinforcements NZEF
2 NZEF
East Coast Hussars (helmet plate)
Army Pay Corps
OH: Otago Hussars
SH: Southland Hussars
PMR: Piako Mounted Rifles
RCV: Rangitikei Cavalry Volunteers
NZTC: New Zealand Torpedo Corps
NZSM New Zealand Submarine Miners
NZVC: New Zealand Veterinary Corps
CYC: Canterbury Yeomanry Cavalry
FR: Forest Rangers (believed to be the first New Zealand military badge)
ASC: New Zealand Army Service Corps
CMR: Canterbury Mounted Rifles
CRV: Canterbury Rifle Volunteers (helmet plate)
TMR: Taranaki Mounted Rifles
MRV: Manawatu Mounted Rifle Volunteers
APC: NZ Army Pay Corps
NZV: New Zealand Volunteers
HMR: Heretaunga Mounted Rifle Volunteers

FLORA

Ponga Tree: 2nd (Wellington West Coast) Mounted Rifles
23rd Reinforcements
Cabbage Tree: 4th Battalion Otago Rifle Volunteers
Thistle: New Zealand Scottish Regiment
Thames Scottish (helmet plate)
Wheat Sheaf: NZ Women's Land Service
Fern Leaf: NZ Staff Corps
King Edward's Horse (N.Z. portion CSqn.)
Boer War Contingents
N.Z. Temporary Staff
Fern Leaves (crossed): New Zealand Intelligence Corps
31st Reinforcements
Three Fern Leaves: 1st, 2nd and 3rd Reinforcements

NUMERALS

6: 6th (Manawatu) Mounted Rifles
Various Numerals: Senior Cadet Corps
Many of these badges are merely the Expeditionary Force badge with the 'NZ' removed and the Cadet Corps number substituted. In some cases a brass bar is placed over the original title.
Various Numbers and Letters: The reinforcements to the Main Body of the 1st NZEF World War I.
IX 9th (Wellington East Coast Rifles) Regiment
XIII: 13th (North Canterbury & Westland) Regiment

XIV:	14th (South Otago Rifles) Regiment
15	15th (North Auckland) Regiment
	15th (Northland) Regiment

ROYAL CYPHER

VR:	New Zealand Armed Constabulary
EVIIR:	Public School Cadets NZ
GVR:	Junior Cadets NZ
EIIR:	Royal New Zealand Provost Corps
	Royal New Zealand Army Service Corps
	Royal New Zealand Engineers

ARMOUR AND WEAPONS

Crossed Swords Behind Globe:	NZ Army Legal Service
Cannon:	NZ Regiment Artillery Volunteers
	NZ Field Artillery
	Royal New Zealand Artillery
	New Zealand Garrison Artillery
	Artillery Volunteers (helmet plate)
	New Zealand Regular Forces (helmet plate)
	Royal New Zealand Artillery (helmet plate)
	New Zealand Garrison Artillery (helmet plate)
	Coast Guard Artillery Volunteers (helmet plate)
Mailed Arm:	1st Battalion Auckland Infantry
	3rd (Auckland) Regiment
Tank:	Royal NZ Armoured Corps
Machine Gun:	NZ Specialists
	New Zealand Machine Gun Corps
Locomotive on Crossed Cannons:	Railway Battalion, New Zealand Engineers
Crossed Rifles and Wheel:	New Zealand Cyclist Corps
Winged Bicycle:	New Zealand Cyclist Corps
Winged Dagger:	Ranger Sqn. NZ Special Air Service
Winged Wheel:	NZ Cyclist Corps
	NZ Motor Service Corps
Wheel:	1st Pattern Volunteer Cycle Corps

MYTHOLOGY

Rod and Serpent:	NZ Field Ambulance
	NZ Field Hospital
	NZ Army Medical Corps
	NZ Medical Corps
	Royal New Zealand Army Medical Corps
Justice:	NZ Army Legal Service
Mercury:	New Zealand Corps of Signals
	Royal NZ Signals
Winged Foot:	NZ Post & Telegraph Corps

MISCELLANEOUS

Harp:	Canterbury Irish (helmet plate)
Post Horn:	New Zealand Volunteers
	Waimea Rifles (helmet plate)

Crossed Flags: New Zealand Signal Corps
New Zealand Specialists
Torch: NZ Army Educational Corps
Maltese Cross: NZ Permanent Staff
RNZChD
NZ Signal Corps (NZ Engineers)
South Canterbury Battalion
2nd (South Canterbury) Regiment
Mount Egmont: 4th Battalion Wellington (Taranaki) Rifle Volunteers
11th (Taranaki Rifles) Regiment
Crossed Trumpets: Featherston Camp Trumpet Band
NZ Outline Map: 32nd Reinforcements

Arm badge for Junior Warrant Officer 1901

Worn by all Warrant Officers Class II in 1938

Warrant Officer Class II 1954

REGIMENTAL MOTTOES

THE FOLLOWING MOTTOES are those which were embossed on the various cap or collar badges of New Zealand units. They do not include those which formed an integral part of the Arms of Royalty or Orders of Knighthood.

Ad unum omnes (Together as one): 17th (Ruahine) Regiment.

Ake ake (Forever and ever): 23rd Reinforcements.

Ake ake kia kaha (Forever and ever be strong): North Canterbury Battalion; 2nd Queen Alexandra's (Wellington West Coast) Mounted Rifles; 1st Canterbury Regiment; 29th Reinforcements.

Ake ake kia maia (Forever be brave): 30th Reinforcements.

Ake ake kia mana (Forever guard your honour): 30th Reinforcements.

Ake kia kaha (Forever be strong): 14th (South Otago Rifles) Regiment.

Arte et marte (By skill and fighting): Royal NZ Electrical and Mechanical Engineers.

Celer et audax (Swift and bold): 7th (Southland) Mounted Rifles; 1st (Canterbury) Mounted Rifles.

Celeritas (Swiftly): NZ Corps of Signals (Post and Telegraph Corps).

Certa cito (Fast and sure): Royal NZ Signals.

Ex malo bonum (From evil comes good): Royal NZ Dental Corps.

Es fidelis (Be faithful): 1st Regiment Otago Mounted Rifles. 5th Mounted Rifles (Otago Hussars).

For King and country: 12th (Otago) Mounted Rifles.

Fortes fortuna juvat (Fortune favours the brave): 9th (Wellington East Coast) Mounted Rifles; Territorial officers unattached to units; Regular Force Cadets.

God guard thee: NZ Legion of Frontiersmen.

He kawau maro (Unyielding as the shag): 6th (Manawatu) Mounted Rifles.

Hoko whitu a tu (War party of Tu): NZ Native Contingent; Maori Pioneer Battalion.

Hold Fast: 24th Reinforcements.

Huia tatau (Let us band together): 33rd Reinforcements.

In this sign conquer: Royal NZ Chaplains Department.

Inga wahi katoa (Everywhere): NZ Tunnellers Corps.

Justitia in armis (Justice in arms): NZ Army Legal Service.

Ka whawhai ake ake tonu (We shall fight for ever and ever): 16th (Waikato) Regiment.

Kia kaha (Be strong): 6th (Hauraki) Regiment.

Kia kaha kia toa (Be strong and Brave): 28th Reinforcements.

Kia mate toa (Die bravely): 8th (Southland Rifles) Regiment; The Otago and Southland Regiment; 23rd Reinforcements (collar badges).

Kia matara (Be watchful): 22nd Reinforcements; The Home Guard.

Kia matenga ururoa te tangata (A man should die like a shark): Orepuki Rifle Volunteers.

Kia pono tonu (Ever faithful): 13th (North Canterbury and Westland) Regiment; 12th and XIIth (Nelson Marlborough and West Coast) Regiment; The Canterbury Regiment.

Kia toa (Be brave): 9th (Wellington East Coast Rifles) Regiment; 25th Reinforcements.

Kia tupato (Be cautious): 3rd Auckland Mounted Rifles; 11th (North Auckland) Mounted Rifles; 19th Reinforcements.

Ko tatou hei tauira (We serve as examples): Royal NZ Provost Corps.

Kokiri kia maia (Attack with confidence): 20th Reinforcements.

Kura takahi puni (We are ready): 1st Battalion NZ Regiment.

Libertas et natale solum (Liberty and homeland): 4th (Waikato) Mounted Rifles.

Mo Rich mo dhuthaich (My King and country): 1st NZ Armoured Car Regiment.

Moveo et profitor (By my actions I am known): 8th (South Canterbury) Mounted Rifles.

Nga marohirohi (The brave): 2nd Regiment Otago Mounted Rifles.

Nil sine labor (Nothing without work): Royal NZ Army Service Corps.

Nulli secundus (Second to none): Hauraki Engineer Volunteers; Hauraki Rifle Volunteers.

Onward: British Section NZEF; 2nd NZ Expeditionary Force (2NZEF); Royal NZ Infantry Regiment.

Pass forward: Canterbury Highland Rifles.

Pour devoir (For right): 15th (North Auckland) Regiment; Northland Regiment.

Primus in armis (First in arms): 11th (Taranaki Rifles) Regiment.

Pro aris et focus (For hearth and home): 1st Canterbury Rifle Battalion.

Pro focus et patria (For home and country): 1st (Canterbury Yeomanry Cavalry) Mounted Rifles: 2nd Battalion Canterbury Mounted Rifles; Southland Hussars; Otago Hussars.

Pro patria (For our country): The South Canterbury Battalion; 3rd Battalion Otago Rifles; 2nd (South Canterbury) Regiment; 10th (North Otago Rifles) Regiment; Women's Auxiliary Army Corps; NZ Woman's Royal Army Corps.

Quo fas et gloria ducunt (Whither right and glory lead): Royal NZ Artillery; NZ Artillery Volunteers; NZ Engineers; NZ Engineers (Tunnellers): Coastguard Artillery Volunteers.

Ready: South Canterbury Rifle Battalion.

Regi adsumus Coloni (As Colonials we stand by the King): King Edward's Horse.

Rem gero strenue (Fight with zeal): 10th (Nelson) Mounted Rifles.

Sisit prudentia (Ever prudent): 1st Battalion Auckland Infantry; 3rd (Auckland) Regiment (Countess of Ranfurly's Own).

Sodales parati (Prepared as comrades together): NZ Signal Corps.

Soyes ferme (Stand fast): NZ Rifle Brigade.

Sua tela tonanti (To the warrior his arms): Royal NZ Ordnance Corps.

Te kaahu mataara (Be like a hawk): 3rd (Auckland) Mounted Rifles.

Te Manaaki tika (Take great care of others); Field Ambulance; Field Hospital.

Ubique (Everywhere): Royal NZ Artillery; NZ Field Artillery; NZ Garrison Artillery; NZ Engineers.

Virtutis fortuna comes (Good fortune is the companion of courage): 5th (Wellington Rifles) Regiment.

Whaka tangata kia kaha (Canoe men be brave): 31st Reinforcements.

Who dares wins: Ranger Squadron NZ Special Air Service.

The above spellings, word divisions and translations into English are those traditionally accepted. Modern usage may in a number of instances, differ somewhat from the versions given here.

Warrant Officer Class I 1918

ROYAL CROWNS

Victorian Crown

This pattern, displaying pronouncedly splayed arches with gems in settings on them, was used in mid-Victorian period, e.g. East Coast Hussars helmet plate 1887. A similar pattern crown but with conventional pearls was introduced at the same period and is the more common pattern, e.g. South Franklin helmet plate 1887.

Tudor Crown

When Edward VII came to the throne an attempt was made to standardise the appearance and shape of the crown, the result becoming known as the Tudor Crown because of the similarity to the crown in use in the Tudor period. This crown with semi-circular arches, nine pearls on each of the lateral quadrant arches and five pearls on the medial arch, was used throughout the reign of four Kings and is generally referred to as the 'King's Crown' (K/C), e.g. 3rd Battalion Otago Rifle Volunteers helmet plate 1901.

St Edward's Crown

On the accession of Queen Elizabeth II the representation of the Crown was altered and it was ordained that the new design would be the St Edward's

ROYAL CYPHER and CROWN

Aides-de-camp general to the sovereign, officers holding similar appointments and ex-appointees, wear the Royal Cypher and Crown in one piece below their badges of rank. Should an officer who has held an appointment to a late sovereign be subsequently re-appointed to the reigning sovereign, he may wear the insigna of both appointments. In this case he would wear the Royal Cypher and Crown of the late sovereign in miniature, and that of the reigning sovereign in full size.

APPOINTMENT	WEARS ROYAL CYPHER AND CROWN IN:
Aides-de-camp general to the sovereign Aides-de-camp to the sovereign Extra equerries to the sovereign	Dull silver metal, $1^{11}/_{40}$ ins high and $1^{3}/_{10}$ ins wide.
Honorary chaplains Honorary surgeons Honorary physicians Honorary dental surgeons Honorary nursing sisters to the sovereign	Gilt metal, $1^{11}/_{40}$ ins high and $1^{3}/_{10}$ ins wide.
Ex aides-de-camp general to the sovereign Ex aides-de-camp to the sovereign Ex honorary chaplains Ex honorary surgeons Ex honorary physicians Ex honorary dental surgeons Ex honorary nursing sisters to the sovereign	Dull silver metal $^4/_5$ ins high and $^{19}/_{20}$ ins wide. Gilt metal, $^4/_5$ ins high and $^{19}/_{20}$ ins wide.

Crown. This pattern is referred to by collectors as the 'Queen's Crown' (Q/C), e.g. RNZA cap badge 1954.

The 'Albert Crown' was used by South Canterbury Infantry Battalion 1885 and appeared on many of the bit-bosses of that period.

The 'Star of India' Crown with only six pearls on the lateral arches was worn by the 1st North Canterbury Battalion 1897.

DRESS REGULATIONS FOR VOLUNTEERS

THE REGULATIONS which were published on 3 February 1866 were formulated on the British 'Dress Regulations for the Army 1864' with the proviso that Colonial Forces were not to wear gold lace.

The significant badges approved for wear on the uniform were: A volunteer classed as 'efficient' wore on the right arm, immediately above the cuff of the sleeve, a distinctive badge consisting of a ring of silver lace ¾ inch wide. A volunteer who obtained highest score in shooting at 300 yards wore an embroidered rifle horizontally above the cuff of the left sleeve. A volunteer who obtained the highest score at a range of up to 600 yards wore a star above the embroidered rifle. A volunteer who obtained 20 points or more at a range of 900 yards wore two stars above the embroidered rifle. A volunteer who obtained the greatest number of points at a range of 900 yards wore three stars above the embroidered rifle. A sergeant instructor in musketry who qualified as proficient in rifle practice wore the embroidered rifle on the right arm between the elbow and the shoulder.

The Army Regulations of 5 November 1867 permitted members of a rifle corps to wear the initials or number of the corps to be placed on the band of the forage cap. This privilege was extended to include engineers and rifle cadets on 11 November 1870.

Naval artillery volunteers wore the same uniform as the Royal Navy Artillery Volunteers, substituting silver lace for gold. This was amended on 28 March 1889 when gold lace was permitted.

BUTTONS: Royal Navy pattern with the letters N.A.V. in Old English characters across an anchor surmounted by a crown. The buttons were gilt.

CAP BADGES: *Officers:* A silver anchor, with the letters N.A.V. above it in silver, on a medallion of black velvet, encircled by an edging of gold lace, surrounded by a laurel wreath of gold embroidery, surmounted by an embroidered gold and silver crown with a crimson velvet centre. *Chief petty officers:* Crown and anchor encircled with oak leaves. Silver embroidery. *First and second class petty officers:* Crown and cross anchor. Silver embroidery. *Leading gunners:* The anchor. Silver embroidery.

CAP BADGE AND HAT RIBBON: Crown and anchor with letters N.A.V. above. *Garrison artillery efficiency badge:* A gun embroidered in silver, worn above right wrist. *Submarine miners efficiency badge:* A Whitehead torpedo embroidered in silver, worn on the right arm above the wrist.

Men who qualified as 'efficient' for three consecutive years wore a badge of two crossed guns, or torpedoes, embroidered in silver above the right wrist.

The Regulations of 22 November 1882 permitted the Rifle Corps to wear the Imperial pattern helmet. The helmet plate was the standard Rifle Corps plate authorised for wear by the British Army on the Home Service pattern helmet in May 1878. This helmet plate consisted of an eight-pointed star, the centre containing the bugle-horn surrounded by the motto of the Order of the Garter, the whole surmounted by a Victorian crown.

The Regulations of 28 March 1889 introduced an Efficiency Star for volunteers who were classed as 'efficient' for three consecutive years. This star, in silk, was worn on the right arm above the Austrian knot. A second star was awarded for an additional period of three years, and after a total of nine years of being classed as efficient, a volunteer wore a silver star on the right arm above the elbow, or if a non-commissioned officer, above the chevrons.

Dress Regulations of 1 September 1895:
Officers of the New Zealand Forces were permitted to wear the letters of the colony 'N.Z.' embroidered in gold on the shoulder strap. On the field service cap, these letters were worn with the letter 'N' in front and 'Z' in rear of the badge of arm of the service. Other ranks wore the letters in brass. *Officers on the Reserve List:* The letter 'R' on the shoulder strap. *Staff-instructor, sergeant-major and regimental sergeant-major:* Four chevrons, point upwards, surmounted by a crown, below the elbow. In gold lace on scarlet. *Regimental quartermaster-sergeants:* Four chevrons, point upwards, surmounted by a star, below the elbow. In gold lace on scarlet ground. *Battery sergeant-major:* Three chevrons, point downwards, surmounted by a gun and crown, above the elbow. In gold lace on scarlet ground. *Battery Quartermaster-sergeants:* Three chevrons, point downwards, surmounted by a gun and star, above the elbow. *Company sergeant-majors and colour sergeants:* Three chevrons, point downwards, surmounted by a crown, above the elbow. *Company quartermaster-sergeants:* Three chevrons, point downwards, surmounted by a star, above the elbow. *Sergeants of artillery:* Three chevrons, point downwards, surmounted by a gun, above the elbow. *Sergeants of Mounted Companies, Engineers and Rifles:* Three chevrons, point downwards, above the elbow. *Corporals:* Two chevrons, point downwards, above the elbow. *Bombardiers, acting bombardiers and lance-corporals:* One chevron, point downwards, above the elbow. *Trumpeters and buglers:* Trumpet or bugle embroidered in scarlet on right arm, above the elbow. *Bandsmen:* A lyre embroidered in scarlet on both arms, below the elbow.

Naval Artillery Volunteers
Chief petty officer: Crown and anchor encircled in oak-leaves, embroidered in gold, above the elbow. *First and second class petty officer:* Crown and cross-anchor, embroidered in gold, above the elbow. *Leading gunner:* The anchor, embroidered in gold, above the elbow.

SERVICE BADGES
Badges for the different arms of the service were worn on the collar of the jacket, embroidered in gold for officers and in brass for other ranks.
Artillery and engineers: A grenade; *Mounted companies and rifles:* A Bugle.

SHOULDER TITLES
Which were known at this time as letter-badges had these straight titles in brass.
N.Z.A. Permanent Force. **N.Z.M.R.** Mounted Corps. **N.Z.A.V.** Artillery Volunteers. **N.Z.E.** Engineer Volunteers. **N.Z.R.** Rifle Corps.

BUTTONS
The Universal-pattern button for all volunteers, except naval volunteers, was brass 15/16 in. diameter with the words 'New Zealand Volunteers' around the edge, and in the shaded field in centre, four stars representing the constellation of the Southern Cross. Smaller buttons fastened the shoulder-straps.

DISTINGUISHING LETTERS
The five districts into which the Colony was divided for military purposes, were represented by brass distinguishing letters worn on the shoulder-strap, above the letter-badge.
A Auckland; **W** Wellington; **N** Nelson; **C** Canterbury; **O** Otago.

EFFICIENCY BADGES
A star of blue silk on scarlet ground for volunteers classed as 'efficient' for

three consecutive years, worn on the right arm above the Austrian knot. After nine years of 'efficient' classification, a volunteer wore a silver star on the right arm above the elbow.

PROFICIENCY BADGES

Gunnery: A gun embroidered in silver worn on the right arm below the elbow, muzzle pointing to the front. *Sub-mining:* A torpedo embroidered in silver worn on the right arm below the elbow, head of torpedo pointing to the front. *Engineering:* Crossed flags with star above, worn on right arm below the elbow; (this qualification was amended on 1 December 1897 as follows: Cross flags with a star above for Signalling and Electricity Branch. Cross pick and shovel for Field Engineering). *Signalling:* Cross flags worn on right arm below the elbow. *Ambulance:* Geneva Cross, worn on right arm below the elbow.

A volunteer who was classed as 'proficient' for three years wore the following: *Gunnery:* Crossed guns; *sub-mining:* Crossed torpedoes; *Engineering:* A Star below the crossed flags or badge (after 1897); *Signalling:* A Star below the crossed flags; *Marksman's badge:* A rifle embroidered in silver mounted by two stars worn horizontally on left forearm. The best shot in each company wore an additional star; *Bandsmen:* The regulations of 1895 were amended as follows: *Bandmasters:* A lyre embroidered in gold on each arm below the elbow. *Non-commissioned bandsmen:* A Lyre embroidered in silver on scarlet ground. *Bandsmen:* A lyre embroidered in scarlet worsted.

The 'Dress Regulations' of 27 October 1897 permitted any volunteer corps to adopt whatever uniform they so desired.

DRESS REGULATIONS OF 31 MAY 1905:

A major revision was promulgated to regulate the wearing of badges, one interesting instruction being that 'Irishmen of all ranks are authorised to wear a sprig of shamrock in their head-dress on St. Patrick's Day'.

Officers on the Retired List to wear the letter 'R' below the badge of rank on the shoulder-strap. In brass on service dress, but in full-dress, if the shoulder-knots were of gold lace the badges in silver, and vice versa.

Permanent staff instructors and inspectors: A helmet plate similar to that worn by the Royal New Zealand Artillery with the exception of the gun and regimental designation, which were omitted. In full dress, the letters 'N.Z. Staff' embroidered in gold on the shoulder-strap. The same in Brass for service dress.

Royal N.Z. Artillery: Initials 'R.N.Z.A.' in silver on shoulder-knots. Brass for other ranks.

Royal New Zealand Engineers: Initials 'R.N.Z.E.' in silver on shoulder-knots. Brass for other ranks.

N.Z. Field Artillery and Garrison Artillery Volunteers: Initial 'N.Z.A.V.' in silver. Brass for other ranks.

N.Z. Engineer Volunteers: Initials 'N.Z.E.V.' in silver on shoulder-knots. Brass for other ranks.

Veterinary Officers: Initials 'N.Z.' in silver on shoulder knots.

Officers of Medical Corps and Bearer Companies: Initials 'N.Z.' in gold on shoulder-knots.

Officers uniforms were to follow the pattern in the British Army 'Dress Regulations for the Army 1904'.

New Zealand rifle clubs which were formed as from 17 April 1901 were embodied in the defence forces of the colony and formed a reserve force of volunteers. They were distinguished by wearing a brass shoulder title with the letters 'N.Z.R.C.'.

Members of the staff and permanent forces wore rank badges on both arms, but other branches wore a rank badge on the right arm only. Four bar chevrons were worn below the elbow with the point upwards; all other chevrons were worn above the elbow with the point downwards. For full dress, the chevrons were of gold lace on scarlet, or of silver lace if the officers of the unit wore silver lace. For service dress, the chevrons were of scarlet braid on khaki-coloured cloth. Other badges were of gold or scarlet worsted:

Staff instructors: A crown, below elbow. *Garrison artillery division* or *battalion sergeant majors:* Four chevrons surmounted by a crown. *Garrison artillery division* or *battery quartermaster sergeants:* Four chevrons surmounted by a star. *Farrier majors:* Four chevrons surmounted by a horseshoe. *Sergeant buglers:* Three chevrons surmounted by crossed bugles. *Battery* or *company sergeant majors* or *colour sergeants:* Three chevrons surmounted by a crown. (In artillery a gun, and in engineers a grenade, were also worn.) *Sergeant artificers:* Three chevrons surmounted by a gun or grenade, and crossed hammer and pincers. *Sergeant:* Three chevrons (in artillery a gun and in engineers a grenade were also worn). *Corporal:* Two chevrons. *Bombardier, second corporal* and *lance corporal:* One chevron. *Farrier:* Horseshoe above elbow. *Trumpeter:* Trumpet, above elbow. *Bugler:* Bugle, above elbow. *Permanent force signallers:* Signalling badge above chevrons on both arms. *Permanent force gymnastic instructors:* Respective badge above chevrons on both arms.

All specialist and proficiency badges were worn on the left arm only, below elbow.

PROFICIENCY BADGES

Signalling (all arms): Crossed flags in worsted, 'distinguished', crossed flags in gold and silk. *Gunnery:* 'G in red, 'distinguished', 'G' in gold. *Gun-laying:* 'L' in red, 'distinguished', 'L' in gold. *Range-finding:* 'R' in red, 'distinguished', 'R' in gold. *Driving:* Snaffle (bridle-bit) in red, 'distinguished', snaffle in gold. *Submarine mining:* Torpedo in red, 'distinguished', torpedo in gold. *Testing:* Outline of a testing key in red, 'distinguished', outline of a testing key in gold. *Electric lighting:* Outline of electric globe in red, 'distinguished', outline of an electric globe in gold. *Field engineering:* Crossed picks in red, 'distinguished', crossed picks in gold. *Bridging sections:* Outline of a trestle in red, 'distinguished', outline of a trestle in gold. *Field telegraph:* Outline of a telegraph pole in red, 'distinguished', outline of a telegraph pole in gold. *Marksmen badges:* A rifle in red, 'distinguished' (best in battalion), a rifle in gold. *Ambulance:* Red cross in worsted, surmounted by a yellow circle, 'distinguished', red cross in silk, surmounted by a circle in gold. *1st class artillery batteries* or *companies:* The notation '1st' surrounded by a wreath in red worsted.

Three years efficiency badge: A red worsted star.

Nine years efficiency badge: A gold star.

School instruction badge: the letters 'P.S.' in gold.

Badge style for volunteer Glengarry cap, cira 1900

Arrangement as used on blue Glengarry cap of 5th Battalion Rifle Volunteers, 1901

RANK BADGES PRE 1927

DURING WORLD WAR I, the rank badges worn within New Zealand by warrant and non-commissioned ranks differed somewhat from those worn overseas by the NZEF.

NEW ZEALAND PERMANENT STAFF:
Warrant officer 1st class: Crown and wreath. *Warrant officer, 2nd class:* Royal Arms. *Sergeant-instructor:* Crown.

TEMPORARY INSTRUCTORS:
Regimental sergeant-major and staff quartermaster-sergeant: 4 chevrons and crown on fore-arm.
Staff sergeant: 3 chevrons and crown on fore-arm.

TERRITORIAL FORCE:
Regimental sergeant-major: 4 chevrons and crown on fore-arm. *Regimental quartermaster-sergeant:* 4 chevrons and star on fore-arm. *Staff quartermaster-sergeant:* 4 chevrons on fore-arm. *Company sergeant-major:* 3 stripes and crown on upper arm. *Company quartermaster-sergeant:* 3 stripes and star on upper arm. *Staff sergeant:* 3 stripes and crown on upper arm.

Temporary instructors were attached to the New Zealand Permanent Staff and wore the regimental badges and puggaree of the New Zealand Permanent Staff.

The following table is reprinted from *Regulations for the Military Forces of the Dominion of New Zealand, 1927.*

Appendix IX.

APPENDIX IX.— BADGES OF RANK, WARRANT OFFICERS AND NON-COMMISSIONED OFFICERS, N.Z. MILITARY FORCES; DISTINGUISHING BADGES.

(a.) BADGES OF RANK.
(1.) Warrant Officers, Class I.

Staff sergeant-major, N.Z. Permanent Staff	Royal Arms and wreath.
Conductor	Royal Arms and wreath.
Master gunner, 1st class	Royal Arms and wreath and gun.
Master gunner, 2nd class	Royal Arms and gun.
Regimental sergeant-major, Royal N.Z. Artillery	Royal Arms, wreath, and crossed guns.
Bandmaster (W.O.I.)	Royal Arms and lyre.
Armament sergeant-major	Royal Arms and crossed hammer and pincers.
Armourer sergeant-major	Royal Arms and crossed hammer and pincers.
Sergeant-major artificer	Royal Arms and crossed hammer and pincers.
Fitter sergeant-major	Royal Arms and crossed hammer and pincers.
Saddler sergeant-major	Royal Arms and bit.
Farrier sergeant-major	Royal Arms and horse-shoe.
Wheeler sergeant-major	Royal Arms and wheel.
Sergeant-major, School of Musketry	Royal Arms and crossed rifles.
Sergeant-major, gymnastic staff	Royal Arms and crossed swords.
All other warrant officers, Class I	Royal Arms.

(2.) Warrant Officers, Class II.

Sergeant-major, N.Z. Permanent Staff	Crown and wreath.
Master gunner, 3rd class	Crown and wreath and gun.
Regimental quartermaster-sergeant	Crown and wreath.
Staff quartermaster-sergeant	Crown and wreath.
Armament quartermaster-sergeant	Crown and wreath and crossed hammer and pincers.
Armourer quartermaster-sergeant	Crown and wreath and crossed hammer and pincers.
Smith quartermaster-sergeant	Crown and wreath and crossed hammer and pincers.
Quartermaster-sergeant artificer	Crown and wreath and crossed hammer and pincers.
Quartermaster-sergeant coxswain	Crown and wreath.
Fitter quartermaster-sergeant	Crown and wreath and crossed hammer and pincers.
Farrier quartermaster-sergeant	Crown and wreath and horseshoe.
Laboratory quartermaster-sergeant	Crown and wreath and crossed guns.
Quartermaster-sergeant instructor in gunnery	Crown and wreath and crossed guns.
Quartermaster-sergeant instructor in small-arms	Crown and wreath and crossed rifles.
Quartermaster-sergeant, School of Musketry	Crown and wreath and crossed rifles.
Quartermaster-sergeant instructor	Crown and wreath.
Quartermaster-sergeant, gymnastic staff	Crown and wreath and crossed swords.

Appendix IX.

(2.) **Warrant Officers, Class II**—*continued.*

Saddler quartermaster-sergeant	Crown and wreath and bit.
Wheeler quartermaster-sergeant	Crown and wreath and wheel.
Quartermaster-sergeant, N.Z. Medical Corps	Crown and wreath.
Battery or company sergeant-major instructor in gunnery	Crown and crossed guns.
Company sergeant-major instructor in gymnastics and fencing	Crown and crossed swords.
Company sergeant-major instructor in small-arms	Crown and crossed rifles.
Company sergeant-major, School of Musketry	Crown and crossed rifles.
Squadron, battery, or company sergeant-major	Crown.

(3.) **Non-commissioned Officers.**

Staff sergeant instructor, N.Z. Permanent Staff	Crown and four inverted chevrons on forearm.

Special Badges to be worn between Chevrons and Crown.

Worn with Crown and three chevrons on upper arm:

Squadron, battery, or company quartermaster-sergeant	Gun for battery quartermaster-sergeant.
Staff sergeant, N.Z. Permanent Staff	Nil.
Staff sergeant artillery clerk	Gun.
Staff sergeant artificer	Crossed hammer and pincers.
Armament staff sergeant	Crossed hammer and pincers.
Armourer staff sergeant	Crossed hammer and pincers.
Staff sergeant fitter	Crossed hammer and pincers.
Engineer clerk staff sergeant	Grenade.
Engineer storekeeper staff sergeant	Grenade.
Farrier staff sergeant	Horse-shoe.
Farrier staff sergeant and carriage-smith	Horse-shoe.
Mechanist staff sergeant	Crossed hammer and pincers.
Saddler staff sergeant	Bit.
Smith staff sergeant	Crossed hammer and pincers.
Wheeler staff sergeant	Wheel.
All other staff sergeants	Nil.

Special Badges to be worn above Chevrons.

Worn with Three chevrons on upper arm:

Sergeant	Nil.
Engineer clerk sergeant	Grenade.
Engineer ledgerkeeper and storeman sergeant	Grenade.
Farrier-sergeant	Horse-shoe.
Farrier-sergeant and carriage-smith	Horse-shoe.
Fitter-sergeant	Crossed hammer and pincers.
Orderly-room sergeant	Nil.
Pioneer-sergeant	Crossed axes.
Saddler-sergeant	Bit.
Sergeant artillery clerk	Gun.
Band sergeant	Lyre.
Sergeant-bugler	Crossed bugles.
Sergeant-cook	Nil.
Sergeant-drummer	Drum.
Armourer-sergeant	Crossed hammer and pincers.
Sergeant-fitter	Crossed hammer and pincers.
Sergeant-artificer	Crossed hammer and pincers.
Sergeant-instructor in gymnastics	Crossed swords.
Sergeant-instructor, School of Musketry	Crossed rifles.
Sergeant-shoemaker	Nil.
Sergeant-tailor	Nil.
Sergeant-piper	Nil.
Sergeant-trumpeter	Crossed trumpets.
Smith-sergeant	Crossed hammer and pincers.
Wheeler-sergeant	Wheel.
Lance-sergeant	Nil.

Appendix IX.

Special Badges to be worn above Chevrons—continued.

Bombardier	⎫	Nil.
Bombardier artillery clerk		Nil.
Bombardier-cook		Nil.
Acting-bombardier		Nil.
Acting-bombardier artillery clerk.. ..		Nil.
Corporal		Nil.
Armourer-corporal		Crossed hammer and pincers.
Artificer-corporal		Crossed hammer and pincers.
Corporal orderly-room clerk	Two chevrons on upper arm.	Nil.
Farrier corporal and carriage-smith ..		Horse-shoe.
Band corporal		Lyre.
Fitter-corporal..		Crossed hammer and pincers.
Saddler-corporal		Bit.
Shoeing-smith corporal		Horse-shoe.
Smith-corporal..		Crossed hammer and pincers.
Engineer clerk corporal		Nil.
Wheeler-corporal		Wheel.
Corporal-cook	⎭	Nil.
Band bombardier	⎫	Lyre.
Engineer clerk lance-corporal	One chevron on upper arm.	Nil.
Lance-corporal..		Nil.
Lance-bombardier	⎭	Nil.

(b.) DISTINGUISHING-BADGES.

Distinguishing-badges will be worn as follows :—

Worn by	Badge.
(a.) Warrant officer instructors of the N.Z. Engineers..	A grenade.
(b.) Warrant officer instructors of the N.Z. Corps of Signals	Crossed flags.
(c.) Non-commissioned officers of N.Z. Artillery above the rank of corporal	A gun.
(d.) Non-commissioned officers of N.Z. Engineers above the rank of corporal	A grenade.
(e.) Non-commissioned officers of N.Z. Corps of Signals above the rank of corporal	Crossed flags.
(f.) Assistant instructors in signalling and trained signallers authorized to wear badges	Crossed flags.
Telegraphists	Crossed flags.
(g.) Warrant officers, non-commissioned officers, and privates employed as artificers :—	
(i.) Saddlers	A bit.
(ii.) Farriers and shoeing-smiths	A horse-shoe.
(iii.) Wheelers and carpenters	A wheel.
(iv.) Armourers, machinery artificers, machinery gunners, and smiths ..	Hammer and pincers.
(v.) Qualified electricians	"E" in wreath.
(vi.) Qualified engine-drivers	Governor in ring.

Qualified electricians and engine-drivers are entitled to wear the distinguishing-badges although they may not necessarily be employed as artificers.

(h.) Roughriders	A spur.
(i.) Bandsmen	A lyre.

Appendix X.

Armlets.

Armlets will be worn as follows :—

(a.) Military Police, Garrison Police, and Regimental Police   ..   ..   Black armlet with letters "M.P.," "G.M.P.," or "R.P." in red.

(b.) N.Z. Corps of Signals (when in training camps or at manoeuvres)   ..   ..   ..   Blue and white armlet.

NOTES.

1. Chevrons, badges of rank, and distinguishing-badges will be worn on both arms of jackets and greatcoats.

2. Chevrons, badges of rank, and distinguishing-badges will be worn below the elbow by warrant officers and staff sergeant instructors. In all other cases they will be worn above the elbow.

3. Chevrons will be worn with the points downwards, except in the case of four-bar chevrons, which will be worn with the points upwards.

4. (a.) The point of the one-bar chevron will be placed 9 in., the two-bar 9½ in., and the three-bar 10½ in. from the top of the sleeve.

(b.) Four-bar chevrons will be worn with the point 9 in. from the bottom of the sleeve on jackets and 11 in. from the bottom of the sleeve on greatcoats.

(c.) Warrant officers' badges will be worn with the lower edges 6½ in. from the bottom of the sleeve.

5. In the case of warrant officers, distinguishing-badges will be worn below the rank-badges, and in the case of non-commissioned officers they will be worn above the chevrons.

6. Distinguishing-badges will be worn by privates with the lower edges 9 in. from the top of the sleeve.

7. Distinguishing-badges will be worn by non-commissioned officers with the lower edge of the badge ¾ in. above the point of the V of the chevron. When the distinguishing-badge consists of a combination of a corps badge (e.g., gun, grenade, &c.) and a trade badge (e.g., horse-shoe, wheel, &c.) the corps badge will be worn ¾ in. above the trade badge.

APPENDIX X.—EFFICIENCY AND SKILL-AT-ARMS BADGES.

Gunnery Badges, N.Z. Artillery.

* Crown and "G" in wreath (first prize)
* Star and "G" in wreath (second prize) } One of each for each battery of Field Artillery or Coast Artillery.
* "G" in wreath (third prize)   ..

Layers' Badges, N.Z. Artillery.

The appointment of layer within the undermentioned establishment carries the right to wear the badge, provided the layer has qualified in the test :—

† "L" in wreath   ..   ..   ..   { Batteries of Field Artillery—eighteen for each battery. Coast Artillery, 15 per cent. of the peace establishment of each battery.

Appendix X.

Musketry Badges.

* Star and crossed rifles in wreath	Best shot in regiment, battalion, or Cadet battalion.
* Star and crossed rifles	Best marksman of a squadron, company, or Cadet company.
* Crossed rifles	Marksmen in Territorial Force and Cadets.

Machine-gun Badge.

‡ "M.G." in wreath	Marksmen machine-gunners.

Light-gun Badge.

‡ "L.G." in wreath	First-class Lewis and Hotchkiss gunners.

Badges for Qualified Range-takers and Range and Position Finders.

† "R" in wreath	Six for each battery of Field Artillery and twelve for each battery Coast Artillery.

Badges for Skill in Driving.

* Crown, crossed whip and spur (first prize)	First, second, third, and fourth prizes, one of each for each horse-drawn battery Field Artillery or depot company, N.Z. Army Service Corps.
* Crossed whip and spur (second, third, and fourth prizes)	First, second, and third prizes, one of each for each depot company, N.Z. Engineers, and N.Z. Corps of Signals.
* Crown, steering-wheel (first prize) * Steering-wheel (second, third, and fourth prizes)	First, second, third, and fourth prizes, one of each for each depot company, N.Z. Army Service Corps.

Engineers, Field Work.

‡ "Q.I." in wreath	For each qualified instructor below the rank of sergeant.

N.Z. Artillery.

‡ Crossed guns	For all non-commissioned officers who have been through the gunnery staff course and are recommended for the badge.
‡ Battery classification badge, "1st" in wreath	Battery classification badges will be awarded to all non-commissioned officers and men in a Field Artillery battery which has been classified as "special," and to all non-commissioned officers and men in a Coast Artillery battery which has been graded "A" and classified as "1st class" at annual practice.

Signallers.

‡ Crossed flags	Qualified signallers of all arms.

Appendix XI.

Judging-distance Badges, Cadets.

‡ Star .. .. Five best non-commissioned officers and Cadets in each company of Cadets. (Where strength exceeds 100 this badge will be awarded on a basis of 5 per cent.)

Attendance, Good-conduct, and Efficiency Badges, Cadets.

* Good attendance : Star, five-pointed, red — For a Cadet who has not been absent from parade without leave and absent with leave not more than four times in the year.

* Good conduct : Star, five-pointed, white — To be awarded to those Cadets who have not merited punishment or censure during one year.

* Efficiency : Star, five-pointed, blue .. To be awarded to 10 per cent. of the most efficient Cadets in each company who hold both the attendance and good-conduct badges.

NOTES.

1. The qualifications for the several badges will be as laid down in the various training-manuals.
2. The expression "Field Artillery" includes all N.Z. Artillery except Coast Artillery batteries.
3. Warrant officers, Class II, are eligible for the following musketry badges : Star and crossed rifles, crossed rifles.
4. Badges for good attendance and good conduct awarded to a Cadet will be forfeited should the Cadet fail to observe the conditions of either.
5. Efficiency badges and badges for skill-at-arms will be worn on the left arm of jackets only, below the elbow, with the lower edge 6½ in. from the bottom of the sleeve.
6. Badges marked * are awarded annually by the O.C. Unit in the Territorial Force or the O.C. Company in the Cadets.
7. Badges marked † are badges of appointment.
8. Badges marked ‡ are awarded as earned.
9. Efficiency badges and badges awarded for skill at arms shall be retained as the personal property of the winners.

The regulations were later amended as follows:

Signallers

Winged orb on forked lightning .... Qualified wireless operators of NZC of Signals.

Medical

M .... Holds Advanced Training Certificate as qualified.
M in wreath .... Holds Advanced Training Certificate as qualified with merit.
M in wreath with crown .... Holds Advanced Training Certificate as qualified with great merit.

BADGES OF RANK AS WORN TODAY

General Officers: CAP BADGE: The Royal Crest, with crossed sword and baton within a laurel wreath, in gold embroidery.
Brigadiers and Colonels: CAP BADGE: The Royal Crest in gold embroidery.
Other officers, warrant officers, non-commissioned officers and soldiers: The corps or regimental cap badge.
Regular Force Cadets: The Regular Force cadet cap badge.
Recruits not posted to a corps or regiment: A brass fern leaf with the letters 'NZ' inscribed centrally.

SHOULDER STRAP OR SHOULDER CORD BADGES:
Lieutenant General: Crossed sword and baton with crown above.
Major General: Crossed sword and baton with star above.
Brigadier: Crown above three stars, the two lower stars side by side.
Colonel, Chaplain 1st Class: Crown with two stars below.
Lieutenant Colonel, Chaplain 2nd class: Crown with one star below.
Major, Chaplain 3rd class: Crown.
Captain, Chaplain 4th class: Three stars.
Lieutenant: Two stars.
Second Lieutenant: One star.
Sergeant Major of the Army: A badge incorporating the New Zealand Coat of Arms.
Regimental Sergeant Major, the Army Schools: A badge incorporating portions of the official crests of the New Zealand Army and the Army Schools, supported by the lion and unicorn.
Warrant Officer Class I: Royal Arms within a wreath.
Warrant Officer Class II: Crown within a wreath.
Staff Sergeant: Three chevrons surmounted by a crown.
Sergeant: Three chevrons.
Bombadier, Corporal: Two chevrons.
Lance Bombadier, Lance Corporal: One chevron.

Officer-pattern badges are of gilt; gilt and silver; gilt, silver and enamel; silver; bronze; anodised aluminium.

Other ranks-pattern badges are of brass; brass and white metal; white metal; anodised aluminium.

Artillery NCO arm badges — guns point forwards on arm

Mounted artillery

Gun layer

Surveyor

Assistant Gunnery instructor

Despatch rider
1914-1918

1st class driver

Wheeler and carpenter

Warrant Officer Class I: As of June 1979 this badge is the New Zealand Coat-of-Arms embroidered on cloth.

BADGES OF APPOINTMENT AND QUALIFICATION AS WORN TODAY

The regulations governing the wearing of badges of appointment or qualification have been changed, especially since World War II. Some of the original badges have been lost, but the distinctions required by a modern army have been maintained.

A Gun — Metal, gilt finish: worn in right and left facing pairs by all staff sergeants and sergeants of RNZA.

A Grenade — Metal, gilt finish: worn by warrant officers class II, and instructors at SME.

Mercury — Metal, gilt and silver finish: worn by all staff sergeants and sergeants of RNZ Signals.

A hammer and pincers, crossed — Metal, gilt finish: worn by all staff sergeants and sergeants of RNZEME.

A lyre surmounted by a crown — Metal, gilt finish: worn by all bandsmen, including drummers (other than drummers of pipe bands).

A drum – (1) Metal, gilt finish; worn by Drum majors of all bands and drummer of pipe bands with service dress.

(2) Gold thread on cloth of the same colour as the jacket: worn by Drum majors of all bands and drummers of pipe bands with dress uniform.

Pipes – (1) Metal, gilt finish: worn by Pipe majors and pipers of pipe bands with service dress.

(2) Gold thread on cloth the same colour as the jacket: worn by Pipe majors, and pipers of pipe bands with dress uniform.

Badges, arm, bandmaster — Embroidered gold and blue thread on cloth the same colour as the jacket: worn by bandmasters in dress uniform.

Badges, arm, RA band — Gold embroidered on cloth the same colour as the jacket; worn by bandsmen, including drummers of bands other than pipe bands when wearing dress uniform.

Chevrons 4-bar (inverted) — (1) Embroidered worsted or drill: worn by Drum majors or Pipe majors in service dress.

(2) Gold embroidered on cloth the same colour as the jacket: worn by Drum majors or Pipe majors wearing dress uniform.

BADGES OF QUALIFICATION

Ammunition Technical Officer/Ammunition Technician — The letter A in a circle from which symbolic flames emanate.

(1) Embroidered: circle, centre flames and A in gold, outer flames in red, the whole on a black background.

(2) Worsted: Circle, centre flames and A in yellow, outer flames in red, the whole on a khaki background.

Assistant Instructors in Gunnery: Warrant officers and NCO's of RNZA wear crossed guns in metal, gilt finish.

Fireman's Badge: Soldiers serving as firemen and volunteer firemen wear a badge in the design of a fireman's helmet over crossed axes with red symbols on a yellow background of embroidered cloth.

RNZASC Driver of the Year Award Badge: RNZASC soldiers who are placed first, second or third in the RNZASC Annual National Driver of the Year Competition wear the badge for one year.

First place: Yellow waggon wheel with numeral '1' placed centrally on the hub.
Second place: Yellow waggon wheel with numeral '2' placed centrally on the hub.

Third place: White waggon wheel with numeral '3' placed centrally on the hub.

Conductor RNZAOC Badge: The appointment of Conductor RNZAOC is denoted by a crimson backing to the metal badge of rank worn by warrant officers. A crimson circle around the Royal Arms within a wreath is worn as a cloth badge. Only five warrant officers class 1 at any one time may be awarded the appointment.

Bomb Disposal: During World War II, those members of 2NZEF in England who were attached to a bomb disposal unit, wore a cloth grenade as a distinguishing badge.

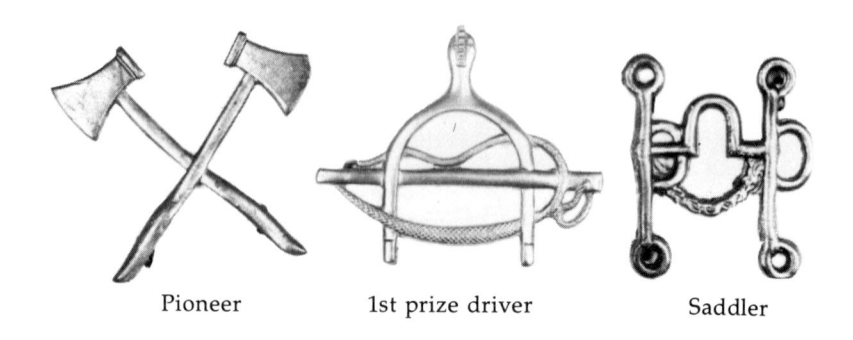

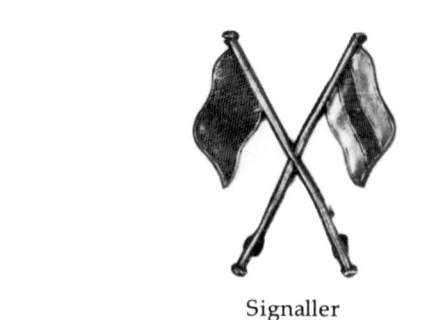

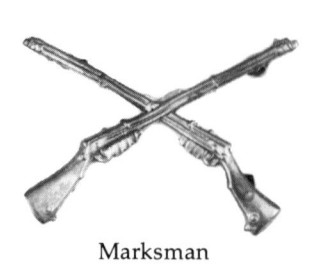

Pioneer   1st prize driver   Saddler

Signaller

Marksman   Qualified instructor

Ammunition
technician

RNZASC
driver of the year

Fireman's
badge

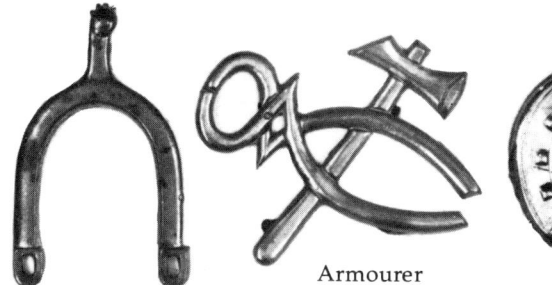

Riding instructor

Armourer

Farrier

BANDSMEN

Piper   Trumpter   Drummer

Camp military bands 1914-1918

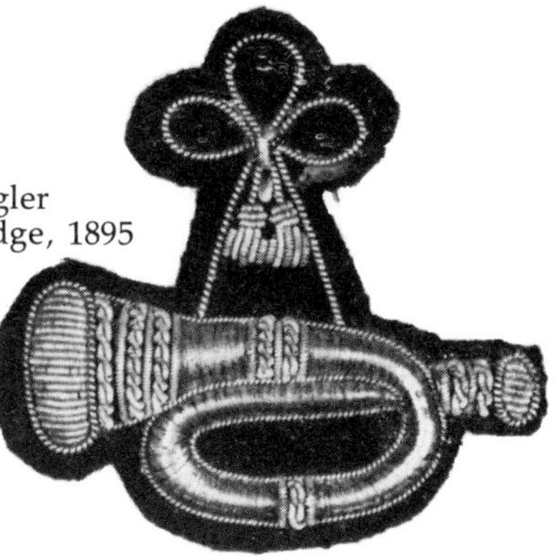

Bugler
cloth badge, 1895

Trumpeter
Boer War period

AUCKLAND MOUNTED RIFLES BAND
The Auckland Mounted Rifles Band became the band of the New Zealand Mounted Rifles Brigade on 10 September 1917 but retained its name. All units of the New Zealand Mounted Rifles Brigade supported the maintenance of the band. Smaller versions of the cap badge were worn as collar badges.

CORPS AND REGIMENTAL DRESS DISTINCTIONS

Royal New Zealand Armoured Corps:
COLOUR PATCH: In honour of 4 (NZ) Armoured Brigade, 2NZEF, a piece of scarlet cloth is worn under the cap and collar badges. As the successor of the N.Z. Divisional Cavalry Regiment 2 (NZ) Division, 2NZEF the officers and men of 1 Armoured Car Regiment (New Zealand Scottish), wore a green cloth patch behind the cap badge.
TANK ARM BADGE: Because of their alliance with the Royal Tank Regiment the RNZAC has permission to wear the RTR Tank Arm badge, in silver embroidery or worsted.
WEBBING: In the tradition of the armoured troops, members of the RNZAC blacken all items of webbing.

Royal New Zealand Artillery:
DISTINGUISHING PATCH: A 2 inch square distinguishing patch worn as a diamond is worn on the corps beret. The upper half in scarlet and the lower half in royal blue, positioned behind the badge.

New Zealand Special Air Service:
WEBBING: to signify the close association with the British SAS members of NZSAS wear black web belts and black anklets.

Royal New Zealand Dental Corps:
CRAVAT: Permission is given to all ranks to wear a cravat in corps colours.

Royal N.Z. Chaplains Department: A strip of purple material ½ inch wide is worn on the shoulder strap, above the shoulder seam and below the badges of rank.

Royal N.Z. Provost Corps: A white lanyard is worn around the left shoulder, this lanyard is attached to a whistle which is worn in the left pocket.

Queen Alexandra's (Waikato/Wellington East Coast) Squadron, Royal New Zealand Armoured Corps: (1) To emphasise the close association between the squadron and the district of Waikato, all ranks of the squadron are permitted to wear a cravat in Waikato colours (red, black and yellow).
(2) As the successor of the Wellington East Coast Mounted Rifles and to perpetuate this association, all ranks are permitted to wear the collar badges of that regiment.

1st and 2nd Squadrons, New Zealand Scottish, RNZAC: (1) Permitted to wear Highland dress, the tartan being that of the Black Watch because of the New Zealand Scottish Squadrons association with that regiment.
(2) Staff sergeant-majors of the New Zealand Scottish squadrons are permitted to wear a grey beret to mark the past affiliation with the Royal Scots Dragoons.

7th Battalion (Wellington (City of Wellington's Own) and Hawke's Bay), RNZIR: The distinctive black blazes of the Rifle Brigade, NZEF worn in WWI, and in WWII by the 19th Battalion 2NZEF, are now worn by the 7th Battalion RNZIR to mark the close association between these corps.

DESCRIPTION	ORIGINAL UNIT	WORN NOW BY
1. An eight pointed star made up of two superimposed squares of 1½ inches	H.Q. NZRB	Battalion HQ and Admin. Company

2. A diamond, 2¼ ins by 1¼ ins with   5th (Reserve)   Support
   longer axis vertical   Battalion NZRB   Company
3. A square with 1½ inch sides worn   1st Battalion NZRB   A Company
   as a diamond
4. A square with 1½ inch sides   2nd Battalion NZRB   B Company
5. An equilateral triangle with   3rd Battalion NZRB   C Company
   height of 1½ inches.
   Apex uppermost
6. An equilateral triangle with   4th Battalion, NZRB   D Company
   height of 1½ inches.
   Base uppermost.

These blazes had originally been inherited by the Wellington Regiment (City of Wellington's Own).

7th Battalion, RNZIR wear the first blaze on their beret, behind the badge.

In addition, in recognition of the Battalion's one hundred years of service, members of the Battalion wear the RNZIR collar badges on all orders of dress (except summer dress), on all occasions.

2nd Battalion (Canterbury and Nelson-Marlborough and West Coast) RNZIR: To mark their alliance with the Royal Irish Fusiliers, members of the 2nd Battalion are permitted to wear the blue bonnet and hackle of the fusiliers.

The Nelson, Marlborough, and West Coast Regiment: To perpetuate a regimental custom dating back to the formation of the 1st Westland Rifles in 1868, members of the regiment were permitted to wear pieces of scarlet cloth behind their cap and collar badges.

1st Battalion, RNZIR and 2nd/1st Battalion, RNZIR: As a symbolic representation of the 22nd Battalion, 2NZEF, members of both battalions wear a 'red diamond'. This diamond is sewn on to the left sleeve, 3½ inches below the epaulette.

FORMATION PATCHES: These patches are circular, one and a half inches in diameter.
   Black: Combat Brigade Group
   Red: Logistic Support Group
   Green: Combat Reserve Brigade Group
   Blue: Home Command Group

EMBLEMS

The wearing of the undermentioned emblems is authorised as follows:
A rose — on Remembrance Sunday.
A poppy — on Anzac Day (25th April).
These emblems will be worn on the left side of the headdress.

COLOURED BERETS
Black: RNZAC.
Blue: RNZA, RNZE, RNZ Signals, RNZASC, RNZAMC, RNZAOC, RNZEME, RNZDC, RNZChD, NZAPC, NZALS, RNZ Pro, RNZAEC, NZAPTC, RF Cadets, NZCC Officers.
Green: RNZIR.
Maroon: NZSAS.
Light blue: NZAAC.
Grey: RNZNC.
Green: NZWRAC.
Distinguishing Patch on the Corps beret (a two-inch square worn as a diamond).

RNZA: A diamond with the upper half in scarlet and the lower half royal blue.
RNZAC: A dark green diamond.
RNZNC: Scarlet diamond.
NZWRAC: Beech brown diamond.

STABLE BELTS

Stable belts may be worn by the following:

Corps

RNZA: RA pattern; red, dark blue and yellow.
RNZAC (except for Queen Alexandra's (Waikato/Wellington East Coast) Squadron) R.T.R. pattern red, brown and green.
RNZE: RE pattern — dark blue and scarlet.
RNZ Sigs: R Sigs pattern — green, dark blue and light blue.
RNZIR: Regular Force personnel — D.L.I. pattern — red and green.
RNZASC: RCT pattern — navy blue with red and white stripes.
RNZAMC: RAMC pattern — cherry, blue and gold.
RNZAOC: RAOC pattern — with RNZAOC badge on the buckle.
RNZEME: REME pattern — dark blue, scarlet and gold.
RNZDC: RADC pattern — green, blue and red.
RNZChD: RAChD pattern — black and purple.
RNZAEC: RAEC pattern — dark blue and light blue.

Regimental

Queen Alexandra's (Waikato/Wellington East Coast) Squadron: 4/7th Royal Dragoon pattern — red, black and yellow.
1st Battalion, RNZIR: DLI pattern — red and green.
2nd Battalion, RNZIR: DLI pattern — red and green.
2nd Canterbury NMWC: Light Infantry pattern — green.
3rd Auckland, Northland: Red, black and white.
4th Otago, Southland: Queen's Own Highlanders pattern — McKenzie tartan.
5th Wellington, West Coast, Taranaki: Royal Hampshire Regiment pattern — black, red, green, purple and yellow.
6th Hauraki: Purple navy, gold and purple navy.
7th Wellington, Hawke's Bay: York and Lancaster Regiment pattern — maroon, white, black and gold.
1st Ranger Squadron: 22nd SAS Regiment pattern — light blue.
RF Cadets School — Post office red.

OFFICERS' GILT BADGES

1st Canterbury Regiment:	Gilt and silver;	K/C or Q/C
3rd Auckland Regiment:	Gilt	K/C or Q/C
5th Wellington Regiment:	Gilt	No crown
6th Hauraki Regiment:	Gilt	No crown
9th Wellington East Coast Regiment:	Gilt	K/C or Q/C
12th and X111th Regiment:	Gilt	K/C or Q/C
13th North Canterbury-Westland Regiment:	Gilt and silver	K/C only
15th Northland Regiment:	Gilt	Q/C only
16th Waikato Regiment:	Gilt and silver	K/C only
Otago-Southland Regiment:	Gilt	No crown
Wellington West Coast Taranaki Regiment:	Gilt and silver	No crown
NZ Army Education Corps:	Gilt and silver	Q/C only
NZ Army Legal Service:	Silver and enamel	Q/C only
NZ Army Nursing Service:	Gilt and enamel	K/C only
	Silver and enamel	K/C only
New Zealand Regiment:	Gilt	K/C only
	Gilt, silver, enamel	Q/C only
New Zealand Staff Corps:	Gilt	K/C only
NZ Women's Royal Army Corps:	Gilt, silver, enamel	Q/C only
RNZ Armoured Crops:	Gilt and silver	K/C or Q/C
RNZ Army Medical Corps	Gilt and silver	K/C or Q/C
RNZ Army Ordnance Corps:	Gilt, silver, enamel	K/C or Q/C
RNZ Army Service Corps:	Gilt, silver, enamel	K/C or Q/C
RNZ Artillery:	Gilt	K/C or Q/C
RNZ Chaplains Department:	Gilt	K/C or Q/C
RNZ Dental Corps:	Gilt and silver	Q/C only
RNZ Electrical Mechanical Engineers:	Gilt and silver	K/C or Q/C
RNZ Engineers:	Gilt, silver, enamel (Collar badges in gilt and silver)	Q/C only
RNZ Nursing Corps:	Gilt and silver	Q/C only
RNZ Provost Corps:	Silver	Q/C only
RNZ Signal Corps:	Gilt and silver	K/C or Q/C

* See page 225 re 12th Nelson-Marlborough Regiment badges.

ANODISED ALUMINIUM BADGES

Produced in England in 1952 and termed 'Staybrite' badges, they eventually replaced the majority of New Zealand badges after 1954. The following list is that of known badges — the term 'gilt' or 'Silver' is used with reference to the colour of the badge, not the metal.

	CAP BADGE	COLLAR BADGE
NZ Army Air Corps:	Silver	Silver
NZ Army Education Corps:	Gilt and silver	Gilt and silver
NZ Regiment:	Gilt	Gilt and silver
NZ Scottish Regiment:		Silver
NZ Special Air Service:		Gilt and silver
NZ Women's Royal Army Corps:	Gilt and silver	Gilt and silver
	Gilt, silver and green	Gilt, silver and green
RNZ Armoured Corps:	Gilt and silver	Gilt and silver
RNZ Army Education Corps:	Gilt and silver	Gilt and silver
RNZ Army Medical Corps:	Gilt	Gilt
	Gilt and silver	Gilt and silver
RNZ Army Ordnance Corps:	Gilt	Gilt
	Gilt, silver, red and blue	As for cap
RNZ Army Service Corps:	Gilt and silver	Gilt and silver
	Gilt, silver, red and blue	As for cap
RNZ Artillery:		Gilt
RNZ Dental Corps:	Gilt and silver	Gilt and silver
NZ Electrical & Mechanical Engineers:	Gilt and silver	Gilt and silver
RNZ Engineers:	Gilt, silver and blue	Gilt
RNZ Infantry Regiment:	Gilt, silver, red and blue	As for cap
RNZ Nursing Corps:	Gilt and silver	
RNZ Provost Corps:	Gilt	Gilt
RNZ Signal Corps:	Gilt and silver	Gilt and silver

CORPS AND REGIMENTAL SHOULDER TITLES (CLOTH)

TITLE	BACKGROUND	LETTERING
Royal New Zealand Artillery	Purple navy	Post Office Red
Royal NZ Armoured Corps	Rifle green	Bunting yellow
New Zealand Scottish	Rifle green	Bunting yellow
New Zealand Scottish Regiment	Rifle green	Bunting yellow
Royal New Zealand Engineers	Post Office red	Purple navy
Royal New Zealand Signals	Spectrum blue	White
Royal New Zealand Infantry Regiment	Post Office red	White
New Zealand Regiment	Post Office red	White
Royal NZ Infantry Corps	Post Office red	White
New Zealand Regiment	Post Office red	White
New Zealand Special Air Service	Maroon	Smalt
New Zealand Army Air Corps	Adonis blue	Indigo
Royal New Zealand Army Service Corps	Midnight blue	Indian Yellow
Royal New Zealand Army Medical Corps	Ruby	Gold
University Medical Unit	Ruby	Gold
Otago University Medical Company	Light blue	Gold
Auckland University Medical Company	Royal blue	White
Royal New Zealand Army Ordnance Corps	Post Office red	Purple navy
Royal NZ Electrical and Mechanical Engineers	Purple navy	Indian yellow
Royal New Zealand Dental Corps	Cossack green	Gold
Royal NZ Chaplains Department	Royal purple	White
NZ Army Pay Corps	Indian yellow	White
NZ Army Legal Service	Maroon	White
Royal New Zealand Provost Corps	Royal blue	White
Royal New Zealand Army Education Corps	Oxford blue	Steel blue
Miles Company, RF Cadets	Black	White
Regular Force Cadets	Post Office red	Black
RF Cadet	Post Office red	Black
Royal New Zealand Nursing Corps	Post Office red	Grebe
New Zealand Women's Royal Army Corps	(1) Beech brown	Dark green
	(2) Tartan Green	White
N.Z. Concert Party	Black	White
Public Relations	Tartan green	Indian yellow
Accredited War Correspondent	Tartan green	Indian yellow
The Band of the New Zealand Army	Red	Yellow
New Zealand Army Band	Red	Yellow
Auckland Regiment (CRO)	Red	White
Hauraki Regiment	Red	White
Northland Regiment	Red	White
Canterbury Regiment	Red	White
Nelson Marlborough and West Coast Regiment	Red	White

YMCA	Black	White
New Zealand YMCA	Black	White
New Zealand Corps of Transport	Navy blue	Yellow
Otago and Southland Regiment	Red	White
Wellington Regiment (CWO)	Red	White
Hawke's Bay Regiment	Red	White
New Zealand	Black	White

This title in a curved form was first worn by the British Section, NZEF in England in 1914.

NZ Women's Land Army	Brown	Bottle green
Cadet Corps		

Secondary School Cadet Corps were given permission to wear a shoulder title; the background and lettering on the title to represent the school colours

Home Guard	Black	White

TITLES WORN OUTSIDE NEW ZEALAND:

New Zealand	Purple navy	Gold
New Zealand	Black	White
New Zealand	Khaki	White

Worn by Nursing Aids (VAD's)

Shoulder titles are normally in a curved pattern, but that of the Home Guard was worn as a straight title.

NEW ZEALAND PUGGAREES

The puggaree was the coloured cloth band worn on the 'lemon-squeezer' hat, the colours of the band identifying the regiment or corps.
Staff Corps: red.
Ceremonial Guards: red.
EIIR Coronation Contingent: red
Artillery: dark blue, scarlet, dark blue.
Mounted Rifles: khaki, green, khaki.
Armoured Corps: khaki, green, khaki.
Engineers: khaki, dark blue, khaki.
Signals: Prior to 1920 wore Engineer pattern. (1) khaki, light blue, khaki; (2) khaki, half white, half light blue, khaki (1935); (3) light blue, dark blue, light blue.
Infantry: khaki, scarlet, khaki.
Army Service Corps: khaki, white, khaki.
Medical Corps: khaki, dull cherry, khaki.
Veterinary Corps: khaki, maroon, khaki.
Ordnance Corps: scarlet, dark blue, scarlet.
Electrical and Mechanical Engineers: (1) red, green, red; (2) dark blue, yellow, scarlet.
Dental Corps: (1) green, khaki, green; (2) dark blue, peacock green, dark blue.
Cyclists Corps: khaki, green, khaki.
Chaplains Department: khaki, edged with black.
Pay Corps: khaki, yellow, khaki.
Provost Corps: dark blue.
Education Corps: dark blue, light blue, dark blue.
Regular Force Cadets: (1) khaki with small black diamond on each side (1949); (2) red, khaki, red (1952).
Unposted Regular Force recruits: black.
Unposted Territorial Force Cadets: khaki, green, khaki.
Officer Cadet Training Unit: white.
Postal Corps: khaki, light blue, khaki.
YMCA: black, white, black.
War Correspondents: green.
Fanning Island Infantry: red, khaki, red.
Cadet Corps: wore the puggaree of the corps to which they were attached. In 1920 they used a green puggaree. In 1927 the Cadet Corps puggaree was khaki. In 1948 the Regular Force Cadets wore a beret with a black diamond. In 1949 when the corps was issued with 'lemon squeezers' they wore a khaki puggaree with a miniature black diamond on each side.
Secondary School Cadets: Approval was given for these cadets to wear a puggaree consisting of the school colours. Because of the expense, many schools elected to wear the universal green puggaree of 1920, with the school badge on the front of the hat and a diamond-shaped patch containing the school colours on each side of the hat.
Home Service Branch, NZEF: khaki, black, khaki.

SERVICE DRESS AND FELT HATS
The Mounted Rifles wore a slouch hat dented with the crease running from front to rear and the brim turned up at the left side. This was the style used in South Africa and when the first troops went overseas in 1914. After the

Gallipoli landing they wore cork helmets for a period but again wore the slouch hat in Sinai and Palestine. After the war it was decided to wear the brim horizontal.

Other units wore the slouch hat dented in the same manner but with the brim horizontal although the Wellington Battalion in 1914 wore their hats peaked. On Gallipoli all troops other than the mounteds wore a peaked forage cap. In the re-organisation after Gallipoli, Major-General Godley issued a directive that all troops, other than the mounteds, would wear their hats with the brim horizontal and the crown peaked, and this began the 'lemon-squeezer' era.

In 1958 the service dress hats on which coloured hatbands were worn, were withdrawn from issue and replaced by a battledress cap as standard New Zealand Army headdress.

The Band of the RNZA was the only unit still wearing (1970) service dress hats and still wears the RNZA puggaree.

The band of the RNZA wore the service dress, hat and RNZA pugaree until 1971.

On 22 February 1977, to commemorate the Royal visit to New Zealand the service dress hat was reintroduced for wear by members of the Honour Guard. The badge was that of the 2NZEF but with a replacement crown of the St. Edward pattern. The pugaree consisted of four bands of pleated scarlet cloth. This badge is now worn by the Officer Cadet Corps at Waiouru Military Camp.

THE NEW ZEALAND MILITIA BATTALIONS

THE MILITIA ACT of 25 March 1845 gave the first official approval of the need to train the European population of New Zealand in the use of arms and the formation of an effective military force with which to defend the lives and property of Her Majesty's subjects within the colony. The Act was in effect a compulsory military system with no provision for volunteers.

In brief, the main clauses of the Act empowered the Governor to:
1. Call and arm the Militia for 28 days in each year.
2. Appoint the officers.
3. Call for service all male inhabitants between the ages of 18 and 60 years, with the exception of judges, members of the Legislative Council, Maoris and clergymen.
4. Call out the Militia for actual service, but the service was limited to a distance of 25 miles from the settlement.
5. Police Magistrates and Justices of the Peace were required to post a militia list in March of each year; the list to be displayed on the door of either the court house or the post office.
6. Militia units could be formed only if the Governor considered that there was a possibility of any emergency in the district.

The Second Militia Act of 28 May 1858 contained a clause which permitted the Governor to define the military districts within the colony. This Act contained the provision for the enrolment of volunteers, as distinct from militia, for military or naval service in the colony.

The Militia Act Amendment of 3 November 1860 defined the classes of militiamen as follows:

FIRST CLASS: Unmarried men or widowers without children; between the ages of 16 years and 40 years.

SECOND CLASS: Married men or widowers with children; between the ages of 16 years and 40 years.

THIRD CLASS: All men between the ages of 40 years and 55 years; these men were to be called 'Reserve men'.

In addition, this Act gave permission for the majority of any company of volunteers to recommend to the Governor, persons to be appointed as officers in such a company. Members of any company of volunteer firemen embodied with the approval of the Governor for this purpose, were exempted from service in the militia.

The Militia Act Amendment of 15 September 1862 allowed officers of volunteers enrolled under the provisions of the Militia Act of 1858 to rank with officers of militia according to the dates of their respective commissions.

The militia units which had been formed after the passing of the Militia Act of 1845 were limited in their activities to a distance of 25 miles from their place of registration and this limitation meant that for the most part they were used for garrison duties, a notable exception being the engagement of the militia in the battle fought at Waireka on 28 March 1860.

In order to have a more mobile force at their disposal, the Government approved the formation of special volunteer forces known as the 'Special Militia' and 'Military Settlers'. This latter defence force was organised on the basis that men could be induced to join the force if they were promised a land grant after the hostilities had ceased. These land grants were given only to

those men who enlisted before 1 April 1865, the grant being reduced to three-quarters of the original amount for those who joined the force after that date. The original land grants were:
> Field Captains: 400 acres; Captains: 300 acres; Surgeons: 250 acres; Subalterns: 200 acres; Sergeants: 80 acres; Corporals: 60 acres; Privates: 50 acres.

The land grant consisted of confiscated Maori land. Each man was given an allotment of one acre on the site where it was proposed to build a township, the remainder of the land grant being for farming allotments in the neighbouring district.

North Island Militia Companies

Auckland Militia: On 12 April 1845, thirty-two officers were appointed to the Auckland Militia. The Auckland Militia Battalion was gazetted on 9 August 1845. Second Battalion was formed on 12 November 1858 and the Auckland Country Battalion was formed on 13 January 1859. With the formation of a Fourth Battalion on 18 April 1860, the title of the Auckland Militia was changed to the Auckland Regiment of Militia.
> 1st Battalion at Albert Barracks; 2nd Battalion at Onehunga; 3rd Battalion at Otahuhu; 4th Battalion at North Shore.

The 1st Battalion was initially divided into five companies and on 10 July 1861 was divided into nine companies, at which time the 2nd Battalion was divided into five companies. On 14 July 1861, the 3rd Battalion was divided into five companies. The Auckland District Militia were called out for training and exercise on 15 January 1863 and were called for service on 23 June 1863. At this time the strength of the Auckland Militia was four hundred men. The Militia were again called for service on 8 July and took part in the actions during July at Papakura (Kirikiri) and at Drury (Pukekiwirika). On 8 August the Third Class Militia were called for service and were in action on 14 September at Pukekohe. Auckland Militia took part in the action at Orakau Pa from 30 March until 2 April 1864.

Bay of Islands District and Militia: Gazetted on 27 February 1860.

Napier Battalion of Militia: Accepted on 13 January 1859, the District being extended on 5 December. The Battalion was called for training on 26 June 1863 and divided into seven companies on 21 July. Napier Militia were released from active service on 3 May 1869.

New Plymouth Battalion of Militia: Gazetted on 12 November 1855 and disbanded on 31 August 1858. The Province of New Plymouth became the Province of Taranaki on 1 January 1858 resulting in the formation of the Taranaki Militia.

Patea District (Taranaki) Militia: Accepted on 5 April 1867 and were called out for active service on the same date.

Rangitikei Militia Battalion: Gazetted on 5 February 1864.

Taranaki Battalion of Militia: Gazetted on 13 January 1859 and on 28 March 1860 fought a battle at Waireka which resulted in the granting of the first battle honour to be awarded to a New Zealand unit. Although the battalion endeavoured to obtain the battle honour 'Waireka' this was not approved but the honour 'New Zealand' was granted and was passed down to the Taranaki Regiment. The battle at Waireka was the first occasion in which a British Volunteer Corps had engaged the enemy on a battlefield. On 6 May 1861 the battalion was designated the Taranaki Regiment of Militia. They were in action on 16 September 1863 at Poutoko, and on 29 September at Bell Block where they were engaged again on 19 January 1864. Further actions took place at Kaitake on 11 March and from 20-26 March at Kaitake, Oakura, Tutu and

Ahu-ahu. Engagements took place at Kaitake on 23 April at Sentry Hill, and at Manutahi on 8 September. On 12 January 1867 the Northern, Middle and Southern Districts of Taranaki were gazetted at which time the Middle District Militia were released from active service.

Waikato Militia: Raised in Australia in September 1863 by Lieut-Colonel G. D. Pitt of the New Zealand Militia. The first draft of 400 men was known as 'Pitt's Militia'.

Some 2,500 men were recruited in Australia and formed the greater part of the four regiments of Waikato Militia. They were in action at Titi Hill on 23 October 1863 and on 21 April 1864 at Waihi. The militia were in the engagement at Pukehinahina (Tauranga) and Te Ranga on 21 June 1864. Major W. V. Herford, 2nd Regiment Waikato Militia, the Senior Colonial Officer, died on 28 June 1864 from wounds received in the attack on Orakau Pa. Each regiment comprised ten companies, each company consisting of one hundred men. The 1st Regiment were to become the first Colonial troops to take part in a charge in line with British Regulars, the 43rd and 68th Regiments, in the assault at Te Ranga on 21 June 1864. Many of the Militia elected to serve with the Imperial Commissariat Corps, serving as clerks, storekeepers, issuers, butchers, bakers, labourers and boatmen. For their service, they were paid by the Imperial Government. Major-General T. J. Galloway who had arrived in New Zealand in 1861 as Colonel of the 70th Regiment was appointed Commander of Militia and Volunteers in the Province of Auckland on 22 July 1863. Colonel T. M. Haultain was appointed Commandant of all Waikato Militia in February 1865.

Wairarapa Militia: Gazetted on 27 February 1860. The militia were called out for training on 26 June 1863 and were designated a regiment on 6 July. The formation of the Wairarapa Battalion had included both the Wairarapa and Castlepoint District Militia but this was altered on 20 November 1868 when a separate Castlepoint District Militia was gazetted.

Wanganui Militia: Gazetted on 27 February 1860. The Wanganui Battalion was formed into a regiment on 6 May 1861 and was called out for training on 26 June 1863. This Militia took part in the engagement at Kaitake on 23 April 1864.

Wellington Militia: Seventeen officers were appointed to the Wellington Militia on 23 July 1845. A second battalion of militia was formed in Wellington on 13 January 1859. This battalion took the title of 2nd (Hutt and Wainuiomata) Battalion of Militia. It was eventually divided into two separate divisions, the Upper Hutt Militia and the Lower Hutt Militia. Wellington Militia were called out for training on 26 June 1863 and again on 23 December. The Wellington District Militia were released from active service on 16 April 1869.

Whangarei Militia: Gazetted on 27 February 1860.

When the Waikato regiments were disbanded on 31 October 1867, their place was taken by new companies which were part of the 4th Battalion, Auckland Militia.

South Island Militia Companies
Christchurch Militia: Gazetted on 28 June 1859. The Battalion was gazetted as a regiment on 6 May 1861.
Dunedin Militia: The Battalion was gazetted as a regiment on 6 May 1861.
Invercargill Militia: Gazetted on 27 February 1860.
Marlborough Militia: Gazetted on 27 February 1860, the Battalion being divided into four companies on 5 September 1861.
No. 1 (Blenheim) Company.
No. 2 (Picton) Company.
No. 3 (Waihopai) Company.
No. 4 (Awatere) Company.
Nelson Militia: Nine officers were appointed to the Nelson Militia on 27 August 1845. This battalion of militia was the first New Zealand army unit to be formed in the South Island. The Battalion consisted of two companies, each of fifty men.
Otago Militia: Gazetted on 27 February 1860.
South Otago Militia: Formed on 6 May 1861 with three companies.
1st (Victoria) Company at Tokomairiro.
2nd (Prince of Wales) Company at Inchclutha.
3rd (Albert) Company at Warepa.
The Defence Act of 1862 had empowered the Government to raise a force of five hundred if necessary, to be sent to any part of the colony. This 'Special Force' was to be capable of dealing with insurrection at any of the trouble spots within the colony. With the enactment of the Armed Constabulary Act of 1 November 1867, most of the men of this 'Special Force' were transferred into the new corps.

With the formation of the Armed Constabulary in 1867 a start was made to disband all militia and by July 1872 all militiamen were released from any further service.

Taranaki Militia pouch badge
A similar badge 'A.M.' was worn by Auckland Militia

New Zealand Militia waist-belt plate

NEW ZEALAND MILITIA

THE PERMANENT FORCE for defence within the colony was the New Zealand Militia. Officers transferring to this corps from either the militia regiments or battalions or from the various volunteer corps had their local rank in these forces converted to substantive rank in the New Zealand Militia. Edward McKenna who had been awarded the Victoria Cross while serving as a colour-sergeant in the 65th Regiment was appointed as ensign in the New Zealand Militia on 14 December 1865.

The Staff Officers wore the uniform as defined in the 'Dress Regulations for Her Majesty's Militia Service' until 1883 when distinctive badges were worn.
FORAGE CAP: Blue cloth, with gold-embroidered drooping peak, and a band of 1¾ inch lace; gold-purl button and braided figure on the crown, with the letters 'N.Z.M.' in gold on the front.
HELMET: White, with gold-gilt front plate, star and Garter surmounted by crown, with *Honi soit qui mal y pense* around Garter, and the letter 'M' in centre. The helmet had a spike on top, and chin chain.
SHOULDER STRAP: A gold embroidery letter 'M' worn below rank badge.
WAIST-BELT PLATE: A mounted device of Royal Arms within a crowned Garter and an open wreath of roses, thistle and shamrock on a scroll bearing the letters 'N.Z.M.'

The designation of the New Zealand Permanent Militia was altered as per the General Order No. 37 of 1903. This order stated that "The New Zealand Permanent Militia is now known as the New Zealand Permanent Force. The No. 1 Service Company will in future be designated the 'Royal New Zealand Artillery' and the No. 2 Service Company will in future be designated the 'Royal New Zealand Engineers', as from 15 October 1902."

This was the first occasion on which the title 'Royal' was granted to a New Zealand army unit and was given with the approval of His Majesty, King Edward VII.

ARMED CONSTABULARY

CAPTAIN D. S. Durie was appointed the first Inspector of Police on 9 April 1846, his previous appointment being that of a captain in the Wellington Militia. Captain Atkyns was appointed inspector when a similar force was authorised for Auckland on 4 May 1846. Thus the Armed Police, the first armed force raised in New Zealand to keep the peace and apprehend offenders, were an effective body before they were duly authorised in October 1846.

The Forest Rangers raised on 31 July 1863 were disbanded in November as the corps proved to be too expensive to maintain. Raised again in December 1863 this corps was absorbed by the Armed Constabulary when it was formed since it was recognised that the Rangers were the undoubted masters in bush fighting in New Zealand.

The Armed Constabulary Act of 1 November 1867 formed a constabulary which was modelled on the Royal Irish Constabulary, a force which had proved to be most effective in the Colony of Victoria, Australia. The Armed Constabulary Field Force with nine divisions of eighty men each, became the fighting force in the colony and were recognised with the award of nine New Zealand Crosses. This force served mainly in the North Island although one division went to the West Canterbury goldfields to restore order. The Arawa Flying Column harried the Maori forces until the war ended on 14 February 1872.

With the formation of this new force, the four regiments of Waikato Militia, ten companies of Taranaki Military Settlers and the Hawke's Bay Military Settlers were disbanded on 31 October 1867. Nos. 4 and 5 Divisions, Armed Constabulary were formed in February 1868 in the Waikato under the command of Lieut-Colonel Moule and Major Von Tempsky, both of whom were given a new title; that of Inspector. No. 5 Division was disbanded on 1 October 1868 for mutinous conduct in the field, after the death of Von Tempsky and their refusal to serve under a British officer.

In 1881 the force was designated 'The New Zealand Constabulary', and all military officers were transferred to the militia.

The defence force was reorganised with the Defence Act of 1886, resulting in all ex-members of the Armed Constabulary serving in the Engineers, Artillery, Rifle or Torpedo Corps being transferred to the Permanent Militia. There were ten companies of rifles (Major Tuke), which were disbanded in 1892.

The Permanent Militia were designated the 'Permanent Force' on 15 October 1902 at which time the two service companies of the Permanent Militia were designated: No. 1 Service Company designated Royal New Zealand Artillery; No. 2 Service Company designated Royal New Zealand Engineers.

The Army Act of 1950 changed the title of the Permanent Force to the Regular Force.

First pattern

Badge worn after 1881

A white metal numeral was worn above the 1st pattern badge as the identification numeral of the constable.

Otago Armed Constabulary wore a badge similar to the first pattern but with the scroll 'Otago Armed Constabulary' and a white metal waist-belt clasp with Victorian Crown surrounded by the words 'Otago Armed Constabulary Force'.

Showing the development or the New Zealand Police badges from the first pattern used by the Armed Constabulary in 1881.

VOLUNTEER CORPS

THE MILITIA ACT of 28 May 1858 gave Government approval for the acceptance of volunteer corps, as distinct from the militia, in order to preserve peace within the colony. Volunteers had been engaged at Kororareka in March 1845, seventy-five Auckland Volunteers took part in the unsuccessful British assaults on Ohaeawai Pa in June-July 1845, and fifty men were raised as a Pioneer Corps in December 1845 to serve with Colonel Despard. These corps were never considered to be more than a token force and although these actions were the beginning of the history of the New Zealand Army, they have since received scant recognition.

The earliest volunteer commission is dated 8 December 1845, the Auckland Rifle Volunteers forming with two companies on 13 December 1845, so these dates should have made these volunteers the senior infantry of the New Zealand Army. The significance of the Volunteer Act of 30 October 1865 was not understood by many volunteer corps. This Act required all volunteer corps to re-register within a period of sixty days or the corps would be disbanded. Seniority of all corps in the New Zealand Army is dated 1 January 1866 and those corps which failed to re-register within the prescribed period lost the recognition they should still have. With the acceptance of Canterbury Rifles and Christchurch City Guards as first to register this gave their descendant Regiment (Canterbury) the right to become the senior infantry regiment.

Taranaki Rifle Volunteers earned the battle honour 'Waireka' for their part in the action at Waireka, New Plymouth, in March 1860. This actual honour was not granted but was later changed to 'New Zealand' and was carried on the colours of the Taranaki Regiment, the only New Zealand infantry unit to be awarded such honour. An officer of the Auckland Rifle Volunteers who held a militia commission was the first colonial officer to be awarded the Victoria Cross.

An engagement at Mangaone, south of Waikaremoana, on 11 February 1872 heralded the end of the wars in New Zealand with the last shot being fired on that date. With a comparative peace descending on the colony there was little need for the volunteers and the majority of the units were disbanded. The Government was not willing to spend money on defence and the volunteer Forces were without guidance. Employers were reluctant to excuse men for military training, so that the men themselves had to make real sacrifices in both time and money, since the capitation grants made by the Government did not pay for all necessary equipment. In 1879 the City Guards was the only surviving rifle company in North Canterbury, so low had the morale of the volunteers fallen due to Government neglect and discouragement. Volunteers were called upon for service during the Parihaka crisis in October 1881. This force under the command of Lieutenant-Colonel Roberts NZC had a strength of nine hundred and fifty Volunteers, six hundred and thirty Armed Constabulary and was supported by the Thames Scottish Corps and the Taranaki Mounted Rifles. Although the incident was resolved without a shot being fired, the Government and the people were made aware of the value of the Volunteer Corps.

Volunteers enlisted in all contingents which were sent to the war in South Africa, a service recognised by the granting of the battle honour 'South Africa' to most regiments when they were formed in 1911.

General issue Helmet plate

The Regulations of 22 November 1882 introduced a general pattern helmet plate known as the 'Bugle Horn' plate. This was worn by all rifle corps with the initials of the corps worked in white worsted on the shoulder straps. *(See opposite page.)*

The 'Bugle Horn' was worn as a pouch badge as from 1889 by the mounted rifles and the rifle corps. From September 1895 all mounted rifles and rifle corps wore the 'Bugle Horn' as a cap badge with smaller matching pairs as collar badges. Many corps wore the bugle collar badges until the introduction of the territorial regiments in 1911.

This helmet plate was worn by Waimea Rifle Volunteers with the circlet bearing the words 'Waimea Rifles' and by Stoke Rifle Volunteers with the circlet bearing the words 'Stoke Volunteer Rifles'.

Volunteer Helmet plates

A standard pattern was introduced in 1895 for those corps which did not apply to have a specific design and as a replacement helmet plate for the British Rifle Corps general pattern which had been worn since 1882. The use of this plate was discontinued in 1911.

59

New Zealand Volunteer Officers' badges

Volunteer Corps glengarry badges

New Zealand Rifle Clubs
Embodied in the Defence Force of New Zealand under the Regulations of 17 April 1901, the Rifle Clubs formed a reserve force for the volunteers and were distinguished by a brass shoulder title with the letters 'NZRC'.

Cross-belt plate, New Zealand Volunteers

Rutland Company, Auckland Rifles

Volunteer badges c1895
(cap badge 95mm)

Volunteer badge c1900
(cap badge 87mm)

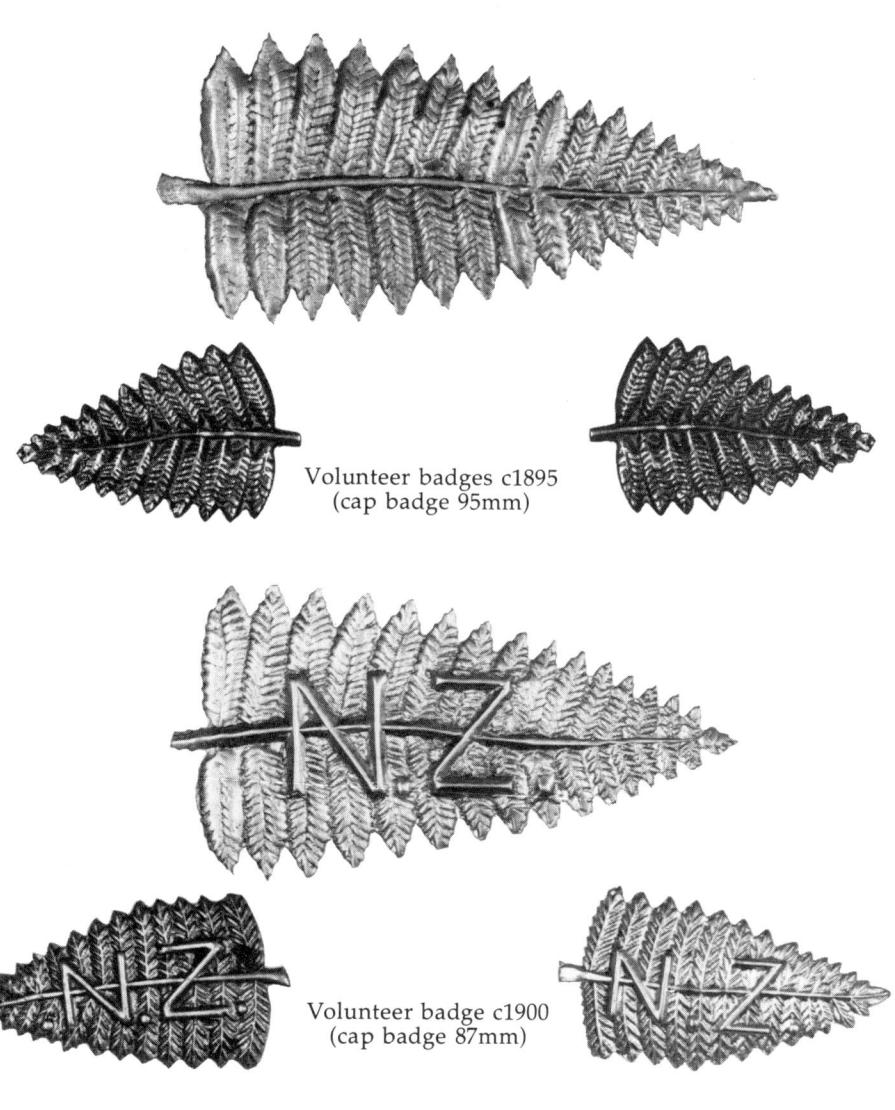

Volunteer pouch badge 1889

1st REGIMENT OF NEW ZEALAND CAVALRY VOLUNTEERS

The several corps of cavalry volunteers in the North Island were formed into the 1st Regiment of New Zealand Cavalry Volunteers on 6 July 1887. They were permitted to wear a uniform after the pattern of the 14th Hussars.
A Troop — Waiuku Cavalry Volunteers
B Troop — Alexandra Cavalry Volunteers
C Troop — Wairoa Light Horse Volunteers
D Troop — Te Awamutu Cavalry Volunteers
E Troop — Heretaunga Cavalry Volunteers
F Troop — Rangitikei Cavalry Volunteers
G Troop — Auckland Cavalry Volunteers (No. 2 Troop). This troop was disbanded on 3 November 1887
H Troop — Auckland Royal Dragoons (added on 13 July 1887)
   The regiment as such was disbanded on 1 January 1889.

WEST COAST (NORTH ISLAND) BATTALION OF RIFLE VOLUNTEERS

Formed on 30 March 1886. Disbanded on 1 January 1889.
Right Wing: Taranaki Rifle Volunteers, Patea Rifle Volunteers, Inglewood Rifle Volunteers, Hawera Rifle Volunteers.
Left Wing: Royal (Rangitikei) Rifle Volunteers, Wanganui Rifle Volunteers, Wanganui City Rifle Volunteers, Palmerston North Rifle Volunteers, Manchester Rifle Volunteers.

Order of Precedence of New Zealand Volunteer Corps

THE VOLUNTEER ACT of 3 February 1866 gave the following pattern in the establishing of the first order of precedence in the Volunteer Force:
Light Horse Volunteers
Artillery Volunteers
Engineer Volunteers
Rifle Volunteers
Naval Volunteers

In 1872 a complete revision to the order of precedence was made, a revision which resulted in the following order:

Artillery Volunteers
Lyttelton Artillery Volunteers
Dunedin Artillery Volunteers
Timaru Artillery Volunteers
Wellington Artillery Volunteers
Christchurch Artillery Volunteers
Auckland Artillery Volunteers
Napier Artillery Volunteers

Engineer Volunteers
No. 1 Company, Canterbury Engineer Volunteers
No. 2 Company, Canterbury Engineer Volunteers
Thames Engineer Volunteers
Auckland Engineer Volunteers

Rifle Volunteers
Hutt Rifle Volunteers
Napier Rifle Volunteers
No. 2 Company, Auckland Rifle Brigade
No. 3 Company, Auckland Rifle Brigade
No. 4 Company, Auckland Rifle Brigade
No. 6 Company, Auckland Rifle Brigade
Featherston Rifle Volunteers
No. 5 Company, Auckland Rifle Volunteers
Wairoa (Auckland) Rifle Volunteers
Greytown Rifle Volunteers
Riverton Rifle Volunteers
No. 4 Company (Rangiora) Canterbury Rifle Volunteers
Masterton Rifle Volunteers
Porirua Rifle Volunteers
No. 1 Company, Auckland Rifle Volunteers
Taita Rifle Volunteers
Carterton Rifle Volunteers
No. 5 Company, Canterbury Rifle Volunteers
City Guards, Canterbury Rifle Volunteers
Union (Rangitikei) Rifle Volunteers
No. 1 Company City Guards, 1st Battalion, Otago Rifle Volunteers
No. 2 Company (Scottish), 1st Battalion, Otago Rifle Volunteers
North Dunedin Company, 1st Battalion, Otago Rifle Volunteers
Waikari Rifle Rangers Company, 1st Battalion, Otago Rifle Volunteers
South District Rifle Rangers Company, 1st Battalion, Otago Rifle Volunteers
Bruce Rifle Volunteers
East Taieri Rifle Volunteers

Oamaru Rifle Volunteers
Royal (Rangitikei) Rifle Volunteers
Turakina Rifle Volunteers
Waimea West (Nelson) Rifle Volunteers
No. 9 Company (Woodend), Canterbury Rifle Volunteers
West Taieri Rifle Volunteers
Wairoa (Hawke's Bay) Rifle Volunteers
Invercargill Rifle Volunteers
No. 1 Company, Wellington Rifle Volunteers
Wellington Veteran Volunteers
Waikouaiti Rifle Volunteers
1st Westland Rifle Volunteers
Greymouth Rifle Rangers
Temuka Rifle Volunteers
Totara Rifle Volunteers
Wairoa (Patea) Rifle Volunteers
Prince Alfred (Marlborough) Rifle Volunteers
Picton Company, Marlborough Rifle Rangers
Wanganui Veteran Volunteers
No. 2 Company, Canterbury Rifle Volunteers
Forest (Waiuku) Rifle Volunteers
Makara Rifle Volunteers
Thames Scottish Rifle Volunteers
No. 1 Company, Waiuku Rifle Volunteers
No. 1 Company, Pukekohe Rifle Volunteers
No. 1 Company, Hauraki Rifle Volunteers
No. 2 Company, Hauraki Rifle Volunteers
Thames Rifle Rangers
Pokeno Rifle Rangers
No. 3 Company, Hauraki Rifle Volunteers
Wainuiomata Rifle Volunteers
Hampden Rifle Rangers
Clutha District Rifle Volunteers
Pauatahanui Rifle Volunteers
Karori Rifle Volunteers
Manukau Rifle Volunteers
Spring Creek Company, Marlborough Rangers
Egmont Rifle Volunteers
Wanganui Rifle Volunteers
Manawatu Rifle Rangers
Nelson (City) Rifle Volunteers
Marton Rifle Volunteers
Onehunga Rifle Volunteers
No. 2 Company, Pukekohe Rifle Volunteers
No. 2 Company, Waiuku Rifle Volunteers
Auckland Scottish Rifle Volunteers
Naval Volunteers
Auckland Naval Volunteers
Dunedin Naval Volunteers
Port Chalmers Naval Volunteers
Thames Naval Volunteers

Order of Precedence of New Zealand Volunteer Corps
(as at July 1903 — giving dates of acceptance)

New Zealand Garrison Artillery
No. 1 Company (Auckland) 20 February 1866
No. 2 Company (Dunedin) 20 February 1866
No. 3 Company (Port Chalmers) 28 February 1866
No. 4 Company (Wellington) 24 March 1879
No. 5 Company (Lyttelton) 6 September 1880
No. 6 Company (Petone) 1 January 1883
No. 7 Company (Lyttelton) 10 April 1885
No. 8 Company (Ponsonby) 22 April 1885
No. 9 Company (Devonport) 10 February 1898
No. 10 Company (Westport) 29 August 1885
Mounted Rifle Volunteers
Canterbury Yeomanry Cavalry 13 February 1866
Alexandra Mounted Rifles 8 December 1868
Wairoa Mounted Rifles 10 February 1871
Otago Hussars 1 January 1883
Heretaunga Mounted Rifles 1 January 1885
Canterbury Mounted Rifles (Christchurch) 11 April 1885
Marlborough Mounted Rifles 8 May 1885
Hawera Mounted Rifles 31 July 1885
North Otago Mounted Rifles (Oamaru) 22 January 1887
No. 1 Company Waikato Mounted Rifles (Hamilton) 22 March 1887
Manawatu Mounted Rifles (Palmerston North) 28 May 1891
Piako Mounted Rifles 15 September 1892
Southland Mounted Rifles (Invercargill) 23 December 1895
Clutha Mounted Rifles (Balclutha) 2 June 1898
No. 2 Company Waikato Mounted Rifles (Te Awamutu) 28 July 1898
Ellesmere Mounted Rifles (Leeston) 5 August 1898
South Canterbury Mounted Rifles (Timaru) 20 September 1898
Auckland Mounted Rifles 31 October 1898
No. 3 Company Waikato Mounted Rifles (Cambridge) 28 October 1899
Wairarapa Mounted Rifles (Papawai) 19 August 1899
Kaikoura Mounted Rifles 28 October 1899
Mataura Mounted Rifles 2 February 1900
East Coast Mounted Rifles (Gisborne) 6 February 1900
Wakatu Mounted Rifles (Nelson) 10 March 1900
Ashburton Mounted Rifles 20 March 1900
Stratford Mounted Rifles 27 March 1900
Pahiatua Mounted Rifles 5 April 1900
Marsden Mounted Rifles (Whangarei) 5 April 1900
Takaka Mounted Rifles 5 April 1900
South Wairarapa Mounted Rifles (Carterton) 5 April 1900
Horowhenua Mounted Rifles 11 April 1900
Otaki Mounted Rifles 11 April 1900
Malvern Mounted Rifles (Waddington) 11 April 1900
Amuri Mounted Rifles (Waiau) 11 April 1900
Maniototo Mounted Rifles (Ranfurly) 11 April 1900
Opunake Mounted Rifles 11 April 1900
Ruahine Mounted Rifles (Dannevirke) 11 April 1900

Pukekohe Mounted Rifles 11 April 1900
Hawke's Bay Mounted Rifles (Hastings) 11 April 1900
Waimakiriri Mounted Rifles (West Melton) 14 April 1900
Cust Mounted Rifles 6 May 1900
Ahuriri Mounted Rifles (Napier) 8 May 1900
Mackenzie Mounted Rifles (Fairlie) 8 May 1900
North Canterbury Mounted Rifles (Tuahiwi) 8 May 1900
Studholme Mounted Rifles (Waimate) 9 May 1900
Seddon Horse Mounted Rifles (Auckland) 9 May 1900
Franklin Mounted Rifles (Clevedon) 16 May 1900
Tuapeka Mounted Rifles (Lawrence) 28 June 1900
Otamatea Mounted Rifles (Maungaturoto) 10 September 1900
Tauranga Mounted Rifles (Tauranga) 10 September 1900
Waiuku Mounted Rifles (Waiuku) 10 September 1900
Raglan Mounted Rifles (Raglan) 10 September 1900
Hokianga Mounted Rifles (Waimamaku) 10 September 1900
Mangonui Mounted Rifles (Mangonui) 10 September 1900
Taieri Mounted Rifles (Outram) 10 September 1900
Eketahuna Mounted Rifles (Eketahuna) 10 September 1900
Motueka Mounted Rifles 10 September 1900
Opotiki Mounted Rifles 10 September 1900
Wakatipu Mounted Rifles (Arrowtown) 10 September 1900
Hunterville Mounted Rifles 10 September 1900
Whakatane Mounted Rifles 10 September 1900
Egmont Mounted Rifles (Okato) 10 September 1900
Kelso Mounted Rifles 10 September 1900
Huramua Mounted Rifles (Wairoa, Hawke's Bay) 10 September 1900
Masterton Mounted Rifles 10 September 1900
Northern Wairoa Mounted Rifles (Aratapu) 22 October 1900
Geraldine Mounted Rifles 9 December 1900
Murihiku Mounted Rifles (Wyndham) 26 March 1901
Wallace Mounted Rifles (Nightcaps) 13 April 1901
Feilding Mounted Rifles 27 July 1901
Waitaki Mounted Rifles (Oamaru) 20 August 1901
Rodney Mounted Rifles (Warkworth) 6 March 1902
New Zealand Field Artillery Volunteers
A Battery, Auckland 20 February 1866
B Battery, Dunedin 28 February 1866
D Battery, Wellington 22 July 1867
E Battery, Christchurch 31 December 1867
H Battery, Nelson 21 March 1873
New Zealand Engineer Volunteers
Canterbury 27 April 1885
Dunedin 30 April 1885
Auckland 8 November 1898
Wellington 1 August 1900
Devonport Naval Submarine Mining Volunteers, Auckland 7 July 1894
Wellington Submarine Mining Volunteers 20 November 1900
Rifle Volunteers
Victoria (Auckland) 15 February 1866
Christchurch City Guards 27 February 1866
Dunedin City Guards 28 February 1866
Bruce (Milton) 28 February 1866

East Taieri (Mosgiel) 28 February 1866
North Dunedin 28 February 1866
Royal (Marton) 28 February 1866
Timaru City 31 October 1866
Invercargill City Guards 23 July 1867
Wellington City 29 October 1867
1st Westland (Hokitika) 13 March 1868
Temuka 28 March 1868
Napier Guards 23 August 1869
No. 1 Company Thames Rifle Volunteers 8 October 1869
Wanganui 6 December 1870
Oreti (Invercargill) 19 January 1872
Stoke 5 April 1873
Queen's (Oamaru) 1 July 1875
Taranaki (New Plymouth) 23 March 1876
Blenheim 23 March 1876
Napier 5 March 1878
Palmerston North 2 January 1879
Waimea 5 May 1879
Manchester (Feilding) 11 June 1879
Wellington Guards 14 July 1879
Ashburton 15 August 1879
Nelson 26 October 1881
Christ's College (Christchurch) 1 January 1883
Christchurch City 11 January 1883
Awarua (Invercargill) 15 January 1883
Greymouth 1 January 1884
Oamaru 19 September 1884
Port Guards (Timaru) 1 January 1885
Dunedin Highland 11 March 1885
Timaru 22 April 1885
Kaiapoi 30 April 1885
Waimate 30 May 1885
Kaitangata 11 August 1885
Gore 13 May 1886
Rangiora 11 November 1886
Hastings 6 June 1887
Woodville 15 June 1896
Kelburne (Wellington) 25 March 1897
No. 1 Company Ohinemuri (Paeroa) 16 June 1897
College (Auckland) 17 June 1897
Hauraki (Thames) 11 October 1897
Imperial (Christchurch) 21 October 1897
No. 1 Company New Zealand Native (Auckland) 23 November 1897
No. 3 Company Ohinemuri (Waihi) 29 November 1897
Coromandel 28 February 1898
No. 2 Company New Zealand Native (Auckland) 14 April 1898
Waipawa 16 April 1898
Dannevirke 16 April 1898
No. 3 Company New Zealand Native (Auckland) 28 April 1898
Gordon (Auckland) 28 April 1898
Dunedin City 9 May 1898
Civil Service (Wellington) 19 May 1898

Wellington Post and Telegraph 21 May 1898
College (Wellington) 30 May 1898
Zealandia (Wellington) 30 May 1898
Dunedin 30 May 1898
Wanganui Guards 25 June 1898
Onehunga 9 July 1898
Sydenham 12 July 1898
Newton (Auckland) 1 October 1898
Linwood (Christchurch) 17 November 1898
Geraldine 21 April 1899
Ashburton Guards 29 June 1899
Hampden 7 July 1899
Palmerston South 1 August 1899
Taranaki Guards (New Plymouth) 22 February 1900
Mercantile Rifles (Invercargill) 27 February 1900
Huntly 10 March 1900
Wakari (Dunedin) 11 April 1900
Wellington Highland 11 April 1900
Wanganui Highland 11 April 1900
Caversham 11 April 1900
Waitohi (Picton) 14 April 1900
Civil Service (Christchurch) 9 May 1900
Winton 16 May 1900
Whangarei 10 September 1900
Rotorua 10 September 1900
Kawakawa 10 September 1900
Denniston 10 September 1900
Waihi 10 September 1900
Foxton 10 September 1900
Masterton 10 September 1900
Reefton 10 September 1900
Canterbury Highland (Christchurch) 10 September 1900
Brunner Rangers (Brunnerton) 10 September 1900
Palmerston Guards (Palmerston North) 10 September 1900
Patea 10 September 1900
Inglewood 10 September 1900
Pahiatua 10 September 1900
Eltham 10 September 1900
Queenstown 10 September 1900
Ranfurly (Napier) 10 September 1900
Canterbury Native (Christchurch) 10 September 1900
Union (Ormondville) 10 September 1900
Hawera 10 September 1900
Waitara 10 September 1900
Gisborne 10 September 1900
Tapanui 10 September 1900
Orepuki 10 September 1900
Bluff Guards 10 September 1900
Owaka 10 September 1900
Colac Bay 10 September 1900
Alexandra South (Otago) 2 October 1900
Greytown (Greytown North) 22 October 1900
Cromwell 22 October 1900

Ellesmere Guards (Doyleston) 31 October 1900
Stratford 12 November 1900
Duntroon 15 May 1901
Castlecliff 10 June 1901
Green Island (Abbotsford) 13 October 1901
Irish (Wanganui) 22 October 1901
Clutha (Balclutha) 22 October 1901
Hikurangi 26 July 1902
Popotunoa (Clinton) 4 August 1902
Ashhurst 8 August 1902
Volunteer Cycle Corps
Wellington 18 May 1898
Dunedin 20 May 1898
Christchurch 20 May 1898
Auckland 14 August 1900
Nelson College 24 May 1902
Volunteer Bearer Corps
Auckland 4 May 1898
Dunedin 20 May 1898
Christchurch 16 March 1899
Wellington 6 November 1899
Nelson 15 May 1901

PRECEDENCE OF CORPS IN NEW ZEALAND MILITARY FORCES 1927

1. The New Zealand Staff Corps and the NZ Permanent Staff
2. The Royal New Zealand Artillery
3. The New Zealand Permanent Air Force
4. The New Zealand Permanent Army Service Corps
5. The New Zealand Army Medical Corps
6. The New Zealand Army Ordnance Corps
7. The New Zealand Army Pay Corps
8. The General Duty Section, NZ Permanent Forces
9. The Regiments of Mounted Rifles
10. The New Zealand Artillery
11. The New Zealand Engineers
12. The New Zealand Corps of Signals
13. The Infantry Regiments
14. The New Zealand Air Force
15. The New Zealand Army Service Corps
16. The New Zealand Medical Corps
17. The New Zealand Chaplains Department
18. The New Zealand Dental Corps
19. The New Zealand Veterinary Corps
20. The New Zealand Army Legal Department
21. The Army Nursing Service
22. The Cadet Battalions
23. The Rifle Clubs

When on parade with aircraft, the New Zealand Air Force was on the right of the Mounted Rifles.

Units of the same arm take precedence among themselves according to the dates of their formation.

Mounted Rifles and Artillery were on the right when mounted on parade, dismounted troops of the Permanent Forces came next and were on the right of the dismounted troops.

NEW ZEALAND ARMY ORGANISATION 1903-1911

Auckland Military District
Detachment Royal New Zealand Artillery
Detachment Royal New Zealand Engineers

New Zealand Field Artillery Volunteers
A Battery (Auckland)

Auckland Division of New Zealand Garrison Artillery Volunteers
Originally in the Auckland District the Companies of Garrison Artillery were as follows:
No. 1 Company (Auckland) Auckland Naval Artillery
No. 8 Company (Ponsonby) Ponsonby Naval Artillery
No. 9 Company (Devonport) Devonport Coastguard Artillery
These were subsequently renamed and became:
No. 1 Company (Auckland Naval Artillery Volunteers)
No. 2 Company (Ponsonby Naval Artillery Volunteers)
No. 3 Company (Devonport Coastguard Artillery Volunteers)

New Zealand Engineer Volunteers
No. 3 Company NZEV (Devonport Naval Submarine Mining Volunteers)
No. 4 Company NZEV (Auckland Engineer Volunteers)

1st Regiment Auckland Mounted Rifle Volunteers
Headquarters: Auckland. 1 May 1901
A Squadron Auckland Mounted Rifle Volunteers
B Squadron Pukekohe Mounted Rifle Volunteers
C Squadron Seddon Horse Mounted Rifle Volunteers (Auckland)
D Squadron Franklin Mounted Rifle Volunteers (Clevedon)
E Squadron Waiuku Mounted Rifle Volunteers
F Squadron Rodney Mounted Rifle Volunteers (Warkworth)

2nd Regiment Auckland Mounted Rifle Volunteers
Headquarters: Cambridge. 1 May 1901
A Squadron No. 1 Squadron Waikato Mounted Rifle Volunteers (Hamilton)
B Squadron Piako Mounted Rifle Volunteers (Te Aroha)
C Squadron No. 2 Squadron Waikato Mounted Rifle Volunteers (Te Awamutu)
D Squadrn No. 3 Squadron Waikato Mounted Rifle Volunteers (Cambridge)
E Squadron Raglan Mounted Rifle Volunteers (Te Mata)

3rd Regiment Auckland Mounted Rifle Volunteers
Headquarters: Kawakawa. 28 January 1902
A Squadron Marsden Mounted Rifle Volunteers (Whangarei)
B Squadron Otamatea Mounted Rifle Volunteers (Paparoa)
C Squadron Hokianga Mounted Rifle Volunteers (Waimaku)*
D Squadron Mangonui Mounted Rifle Volunteers (Kaitaia)
E Squadron Northern Wairoa Mounted Rifle Volunteers (Aratapu)*
F Squadron Bay of Islands Mounted Rifle Volunteers (Ohaewai)
G Squadron Scottish Horse Mounted Rifle Volunteers (Waipu) 14 April 1906

H Squadron Mangakahia Mounted Rifle Volunteers (Mangatapere) 16 November 1906
*C Squadron disbanded 20 August 1908
E Squadron were disbanded 24 July 1908.

4th Regiment Auckland Mounted Rifle Volunteers
Headquarters: Te Puke. 28 January 1902
A Squadron Tauranga Mounted Rifle Volunteers
B Squadron Opotiki Mounted Rifle Volunteers
C Squadron Whakatane Mounted Rifle Volunteers (Taneatua)
D Squadron Te Puke Mounted Rifle Volunteers 4 July 1903
E Squadron Matata Mounted Rifle Volunteers 21 January 1905

1st Battalion Auckland Infantry Volunteers − 'Countess of Ranfurly's Own'
Headquarters: Auckland. 20 May 1898
A Company Victoria Rifle Volunteers (Auckland)
B Company College Rifle Volunteers (Auckland)
C Company No. 1 Company New Zealand Native Rifle Volunteers (Auckland)
D Company No. 2 Company New Zealand Native Rifle Volunteers (Auckland)
E Company No. 3 Company New Zealand Native Rifle Volunteers (Auckland)
F Company Gordon Rifle Volunteers (Auckland)
G Company Newton Rifle Volunteers (Auckland)
H Company Whangarei Rifle Volunteers
I Company Kawakawa Rifle Volunteers
J Company Hikurangi Rifle Volunteers

2nd Battalion Auckland (Hauraki) Infantry Volunteers
Headquarters: Paeroa. 9 July 1898
A Company No. 1 Company Thames Rifle Volunteers
B Company No. 1 Company Ohinemuri Rifle Volunteers (Paeroa)
C Company Hauraki Rifle Volunteers (Thames)
D Company No. 3 Company Ohinemuri Rifle Volunteers (Waihi)
E Company Coromandel Rifle Volunteers
F Company Huntly Rifle Volunteers
G Company Waihi Rifle Volunteers
Three additional companies which had been disbanded by 1907 were:
Onehunga Rifle Volunteers 8 April 1905
Rotorua Rifle Volunteers 6 June 1905
No. 2 Company Ohinemuri 30 November 1901

New Zealand Field Hospital and Bearer Corps
No. 1 Company (Auckland)

Volunteer Cycle Corps
Auckland

Wellington Military District
Detachment Royal New Zealand Artillery
Detachment Royal New Zealand Engineers

New Zealand Field Artillery Volunteers
D Battery (Wellington)

Wellington Division of Garrison Artillery Volunteers
Originally in the Wellington District the companies of Garrison Artillery were as follows:
No. 4 Company (Wellington) Wellington Naval Artillery
No. 6 Company (Petone) Petone Naval Artillery
These were renamed to become Nos. 1 and 2 Company as follows:
No. 1 Company (Wellington Naval Artillery Volunteers)
No. 2 Company (Petone Naval Artillery Volunteers)
No. 3 Company (Electric Light Section) 18 November 1907

New Zealand Engineer Volunteers
No. 5 Company NZEV (Wellington Engineer Volunteers)
No. 6 Company NZEV (Wellington Submarine Mining Volunteers), disbanded 18 November 1907

1st Regiment Wellington (West Coast) Mounted Rifle Volunteers
Headquarters: Wanganui. 1 May 1901
A Squadron Alexandra Mounted Rifle Volunteers (Wanganui)
B Squadron Wairoa Mounted Rifle Volunteers (Waverley)
C Squadron Hawera Mounted Rifle Volunteers
D Squadron Stratford Mounted Rifle Volunteers
E Squadron Opunake Mounted Rifle Volunteers
F Squadron Waimarino Mounted Rifle Volunteers June 1909
Disbanded 1907 was:
F Company Egmont Mounted Rifle Volunteers (Okato) 11 June 1907

2nd Regiment Wellington (Wairarapa) Mounted Rifle Volunteers
Headquarters: Wellington. 1 May 1901
A Squadron Heretaunga Mounted Rifle Volunteers (Wellington) transferred to 3rd Wellington Mounted Rifles 16 March 1911
B Squadron Pahiatua Mounted Rifle Volunteers
C Squadron Eketahuna Mounted Rifle Volunteers
D Squadron Masterton Mounted Rifle Volunteers
Disbanded were:
B Company Wairarapa Mounted Rifle Volunteers (Papawai) — the only known Maori mounted unit 27 September 1906
D Company South Wairarapa Mounted Rifle Volunteers (Carterton) 15 March 1905

3rd Regiment Wellington (Manawatu) Mounted Rifle Volunteers
Headquarters: Palmerston North. 1 May 1901
A Squadron Manawatu Mounted Rifle Volunteers (Palmerston North)
B Squadron Hunterville Mounted Rifle Volunteers
C Squadron Feilding Mounted Rifle Volunteers
Disbanded were:
B Company Horowhenua Mounted Rifle Volunteers (Levin) 10 October 1905
C Company Otaki Mounted Rifle Volunteers 18 January 1905

4th Regiment Wellington (East Coast) Mounted Rifle Volunteers
Headquarters: Napier. 1 May 1901
A Squadron East Coast Mounted Rifle Volunteers (Gisborne)
B Squadron Hawke's Bay Mounted Rifle Volunteers (Hastings)
C Squadron Huramua Mounted Rifle Volunteers (Wairoa, Hawke's Bay)
Disbanded were:
B Company Ruahine Mounted Rifle Volunteers (Dannevirke) 16 December 1905
D Company Ahuriri Mounted Rifle Volunteers (Napier) 21 September 1904

1st Battalion Wellington Rifle Volunteers
Headquarters: Wellington. 9 July 1898
A Company Wellington City Rifle Volunteers
B Company Wellington Guards Rifle Volunteers
C Company Kelburne Rifle Volunteers (Wellington)
D Company Civil Service Rifle Volunteers (Wellington)
E Company Wellington Post and Telegraph Rifle Volunteers
F Company College Rifle Volunteers (Wellington)
G Company Zealandia Rifle Volunteers (Wellington)
H Company Wellington Highland Rifle Volunteers
I Company Hutt Valley Rifle Volunteers (Lower Hutt) 24 September 1904
J Company Johnsonville Rifle Volunteers (Johnsonville) 13 May 1907

Volunteer Cycle Corps
Wellington

2nd Battalion Wellington (West Coast) Rifle Volunteers
Headquarters: Wanganui. 1 May 1901
A Company Royal Rifle Volunteers (Marton)
B Company Wanganui Rifle Volunteers
C Company Palmerston North Rifle Volunteers
D Company Manchester Rifle Volunteers (Feilding)
E Company Wanganui Guards Rifle Volunteers
F Company Wanganui Highland Rifle Volunteers
G Company Palmerston Guards Rifle Volunteers (Palmerston North)
H Company Irish Rifle Volunteers (Wanganui)
Disbanded were the earlier units:
G Company Foxton Rifle Volunteers 21 September 1904
I Company Castlecliff Rifle Volunteers 27 July 1905

3rd Battalion Wellington (East Coast) Rifle Volunteers
Headquarters: Napier. 1 May 1901
A Company Napier Guards Rifle Volunteers
B Company Napier Rifle Volunteers
C Company Hastings Rifle Volunteers
D Company Waipawa Rifle Volunteers
E Company Ranfurly Rifle Volunteers (Napier)
F Company Gisborne Rifle Volunteers
Reserve Corps 26 October 1907

4th Battalion Wellington (Taranaki) Rifle Volunteers
Headquarters: New Plymouth. 1 May 1901
A Company Taranaki Rifle Volunteers (New Plymouth)
B Company Taranaki Guards Rifle Volunteers

C Company Patea Rifle Volunteers
D Company Inglewood Rifle Volunteers
E Company Eltham Rifle Volunteers
F Company Hawera Rifle Volunteers
G Company Stratford Rifle Volunteers
H Company Waitara Rifle Volunteers

5th Battalion Wellington (Centre or Ruahine) Rifle Volunteers
Headquarters: Woodville. 1 May 1901
A Company Woodville Rifle Volunteers
B Company Dannevirke Rifle Volunteers
C Company Masterton Rifle Volunteers
D Company Pahiatua Rifle Volunteers
E Company Greytown Rifle Volunteers (Greytown North)
F Company Carterton Rifle Volunteers 31 October 1907
G Company Ashhurst Rifle Volunteers 8 August 1902
Disbanded were:
F Company Union Rifle Volunteers (Ormondville) 20 February 1905
G Company Ashhurst Rifle Volunteers 13 June 1907

New Zealand Field Ambulance and Bearer Corps
No. 5 Company (Wellington) 21 April 1906

Nelson Military District
New Zealand Field Artillery Volunteers
H Battery (Nelson) 21 March 1873

New Zealand Garrison Artillery Volunteers
Westport Garrison Artillery Volunteers (Westport)

1st Regiment Nelson Mounted Rifle Volunteers
Headquarters: Nelson. 1 October 1901
A Squadron Marlborough Mounted Rifle Volunteers (Blenheim)
B Squadron Wakatu Mounted Rifle Volunteers (Nelson)
C Squadron Takaka Mounted Rifle Volunteers
D Squadron Motueka Mounted Rifle Volunteers

1st Battalion Nelson Infantry Volunteers
Headquarters: Nelson. 1 October 1901
A Company Stoke Rifle Volunteers
B Company Blenheim Rifle Volunteers
C Company Waimea Rifle Volunteers (Wakefield)
D Company Nelson Rifle Volunteers
E Company Waitohi Rifle Volunteers (Picton)

2nd Battalion Nelson Infantry Volunteers
Headquarters: Greymouth. 1 October 1901
A Company 1st Westland Rifle Volunteers (Hokitika)
B Company Greymouth Rifle Volunteers
C Company Denniston Rifle Volunteers
D Company Reefton Rifle Volunteers
F Company Millerton Rifle Volunteers 12 May 1904
Disbanded was the former E Company:
E Company Brunner Ranger Rifle Volunteers (Brunnerton) 12 August 1904

Volunteer Cycle Corps
Nelson College

New Zealand Field Hospital and Bearer Corps
No. 4 Company (Nelson)

Canterbury Military District
Detachment Royal New Zealand Artillery

New Zealand Field Artillery Volunteers
E Battery (Christchurch)

Canterbury Division of Garrison Artillery Volunteers
In 1903 the New Zealand Garrison Artillery was positioned in the Canterbury Military District as follows:
No. 5 Company (Lyttelton) Lyttelton Naval Artillery
No. 7 Company (Lyttelton) N Battery (Lyttelton)
No. 10 Company (Westport) Westport Position Artillery
The latter Company was disbanded but was reformed in the Nelson Military District as the Westport Garrison Artillery Volunteers (Westport) on 12 July 1907. The other two Companies were renamed and became:
No. 1 Company (Lyttelton Naval Artillery Volunteers)
No. 2 Company (N Battery)

New Zealand Engineer Volunteers
No. 1 Company NZEV (Christchurch Engineer Volunteers)

1st Regiment North Canterbury Mounted Rifle Volunteers
Headquarters: Christchurch. 1 May 1901
A Squadron Canterbury Yeomanry Cavalry Volunteers (Christchurch)
B Squadron Canterbury Mounted Rifle Volunteers (Christchurch)
C Squadron Ellesmere Mounted Rifle Volunteers (Leeston)
D Squadron Malvern Mounted Rifle Volunteers (Waddington)
E Squadron Waimakariri Mounted Rifle Volunteers (West Melton)
Reserve Corps:
Canterbury Scout Volunteers Reserve (Christchurch) 15 August 1907
South Canterbury Volunteers Reserve (Timaru) 9 November 1907

2nd Regiment North Canterbury Mounted Rifle Volunteers
Headquarters: Culverdon. 1 May 1901
A Squadron Kaikoura Mounted Rifle Volunteers (Kaikoura)
B Squadron Amuri Mounted Rifle Volunteers (Waiau)
C Squadron Cust Mounted Rifle Volunteers
D Squadron North Canterbury Mounted Rifle Volunteers (Tuahiwi)

1st Regiment South Canterbury Mounted Rifle Volunteers
Headquarters: Temuka. 1 May 1901
A Squadron South Canterbury Mounted Rifle Volunteers (Timaru)
B Squadron Ashburton Mounted Rifle Volunteers
C Squadron Mackenzie Mounted Rifle Volunteers (Fairlie), disbanded 24 October 1907
D Squadron Studholme Mounted Rifle Volunteers (Waimate)
E Squadron Geraldine Mounted Rifle Volunteers (Temuka)

1st North Canterbury Battalion of Infantry Volunteers
Headquarters: Christchurch. 8 October 1895
A Company Christchurch City Guards Rifle Volunteers
B Company Christ's College Rifle Volunteers (Christchurch)
C Company Christchurch City Rifle Volunteers
D Company Kaiapoi Rifle Volunteers

E Company Rangiora Rifle Volunteers
F Company Imperial Rifle Volunteers (Christchurch)
Christchurch Volunteer Cycle Corps

2nd North Canterbury Battalion of Infantry Volunteers
Headquarters: Christchurch. 7 October 1903
A Company Sydenham Rifle Volunteers
B Company Linwood Rifle Volunteers (Christchurch)
C Company Civil Service Rifle Volunteers (Christchurch)
D Company Canterbury Highland Rifle Volunteers (Christchurch)
E Company Canterbury Native Rifle Volunteers (Christchurch)
Disbanded: Ellesmere Guards Rifle Volunteers (Doyleston) 23 October 1906

South Canterbury Battalion of Infantry Volunteers
Headquarters: Timaru. 10 June 1897
A Company Timaru City Rifle Volunteers
B Company Temuka Rifle Volunteers
C Company Ashburton Rifle Volunteers
D Company Port Guards Rifle Volunteers (Timaru)
E Company Timaru Rifle Volunteers
F Company Waimate Rifle Volunteers
G Company Geraldine Rifle Volunteers
H Company Ashburton Guards Rifle Volunteers

New Zealand Field Hospital and Bearer Corps
No. 3 Company (Christchurch)

Otago Military District
Detachment Royal New Zealand Artillery

New Zealand Field Artillery Volunteers
B Battery (Dunedin)

Otago Division of Garrison Artillery Volunteers
There were two Garrison Artillery Companies in Dunedin:
No. 2 Company (Dunedin) Dunedin Naval Artillery
No. 3 Company (Port Chalmers) Port Chalmers Naval Artillery
These Companies were renamed to become:
No. 1 Company (Dunedin Naval Artillery Volunteers)
No. 2 Company (Port Chalmers Naval Artillery Volunteers)

New Zealand Engineer Volunteers
No. 2 Company NZEV (Dunedin Engineer Volunteers)

1st Regiment Otago Mounted Rifle Volunteers
Headquarters: Dunedin. 1 May 1901
A Squadron Otago Hussar Volunteers (Dunedin)
B Squadron North Otago Mounted Rifle Volunteers (Oamaru)
C Squadron Clutha Mounted Rifle Volunteers (Balclutha)
D Squadron Maniototo Mounted Rifle Volunteers (Ranfurly)
E Squadron Tuapeka Mounted Rifle Volunteers (Lawrence)
F Squadron Taieri Mounted Rifle Volunteers (Outram)
G Squadron Waitaki Mounted Rifle Volunteers (Oamaru)

2nd Regiment Otago Mounted Rifle Volunteers
Headquarters: Invercargill. 1 May 1901
A Squadron Southland Mounted Rifle Volunteers (Invercargill)
B Squadron Mataura Mounted Rifle Volunteers (Gore)
C Squadron Wakatipu Mounted Rifle Volunteers (Arrowtown)
D Squadron Kelso Mounted Rifle Volunteers (Kelso)
E Squadron Murihiku Mounted Rifle Volunteers (Wyndham)
F Squadron Wallace Mounted Rifle Volunteers (Otautau)

1st Battalion Otago Rifle Volunteers
Headquarters: Dunedin. 20 May 1898
A Company Dunedin City Guards Rifle Volunteers
B Company North Dunedin Rifle Volunteers
C Company Dunedin Highland Rifle Volunteers
D Company Dunedin City Rifle Volunteers
E Company Dunedin Rifle Volunteers
F Company Waikari Rifle Volunteers (Dunedin)
G Company Caversham Rifle Volunteers
H Company Green Island Rifle Volunteers (Abbotsford)
Originally there were fourteen companies of the 1st battalion but on 2 March 1904 the Battalion was reorganised, six Companies being formed into 4th Battalion and the remainder being renumbered. Those Companies which were transferred the 4th Battalion were:
B Company Bruce Rifle Volunteers (Milton)
C Company East Taieri Rifle Volunteers (Mosgiel)
F Company Kaitangata Rifle Volunteers

K Company Owaka Rifle Volunteers
L Company Clutha Rifle Volunteers (Balclutha)
N Company Popotunoa Rifle Volunteers (Clinton)

2nd Battalion Otago Rifle Volunteers
Headquarters: Invercargill. 1 May 1901
A Company Invercargill City Guards Rifle Volunteers
B Company Oreti Rifle Volunteers (Invercargill)
C Company Awarua Rifle Volunteers (Invercargill)
D Company Gore Rifle Volunteers
E Company Mercantile Rifle Volunteers (Invercargill), disbanded 20 June 1907
F Company Winton Rifle Volunteers
G Company Orepuki Rifle Volunteers
H Company Bluff Guards Rifle Volunteers
I Company Colac Bay Rifle Volunteers
Reserve Corps
Tapanui Rifle Volunteers Reserve (Tapanui) 22 June 1907

3rd Battalion Otago Rifle Volunteers
Headquarters: Oamaru. 1 May 1901
A Company Queen's Rifle Volunteers (Oamaru)
B Company Oamaru Rifle Volunteers
C Company Hampden Rifle Volunteers
D Company Palmerston South Rifle Volunteers
E Company Alexandra South Rifle Volunteers
F Company Queenstown Rifle Volunteers
G Company Cromwell Rifle Volunteers
H Company Duntroon Rifle Volunteers
I Company King's Rifle Volunteers (Oamaru) 20 July 1904

4th Battalion Otago Rifle Volunteers
Headquarters: Milton. 2 March 1904
A Company Bruce Rifle Volunteers (Milton)
B Company Kaitangata Rifle Volunteers
C Company Owaka Rifle Volunteers
D Company Clutha Rifle Volunteers (Balclutha)
E Company Popotunoa Rifle Volunteers (Clinton)
Disbanded: C Company East Taieri Rifle Volunteers 31 December 1906

New Zealand Field Hospital and Bearer Corps
No. 2 Company (Dunedin)

Railway Pioneer Corps
1st Railway Pioneer Volunteers (Dunedin) 30 October 1907

Volunteer Cycle Corps
Dunedin

THE DEFENCE ACT OF 1911

THE 1911 ACT saw the abolition of the Volunteers and the creation of the Territorials by dividing New Zealand into four Military Districts, each of which had four Infantry Regiments. In this military reformation, the new titles of the Mounted Rifles and Infantry Regiments to be borne by regiments of Mounted Rifle and Infantry of the New Zealand Territorial Force at 17 March 1911 were:

Auckland Military District
1st Regiment, Auckland Mounted Rifles, to be the 3rd (Auckland) Mounted Rifles, with HQ at Auckland.
4th Regiment, Auckland Mounted Rifles, to amalgamate with the 2nd Regiment, Auckland Mounted Rifles, and to be designated the 4th (Waikato) Mounted Rifles with HQ at Hamilton.
3rd Regiment, Auckland Mounted Rifles, to be the 11th (North Auckland) Mounted Rifles with HQ at Kawakawa.
1st Battalion, Auckland Infantry (Countess of Ranfurly's Own) to be the 3rd (Auckland) Regiment (Countess of Ranfurly's Own) with HQ at Auckland.
2nd Battalion, Auckland (Hauraki) Infantry to be the 6th (Hauraki) Regiment with HQ at Paeroa.

Wellington Military District
1st Regiment, Wellington (West Coast) Mounted Rifles to be the 2nd (Wellington West Coast) Mounted Rifles with HQ at Wanganui.
3rd Regiment, Wellington (Manawatu) Mounted Rifles to be the 6th (Manawatu) Mounted Rifles with HQ at Palmerston North.
2nd Regiment, Wellington (Wairarapa) Mounted Rifles to amalgamate with the 4th Regiment, Wellington (East Coast) Mounted Rifles and to be designated the 9th (Wellington East Coast) Mounted Rifles with HQ at Napier.
1st Battalion, Wellington Rifles to be the 5th Regiment (Wellington Rifles) with HQ at Wellington.
2nd Battalion, Wellington (West Coast) Rifles to be the 7th Regiment (Wellington West Coast Rifles) with HQ at Wanganui.
5th Battalion, Wellington (Centre or Ruahine) Rifles to amalgamate with the 3rd Battalion, Wellington (East Coast) Rifles and to be designated the 9th Regiment (Wellington East Coast Rifles) with HQ at Napier.
4th Battalion, Wellington (Taranaki) Rifles to be the 11th Regiment (Taranaki Rifles) with HQ at Stratford.

Canterbury Military District
2nd Regiment, North Canterbury Mounted Rifles, to amalgamate with the 1st Regiment North Canterbury Mounted Rifles, and to be designated the 1st Mounted Rifles (Canterbury Yeomanry Cavalry) with HQ at Christchurch.
1st Regiment, South Canterbury Mounted Rifles to be the 8th (South Canterbury) Mounted Rifles with HQ at Timaru.
1st Regiment, Nelson Mounted Rifles to be the 10th (Nelson) Mounted Rifles with HQ at Blenheim.
1st North Canterbury Battalion of Infantry to be the 1st (Canterbury) Regiment with HQ at Christchurch.
2nd North Canterbury Battalion of Infantry to be the 13th (North Canterbury) Regiment with HQ at Rangiora.

South Canterbury Battalion of Infantry to be the 2nd (South Canterbury) Regiment with HQ at Timaru.
2nd Battalion Nelson Infantry to amalgamate with the 1st Battalion Nelson Infantry and to be designated the 12th (Nelson) Regiment with HQ at Nelson.
1st Regiment, Canterbury Mounted Rifles to be the 1st Mounted Rifles (Canterbury Yeomanry Cavalry) with HQ at Christchurch.

Otago Military District
1st Regiment, Otago Mounted Rifles to be the 5th Mounted Rifles (Otago Hussars) with HQ at Dunedin.
2nd Regiment, Otago Mounted Rifles to be the 7th (Southland) Mounted Rifles with HQ at Invercargill.
1st Battalion, Otago Rifles to be the 4th Regiment (Otago Rifles) with HQ at Dunedin.
2nd Battalion, Otago Rifles to be the 8th Regiment (Southland Rifles) with HQ at Invercargill.
3rd Battalion, Otago Rifles to be the 10th Regiment (North Otago Rifles) with HQ at Oamaru.
4th Battalion, Otago Rifles to be the 14th Regiment (South Otago Rifles) with HQ at Milton.

Additional units, new formations and groupings, disbandings, transfers and affiliations, were set out in the General Orders numbered below:

GO 84
One additional regiment of Mounted Rifles in the Otago Military District to be designated the 12th (Otago) Mounted Rifles with HQ at Balclutha.
Two regiments of Infantry in the Auckland Military District to be designated the 15th (North Auckland) and the 16th (Waikato) Regiments with HQ at Whangarei and Hamilton.

GO 122 Territorial Regiments grouped into Brigades
The undermentioned regiments have been grouped into brigades as shown below, in accordance with section 6 (a) of the Defence Act 1909, and with effect from 17 March 1911:
Auckland Mounted Brigade
3rd (Auckland) Mounted Rifles
4th (Waikato) Mounted Rifles
11th (North Auckland) Mounted Rifles
Wellington Mounted Brigade
2nd (Wellington West Coast) Mounted Rifles
6th (Manawatu) Mounted Rifles
9th (Wellington East Coast) Mounted Rifles
Canterbury Mounted Brigade
1st Mounted Rifles (Canterbury Yeomanry Cavalry)
8th (South Canterbury) Mounted Rifles
10th (Nelson) Mounted Rifles
Otago Mounted Brigade
5th Mounted Rifles (Otago Hussars)
7th (Southland) Mounted Rifles
12th (Otago) Mounted Rifles
Auckland Infantry Brigade
3rd (Auckland) Regiment ('Countess of Ranfurly's Own')
6th (Hauraki) Regiment

15th (North Auckland) Regiment
16th (Waikato) Regiment
Wellington Infantry Brigade
5th Regiment (Wellington Rifles)
7th Regiment (Wellington West Coast Rifles)
9th Regiment (Wellington East Coast Rifles)
11th Regiment (Taranaki Rifles)
Canterbury Infantry Brigade
1st (Canterbury) Regiment
2nd (South Canterbury) Regiment
12th (Nelson) Regiment
13th (North Canterbury) Regiment
Otago Infantry Brigade
4th Regiment (Otago Rifles)
8th Regiment (Southland Rifles)
10th Regiment (North Otago Rifles)
14th Regiment (South Otago Rifles)

GO 123
A Company, 9th Regiment (Wellington East Coast Rifles) to be F Battery New Zealand Field Artillery with HQ at Napier. 17 April 1911
E Company, 5th Regiment (Wellington Rifles) to be the Wellington Infantry Brigade Signal Company with HQ at Wellington. 17 March 1911

GO 124
Formation of Mounted Brigade Signal Company. Otago Mounted Brigade Signal Company. HQ at Oamaru. 17 March 1911

GO 143
Corps disbanded.
The Canterbury Scouts Reserve with HQ at Christchurch has been disbanded as from 4 May 1911.

GO 157
Formation of Field Batteries.
B Company, 8th Regiment (Southland Rifles) has been disbanded and re-formed into a field battery, designated 'J Battery New Zealand Field Artillery' with HQ at Invercargill has been approved. 18 April 1911

GO 172
Organisation.
Auckland Field Artillery Brigade (Auckland)
A Battery NZFA
G Battery NZFA
K Battery NZFA (Hamilton)
Canterbury Field Artillery Brigade (Christchurch)
E Battery NZFA
H Battery NZFA
Otago Field Artillery Brigade (Dunedin)
B Battery NZFA
C Battery NZFA
J Battery redesignated C Battery 19 April 1911
K Battery redesignated G Battery 19 April 1911
Wellington Field Artillery Brigade (Wellington)

D Battery NZFA
F Battery NZFA
The abovementioned batteries have been grouped into Field Artillery Brigades with effect from 1 May 1911.

GO 220
Redesignation of companies of the New Zealand Garrison Artillery.
Nos. 1, 2 and 3 Companies, Auckland Division to be redesignated Nos. 1, 6 and 7 Companies of the New Zealand Garrison Artillery.
Nos. 1, 2 and 3 Companies, Wellington Division to be redesignated Nos. 3, 5 and 9 Companies of the New Zealand Garrison Artillery.
Nos. 1 and 2 Companies, Canterbury Division to be amalgamated and designated 'No. 4 Company, New Zealand Garrison Artillery' with HQ at Lyttelton.
The Westport Garrison Artillery, to be redesignated 'No. 8 Company, New Zealand Garrison Artillery' with HQ at Port Chalmers. 17 March 1911

GO 221
Transfer of an Infantry Company.
The Whangarei Rifles have been transferred from the 3rd (Auckland) Regiment ('Countess of Ranfurly's Own') to the 15th (North Auckland) Regiment. 17 June 1911

GO 222
No. 4 Field Ambulance (Nelson) has been disbanded. 17 March 1911

GO 223
No. 5 Field Ambulance (Wellington) has been redesignated 'No. 4 Field Ambulance'. Dated 17 March 1911

GO 224
Formation of Mounted Field Ambulances. 17 March 1911
No. 5 Mounted Field Ambulance with HQ at Hamilton.
No. 6 Mounted Field Ambulance with HQ at Christchurch.
No. 7 Mounted Field Ambulance with HQ at Invercargill.
No. 8 Mounted Field Ambulance with HQ at Palmerston North.

GO 271
Affiliation of Imperial and New Zealand Regiments.
1st Mounted Rifles (Canterbury Yeomanry Cavalry).
2nd (Wellington West Coast) Mounted Rifles.
3rd (Auckland) Mounted Rifles.
5th Mounted Rifles (Otago Hussars).
Allied to King Edward's Horse (The King's Oversea Dominions Regiment).

GO 272
The Otago Mounted Brigade Signal Corps formed 17 March 1911. Redesignated the Otago Mounted Signal Company on 18 March 1911.

GO 273
Formation of Mounted Signal Companies. 17 March 1911
Auckland Mounted Signal Company with HQ at Matangi.
Canterbury Mounted Signal Company with HQ at Ashburton.
Wellington Mounted Signal Company with HQ at Pahiatua.

NEW ZEALAND STAFF CORPS

CAP BADGE: Fern-leaf with the letters 'NZ' superscribed.
COLLAR BADGES: Similar to cap badge with the fern-leaves facing inwards.
SHOULDER TITLES: 'NZSC' and 'NZ Staff'.

This badge in brass was adopted as the badge of the NZ Staff Corps and the New Zealand Permanent Staff in April 1911. From this date it ceased to be worn by any other members of the forces. The shape of the badge varies, dependent upon the manufacturer, and may be seen with and without a dot between the N and the Z.

Second pattern: The constellation of the Southern Cross within a garter inscribed 'N.Z. Staff Corps' flanked by fern fronds and surmounted by a crown. Bronze cap and collar badges the same size. Worn in gilt for mess dress.

With the formation of the New Zealand Army in 1947 the Staff Corps was disbanded on 9 January 1947.

The fern-leaf badge was used during World War II by the New Zealand Temporary Staff.

In 1969 the Regular Force Cadets not assigned to regiments or corps wore this badge as a cap badge.

Formed originally as a separate Corps of 100 officers. The Staff Corps was recruited from ex-regular and volunteer personnel and later from university graduates, ex-officer cadets from Duntroon and Sandhurst, officers who had distinguished careers in World War I and the Permanent Staff.

Variations in the sizes of shoulder titles occurs in all corps. Note the difference between the designs of the ferns used in World War I and World War II.

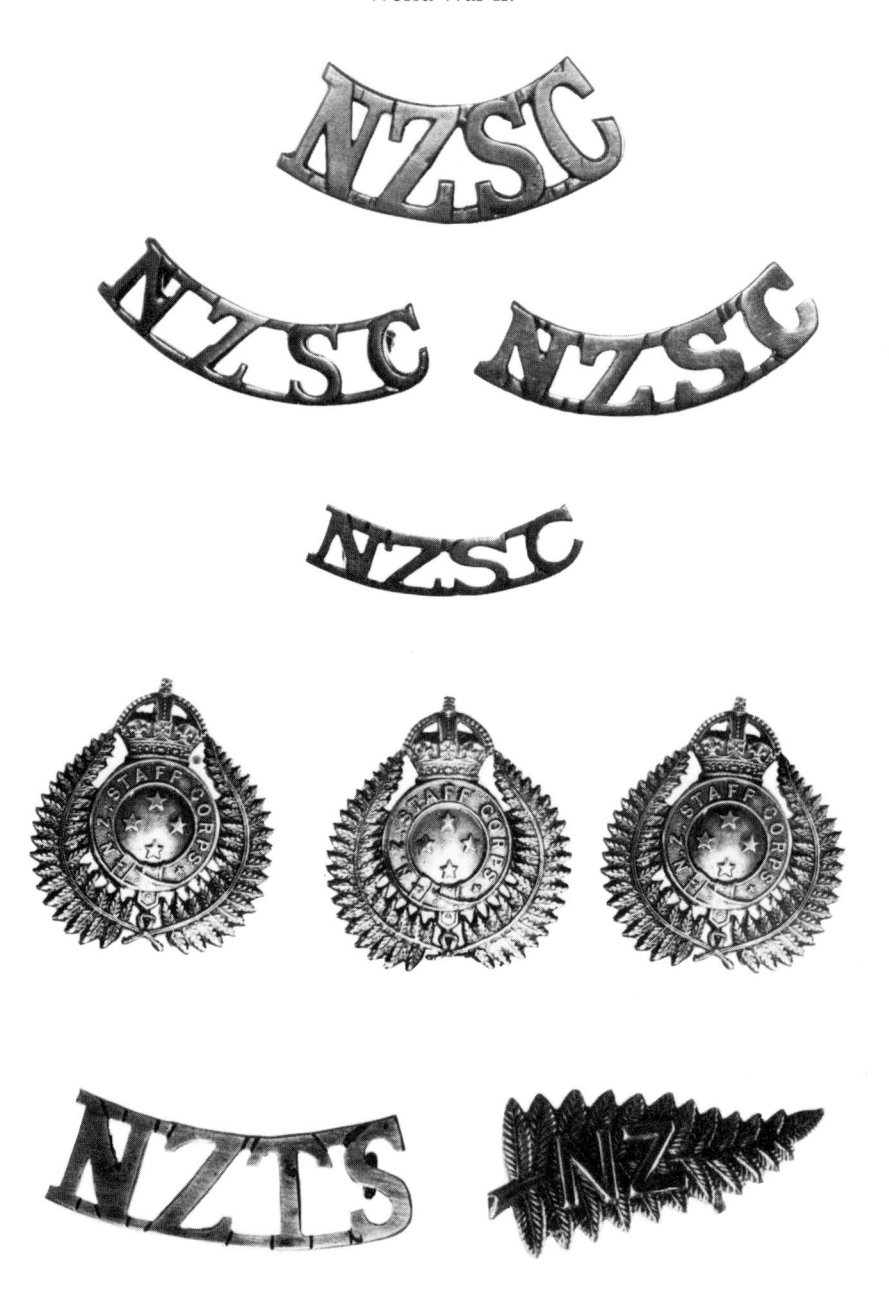

New Zealand Temporary Staff 1939-1945

NEW ZEALAND PERMANENT STAFF

BADGE: A fern-leaf with the letters 'NZ' superscribed.
During WW1 the cap badge of both the Staff Corps and the Permanent Staff was changed to the Crown and Lion in keeping with the badge worn by the British Army, but as of June 1917 permission to wear this badge was withdrawn.
In October 1921 a new badge was approved for members of the NZ Permanent Forces.
BADGE: An eight-pointed bronze-chipped star, superimposed by a Maltese cross of eight points upon which is laid a ring bearing the words 'N.Z. Permanent Staff' and in the centre of which is the representation of a kiwi; the whole surmounted by an Imperial Crown.
COLLAR BADGES: Smaller versions of the cap badge.
SHOULDER TITLE: N.Z.P.S.

Formed in 1911 as a training corps of two hundred non-commissioned officers. The Permanent Staff subsequently recruited personnel from private soldiers. The Corps was disbanded on 9 January 1947 when a New Zealand Infantry Corps was created with all the existing territorial infantry regiments and the regular force New Zealand Regiment becoming integrated.

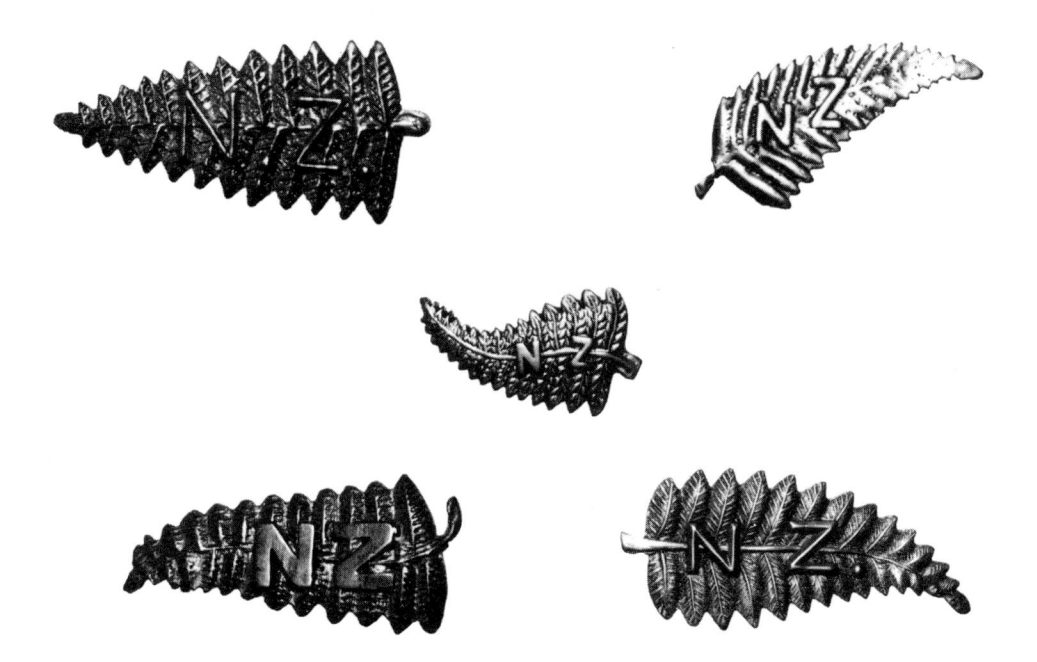

Variations found in the fern-leaf patterns. These were worn both as cap and collar badges by the New Zealand Staff Corps and the New Zealand Permanent Staff.

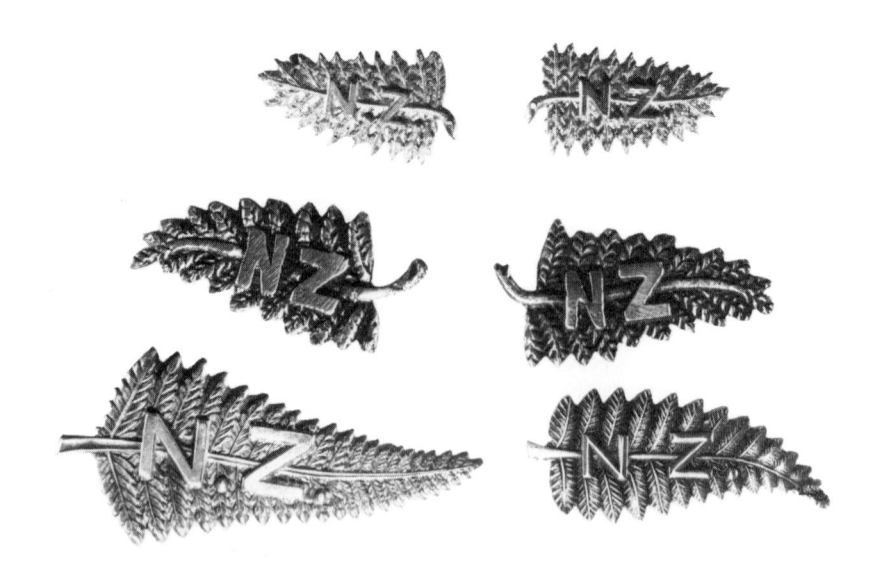

Cap and collar fern-leaf badges worn by New Zealand Staff Corps and New Zealand Permanent Staff. For other variations see page 91

Fern leaf pattern 1939-45 for Temporary Staff

Staff Instructors and Inspectors

The Central School of Instruction was established at Mount Cook, Wellington, in 1882. The complement of the school was small, a Commanding Officer, one Drill Instructor (Rifles), one Musketry Instructor, one Field Artillery Instructor, and one Cavalry Instructor. The school lapsed for want of support but was re-established on 1 April 1902. In 1938 the school was transferred to Trentham Camp and in 1952 to Waiouru Military Camp.

1882-1902

1902-1911

Staff Instructors

Physical Training Staff

Members of the Permanent Staff wore this badge on cap or hat.

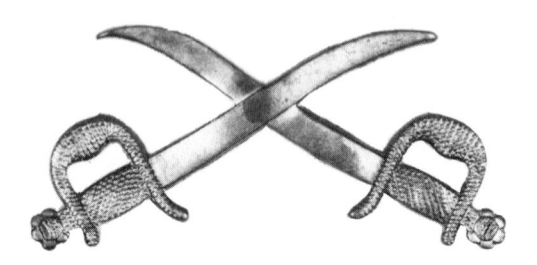

NCO's qualified as instructors in physical training and bayonet training. The badge was worn on the right sleeve above chevrons.

Staff Instructors

NZ Officers School of Musketry 1914-1918

School of Musketry, badge for other ranks.

NEW ZEALAND NAVAL ARTILLERY VOLUNTEERS

THE FIRST GUNNERS in New Zealand were naval personnel from British warships. They were ill-equipped for fighting on the land, but still managed to drag their ship's heavy cannon far inland to bombard rebel stockades during the Maori Wars. Volunteer units were formed by the settlers and forts were erected at strategic points throughout the country, the armament being ships' cannons.

Auckland Military District
Auckland Naval Artillery Volunteers: 17 April 1858, known as the Coastguards. Re-accepted on 20 February 1866. Designated Auckland Naval Artillery Volunteers on 16 January 1868. Designated Auckland Artillery Volunteers on 12 November 1870.
Auckland Naval Coastguard Volunteers: 30 April 1885. Accepted as an Honorary Corps. Designated Waitemata Naval Artillery Volunteers on 21 August 1886. Disbanded on 1 August 1889.
Auckland Naval Volunteers: No. 1 Company: 1862. Became part of the Auckland Volunteer Naval Brigade on 13 May 1873. Designated Auckland Naval Artillery Volunteers on 28 February 1883. No. 2 Company: 3 May 1871. Disbanded on 11 December 1872.
Devonport Coast Guard Artillery Volunteers: 10 February 1898. Formed with the change of title of Devonport Garrison Artillery Volunteers.
Devonport (Auckland) Naval Artillery Volunteers: 1 January 1884 until 5 August 1887. Reformed on 8 September 1887.
Onehunga Naval Artillery Volunteers: 2 May 1885 until 1 August 1889.
Onehunga Naval Volunteers: 1863. Disbanded 23 March 1866.
Ponsonby Naval Artillery Volunteers: 22 April 1885. Formed by members of the Ponsonby Rowing Club. Amalgamated with Devonport Naval Artillery Volunteers under the title of Ponsonby Naval Artillery Volunteers on 30 January 1889.
Thames Naval Volunteers: 8 October 1869. Mobilised on 27 October 1881. Designated Thames Naval Artillery Volunteers on 28 February 1883. Became No. 1 Company, Thames Rifle Volunteers on 16 October 1900.
Waitemata Naval Artillery Volunteers: 21 August 1886. Formed from Auckland Naval Coastguard Volunteers. Disbanded on 1 August 1889.
All Naval Volunteers in New Zealand were formed into a Corps on 17 June 1885 as the New Zealand Naval Artillery Volunteers under the command of Rear Admiral R. A. E. Scott, R.N.
1st Battalion, Auckland (Naval) Volunteers: 26 January 1886 until 1 January 1889. This was the Auckland Division, Naval Artillery Volunteers.
Auckland Naval Artillery Volunteers
Thames Naval Artillery Volunteers
Devonport Naval Artillery Volunteers
Ponsonby Naval Artillery Volunteers
Onehunga Naval Artillery Volunteers
Auckland Naval Coastguard Volunteers

Wellington Military District
Napier Naval Artillery Volunteers: 8 January 1885.
Petone Naval Artillery Volunteers: 18 January 1883. Formed from the Petone

Contingent of the Wellington Naval Brigade. Absorbed the Kaiwharawhara Rifle Volunteers on 26 October 1886.

Star Boating Club Naval Artillery Volunteers: 2 June 1898. The Star Boating Club formed in 1866 was the second such club formed in New Zealand. Designated Star Boating Club Submarine Mining Volunteers on 1 May 1899.

Wanganui Naval Brigade Volunteers: 2 November 1881. Designated Wanganui Naval Artillery Volunteers on 28 February 1883.

Wellington Naval Artillery Volunteers: 28 February 1883. Formed from part of the Wellington Naval Brigade. No. 2 Company: 2 October 1900. Nos. 1 and 2 Company, Wellington Naval Artillery Volunteers were formed into one Company and designated No. 4 Company, New Zealand Garrison Artillery Volunteers on 19 December 1902.

Wellington Naval Artillery Volunteer Brigade: 7 November 1895. A Battery: Wellington Naval Artillery Volunteers. B Battery: Petone Naval Artillery Volunteers. When the Brigade was disbanded on 23 December 1902, the Petone Battery was designated No. 6 Company, Regiment of New Zealand Artillery Volunteers.

Wellington Naval Brigade: 24 March 1879. Mobilised on 27 October 1881. The Petone Contingent of this Brigade became Petone Naval Artillery Volunteers on 18 January 1883.

The remainder of the Brigade was designated Wellington Naval Artillery Volunteers on 28 February 1883. The Brigade was disbanded on 1 January 1889.

Nelson, Marlborough and Westland Military Districts

Greymouth Naval Artillery Volunteers: 13 May 1885. Accepted as an Honorary Corps. Designated Mawhera Rifle Volunteers on 23 August 1897.

Nelson Naval Artillery: 1860.

Nelson Naval Brigade: January 1875. Designated Nelson Naval Brigade Volunteers on 2 November 1881. Designated Nelson Naval Artillery Volunteers on 28 February 1883. Designated Nelson Coast Guard Rifle Volunteers on 23 November 1897.

Nelson (Port) Naval Volunteers: 19 January 1875 until 19 October 1881.

Westport Naval Artillery Volunteers: 29 August 1885. Formed as a Garrison Corps. Designated Westport Rifle Volunteers on 9 April 1895.

Canterbury Military District

Lyttelton Naval Brigade: 6 September 1880. Designated Lyttelton Naval Artillery Volunteers on 28 February 1883.

Timaru Naval Artillery Volunteers: 1 January 1885. Designated Port Guards Rifle Volunteers on 17 August 1897.

Otago Military District

Bluff Naval Artillery Volunteers: 15 January 1883. Designated Awarua Rifle Volunteers on 2 June 1898.

Dunedin Naval Volunteers: 12 February 1864. Re-accepted 20 February 1866. Raised as Dunedin Volunteer Naval Brigade. Designated Dunedin Naval Artillery Volunteers on 28 February 1883.

Oamaru Naval Artillery Volunteers: 19 September 1884. Designated Oamaru Rifle Volunteers on 19 October 1895.

Peninsula (Dunedin) Naval Artillery Volunteers: 30 April 1885. Formed as a Country Corps. Became a Garrison Corps 17 June 1885. Disbanded on 12 April 1893.

Port Chalmers Naval Brigade: 1864. Re-accepted 28 February 1866 as Port Chalmers Naval Volunteers. Designated Port Chalmers Naval Artillery Volunteers 28 February 1883.

SHOULDER TITLES:
Auckland Navals wore 'AN' in white metal.
Naval Artillery Volunteers 'N.A.V.' in white metal and also brass.

Gunnery proficiency badge

Coast Guard Artillery Volunteers
Helmet plate worn by Devonport Coast Guard Artillery Volunteers when the corps was formed in Auckland on 10 February 1898. Designated No. 9 Company, Regiment of New Zealand Garrison Artillery Volunteers on 19 December 1902.

Waist-belt centres

NEW ZEALAND REGIMENT OF VOLUNTEER ARTILLERY

The Volunteer Artillery Companies in New Zealand were formed into an administrative battalion on 3 December 1878 under the designation of 'New Zealand Regiment of Volunteer Artillery'. This Regiment was established as follows:

A Battery — Formerly Auckland Artillery Volunteers.
B Battery — Formerly Dunedin Artillery Volunteers.
C Battery — Formerly Timaru Artillery Volunteers.
D Battery — Formerly Wellington Artillery Volunteers.
E Battery — Formerly Christchurch Artillery Volunteers.
F Battery — Formerly Napier Artillery Volunteers.
G Battery — Formerly Invercargill Artillery Volunteers. Amalgamated with K Battery and designated G Battery on 6 June 1883.
H Battery — Formerly Nelson Artillery Volunteers.
I Battery — Formerly Oamaru Artillery Volunteers.
J Battery — Formerly Cook County Artillery Volunteers.
K Battery — Formed 6 December 1878 from Invercargill Engineer Volunteers.
L Battery — Formed 14 June 1879 from Port Chalmers Artillery Volunteers.
M Battery — Formed 11 November 1879 by redesignation of Queenstown Rifle Volunteers.
N Battery — Formed 17 June 1885 by redesignation of Lyttelton Artillery Volunteers.
O Battery — Formed 17 June 1885 by redesignation of Parnell Artillery Volunteers.

Two Brigades were formed on 8 March 1886:
1st (North Island) Brigade: A, D, F, J and O Battery. H. Battery was transferred to this Brigade on 20 April 1886.
2nd (South Island) Brigade: B, C, E, G, H, I, L and N Batteries. M. Battery was added to this Brigade on 19 August 1887.

During the Boer War, volunteers were selected from the 4th and 5th Contingents from New Zealand to form the 1st New Zealand Battery of the Rhodesian Field Force Artillery. This was the first New Zealand artillery unit to take part in active service overseas.

On 26 January 1903 the New Zealand Regiment of Artillery Volunteers disbanded and the remaining Field Batteries reformed into the Regiment of New Zealand Field Artillery Volunteers.

A Battery, Auckland   B Battery, Dunedin   D Battery, Wellington
E Battery, Christchurch H Battery, Nelson

This body never formally disbanded but lapsed on the change from the volunteer to territorial organization in 1910 and the grouping of batteries into local brigades on 1 May 1911.

As an example of the changing titles of the Volunteer Artillery, the Westport Rifle Volunteers formed on 29 August 1885, became No. 10 Company, New Zealand Garrison Artillery Volunteers on 27 July 1901 and were known as the Westport Position Artillery Volunteers. They became I Battery, New Zealand Artillery Volunteers on 26 April 1904, formed their own brass band on 1 May 1905 and disbanded on 12 June 1907. Reformed on 12 July 1907 as the Westport Garrison Artillery Volunteers they were redesignated No. 8 Company, New Zealand Garrison Artillery on 17 March 1911.

New Zealand Regular Forces 1897   Royal New Zealand Artillery 1902

No. 7 Company, New Zealand Garrison Artillery Volunteers
Lyttelton Artillery Volunteers formed in 1864 with the reorganisation of the Lyttelton Volunteers. Disbanded 30 June 1875, reformed as a garrison corps on 10 April 1885. On 17 June 1885 part of the corps became N Battery, N.Z. Regiment of Artillery Volunteers. Designated No. 7 Company, Regiment of N.Z. Garrison Artillery Volunteers on 19 December 1902.

NEW ZEALAND FIELD ARTILLERY

BADGE (1903): White metal. A gun surmounted by the word 'Volunteers' and a crown. Below, a scroll bearing the words 'Field N.Z. Artillery'.
COLLAR BADGES: White metal grenades.
BADGE (1904): Brass. A gun surmounted by the word *Ubique* and a crown. Below, a scroll bearing the words 'A Battery N.Z.F.A.' Applicable to each Battery.
COLLAR BADGES: Bronze. 10-flame grenade above scroll 'N.Z.F.A.'
BADGE (1907): Bronze, brass or bi-metal. A gun surmounted by the words 'A Battery' and a crown. Below, a scroll with the words 'Field N.Z. Art'y.' Applicable to each Battery.
COLLAR BADGES: A 7-flame grenade above a scroll 'N.Z.F.A.'
BADGE (1911): Bronze, brass. A gun surmounted by a scroll *Ubique* and a crown. Below, a scroll bearing the words 'Field N.Z. Art'y.'

Regiment, New Zealand Field Artillery Volunteers

Formed on 26 January 1903 from the following Batteries:
A Battery (Auckland) — Formerly Auckland Artillery Volunteers (20.2.66)
B Battery (Dunedin) — Formerly Dunedin Artillery Volunteers (28.2.66)
D Battery (Wellington) — Formerly Wellington Artillery Volunteers (22.7.67)
E Battery (Christchurch) — Formerly Christchurch Artillery Volunteers (31.12.67)

H Battery (Nelson) — Formerly Nelson (City) Artillery Volunteers (21.3.73)
I Battery (Westport Position) — This Battery was added with the change of title of No. 10 Company N.Z.G.A.V. on 26 April 1904. Disbanded 12 June 1907.

The helmet plate of the Nelson Battery consisted of the standard British Artillery plate, Victorian Crown, 'N.Z' on plinth, a scroll beneath bearing the words 'H Battery Field Artillery'.

NEW ZEALAND FIELD ARTILLERY
Auckland Field Artillery Brigade
A Battery (Auckland)
G Battery (Hamilton)
Auckland Brigade Ammunition Column (Auckland)
Canterbury Field Artillery Brigade
E Battery (Christchurch)
H Battery (Nelson)
Canterbury Brigade Ammunition Column (Christchurch)
Otago Field Artillery Brigade
B (Howitzer) Battery (Dunedin)
C Battery (Invercargill)
Otago Brigade Ammunition Column (Dunedin)
Wellington Field Artillery Brigade
F Battery (Napier)
J (Howitzer) Battery (Palmerston North)
Wellington Brigade Ammunition Column (Palmerston North)
D (Mountain) Battery (Wellington)

Note the difference of the centre 'N.Z' plinth.

NEW ZEALAND GARRISON ARTILLERY

BADGE (1902): A gun surmounted by a scroll 'N.Z' and a crown. Below, a scroll bearing the words 'No. 2 Coy. Garrison Artillery'. Applicable to each company except Westport. This badge has a lower scroll 'Westport Garrison Artillery'.

COLLAR BADGES: A 7-flame grenade above a scroll 'N.Z.G.A.'

Regiment, New Zealand Garrison Artillery Volunteers

Formed on 19 December 1902 from the following Volunteer Corps:
No. 1 Company, NZGAV — Auckland Naval Artillery Volunteers
No. 2 Company, NZGAV — Dunedin Naval Artillery Volunteers
No. 3 Company, NZGAV — Port Chalmers Naval Artillery Volunteers
No. 4 Company, NZGAV — Wellington Naval Artillery Volunteers
No. 5 Company, NZGAV — Lyttelton Naval Brigade
No. 6 Company, NZGAV — Petone Naval Artillery Volunteers
No. 7 Company, NZGAV — N Battery, formerly Lyttelton Artillery Volunteers
No. 8 Company, NZGAV — Ponsonby Naval Artillery Volunteers
No. 9 Company, NZGAV — Devonport Coastguard Artillery Volunteers
No. 10 Company, NZGAV — Westport Position Artillery Volunteers

Auckland Division: Nos. 1, 8 and 9 Company, NZGAV.
Wellington Division: Nos. 4 and 6 Company, NZGAV. A No. 3 Company was added to this Division on 18 November 1907 and designated 'Electric Light Section'.
Lyttelton Division: Nos. 5 and 7 Company, NZGAV.
Dunedin Division: Nos. 2 and 3 Company, NZGAV.

The helmet plate of No. 7 Company consisted of the standard British Artillery plate but with 'Defence' on the plinth and the lower scroll bearing the words 'No. 7 Coy. New Zealand Garrn. Arty Vols':

106

107

REGIMENT OF NEW ZEALAND ARTILLERY

BADGE: A gun surmounted by a scroll 'N.Z' and a crown. Below a scroll bearing the words *Quo fas et gloria ducunt*.

COLLAR BADGES: A 7-flame grenade above a scroll 'N.Z.A'.

A 7-flame grenade above a scroll *Ubique*.

A 7-flame grenade.

On the cap badge, the upper scroll can be found with a number of varieties: 'N.Z' '.N.Z.' 'N.Z.'

The badges were made in bronze for officers and brass for other ranks.

In 1921 the Territorial Artillery was designated 'New Zealand Artillery'. The badge worn at this time was a gun surmounted by a scroll 'New Zealand' and a crown. Below, a scroll bearing the words *Quo fas et gloria ducunt'*.

COLLAR BADGES: A 7-flame grenade above a scroll 'New Zealand'.

All Artillery (Permanent Force and Territorial) wore the standard British collar badges — a 7-flame grenade above a scroll *Ubique* — at times when the specific collar badge of the corps was not available.

On 9 January 1947 the Regiment of New Zealand Artillery was combined with the Regiment of Royal New Zealand Artillery to become the Royal New Zealand Artillery.

ROYAL REGIMENT OF NEW ZEALAND ARTILLERY

BADGE: A gun surmounted by a scroll *Ubique* and a crown. Below, a scroll bearing the words 'Royal N.Z. Artillery'.
COLLAR BADGES: A 7-flame grenade above a scroll 'R.N.Z.A'.
BADGE (1921): A gun surmounted by a scroll *Ubique* and a crown. Below, a scroll bearing the words 'Royal New Zealand Artillery'.
COLLAR BADGES: A 7-flame grenade above a scroll 'New Zealand.'
BADGE (1954): A gun surmounted by a scroll 'R.N.Z.A' and a crown. Below, a scroll bearing the words *Quo fas et gloria ducunt.*
COLLAR BADGES: A 7-flame grenade above a scroll 'R.N.Z.A'.
BADGE (1956): A gun surmounted by a scroll *Ubique* and a crown. Below, a scroll bearing the words 'Royal N.Z. Artillery'.
COLLAR BADGES: A 7-flame grenade above a scroll 'Royal N.Z. Artillery'.
BERET BADGES: Small type, scroll 'Royal N.Z. Artillery'. Both K/C and Q/C.

When the Permanent Militia became the Permanent Force on 15 October 1902, the No. 1 Service Company was designated the Royal New Zealand Artillery.

Volunteer Artillery had worn a variety of British helmet-plates during their existence. These were the Royal Artillery helmet-plates but without the scroll *Ubique*.
White metal helmet-plate Laurel plinth. Lower scroll *Artillery Volunteers*.
White metal helmet-plate Laurel plinth. Lower scroll *Quo fas et gloria ducunt*.
White metal helmet-plate Laurel plinth. Lower scroll *Volunteer Artillery*.
White metal helmet-plate 'N.Z' on plinth. Lower scroll *Quo fas et gloria ducunt*.
Brass helmet-plate Laurel plinth. Lower scroll *New Zealand Regular Forces*.
Brass helmet-plate 'N.Z' on plinth. Lower scroll *Coast Guard Artillery Volunteers*.
Brass helmet-plate. Lower scroll *Militia Artillery*.
After 1902 the helmet-plate was in brass, *Ubique* was permitted to be worn on the plinth as the Regiment had received Royal sanction, the lower scroll bearing the words *Royal New Zealand Artillery*.

CORPS DRESS DISTINCTION
No. 1 dress blues and tropical whites: embroidered, gold lace collar badges. No collar badges with mess kit.

A two-inch square distinguishing patch may be worn diagonally as a diamond, with the upper half in scarlet and the lower half royal blue. Worn on the beret under the cap badge.

R.N.Z.A.
QUO FAS ET GLORIA DUCUNT

UBIQUE
ROYAL N.Z. ARTILLERY

NEW ZEALAND

R.N.Z.A.

UBIQUE

RNZA

RNZA

CORPS OF ROYAL NEW ZEALAND ENGINEERS

BADGES: The Royal Cypher EVIIR and Garter enclosed in laurel wreath above a scroll 'N.Z. Engineer Vols'.
A similar badge above a scroll 'Royal N.Z. Engineers'.
The Royal Cypher EVIIR enclosed in a circle 'No. 1 N.Z. Engineers'.
The Royal Cypher GVR and Garter enclosed in laurel wreath above a scroll 'N.Z. Engineer Vols'.
COLLAR BADGES: Up to 1922 there were three distinct grenades with 8 flames, 9 flames or 10 flames. The grenade was above a scroll 'N.Z.E.' or *Ubique*. After 1922, a 9-flame grenade became the standard pattern.

Operational military engineering started in 1845 when two New Zealand officers and eighty men were enlisted to work under a Royal Engineer officer in the Maori War at the Bay of Islands. The first New Zealand soldier to be killed in action was a member of that unit.

Military engineering on a voluntary basis in New Zealand commenced with the formation of the Canterbury Volunteer Engineers in 1866. Although the name of that unit has been changed a number of times in the past, it exists still and is now known as 5 Independent Field Squadron RNZE, which appropriately was one of the units on parade when the RNZE received the freedom of the Borough of Levin, on 7 February 1959.

During the Tauranga Bush Campaign against the Hau Hau in 1867-68, the Armed Forces included a Volunteer Engineer Company.

In 1873-75 the Engineer Volunteer Militia of three companies, each about one hundred strong, were enlisted and placed on active service to construct the North Island Main Trunk Railway between Rangiriri and Ngaruawahia, because that area was still very unsettled after the Maori Wars.

New Zealand Engineer Volunteers

Formed into a regiment on 26 January 1903 from the various volunteer corps:
No. 1 Company, NZEV (Canterbury Engineer Volunteers 27.4.85)
No. 2 Company, NZEV (Dunedin Engineer Volunteers 30.4.85)
No. 3 Company, NZEV (Devonport Naval Submarine Mining Volunteers 7.7.94). Disbanded 8 July 1908
No. 4 Company, NZEV (Auckland Engineer Volunteers 8.11.98)
No. 5 Company, NZEV (Wellington Engineer Volunteers 1.8.1900)
No. 6 Company, NZEV (Wellington Submarine Mining Volunteers 20.11.1900). Disbanded on 18 November 1907.

The order to form the regiment was revoked on 17 June 1909 with the formation on that date of the 'New Zealand Engineer Volunteers Regiment'.
No. 1 Company, NZEV — Canterbury Engineer Volunteers
No. 2 Company, NZEV — Dunedin Engineer Volunteers
No. 3 Company, NZEV — Auckland Engineer Volunteers
No. 4 Company, NZEV — Wellington Engineer Volunteers

Hauraki Engineer Volunteers
Formed 10 July 1878 with the change of title of No. 2 Company, Hauraki Rifle Volunteers. Mobilised for service on 27 October 1881. Designated Hauraki Rifle Volunteers on 17 January 1883. Disbanded 10 October 1883.

New Zealand Engineer Volunteers Regiment
The Volunteer Engineer Corps and Submarine Mining Volunteers throughout New Zealand were formed into a regiment on 26 January 1903. The regiment was reformed on 17 June 1909 with a revised strength.

Engineer Volunteers wore the general pattern helmet plate of the British Engineer Volunteers, the Royal Arms with a blank scroll below, below this a scroll with the words *Quo fas et gloria ducunt*. This was in white metal for other ranks.

A similar helmet plate in silver plate was worn by officers. This plate had an ornamental scroll below and beneath this a scroll 'Engineer Volunteers' with an ornamental scroll section between the two words.

The waist-belt plate was similar to the British badge but with a scroll below 'N.Z. Engineer Volunteers'.

The cross-belt plate was the white metal British pattern prior to 1902.

After 1902 the plate was similar with a scroll below 'Engineer Volunteers' and the letters N.Z' on the plinth.

The helmet plate after 1902 was in brass with 'N.Z' on the plinth, below a scroll bearing the words 'Engineer Volunteers'.

The New Zealand Armed Constabulary, in 1885, included both Field Engineers and Torpedo Engineers. The latter became the nucleus of the New Zealand Torpedo Corps formed by the 1886 Defence Act. The Field Engineers were absorbed into the Torpedo Corps in 1888. The Torpedo Corps in conjunction with volunteers also looked after the submarine mine defences of Auckland and Wellington and were renamed No. 2 Service Company, New Zealand Permanent Forces. On 15 October 1902 they were redesignated Royal New Zealand Engineers. The anniversary of this date is now commemorated as 'Sappers Day'.

The RNZE were then absorbed into the RNZA in 1907.

Shoulder-belt plate

SUBMARINE MINING VOLUNTEERS and NZ TORPEDO CORPS

BADGE: Monogrammed letters (NZSM or NZTC in brass)

The 1886 Defence Act formed the New Zealand Torpedo Corps which looked after four second class torpedo boats based at the main ports in New Zealand and was responsible for removing obstructions from the harbours. This Corps, in conjunction with volunteers became responsible for the Submarine Mine Defences of Auckland and Wellington.

Devonport Torpedo Corps Volunteers: 7 July 1894. Designated Devonport Naval Artillery Volunteers on 9 March 1895. Designated Devonport Naval Submarine Miners Volunteers on 25 May 1900. Became No. 3 Company, Regiment of New Zealand Engineer Volunteers on 26 January 1903. Disbanded on 8 July 1908.

New Zealand Torpedo Corps: 1 September 1879. Designated New Zealand Engineer Corps of Sub-Marine Miners on 2 March 1881. Mobilised for service on 27 October 1881. Disbanded on 20 June 1883.

Star Boating Club Submarine Mining Volunteers: 1 May 1899. Formed by change of title of Star Boating Club Naval Artillery Volunteers. Designated Wellington Submarine Mining Volunteers on 18 June 1900.

Wellington Submarine Mining Volunteers: 18 June 1900. Disbanded on 15 August 1900. Reformed on 20 November 1900. Became No. 6 Company, Regiment of New Zealand Engineer Volunteers on 26 January 1903. Disbanded on 18 November 1907.

The corps was renamed No. 2 Service Company New Zealand Permanent Forces and on 15 October 1902 were redesignated Royal New Zealand Engineers. Submarine mining was abandoned by the New Zealand Army in 1907 after the Navy had taken over the responsibility from the Engineers.

The Torpedo Branch was equipped with Thorneycroft Torpedo Boats of 170 hp and fired small Whitehead torpedos. The boats were disposed of in 1910. Each boat was 63 feet long, having in the forward section an oval conning tower upon which was mounted a one-inch Nordenfeldt gun.

Defender Lyttelton Harbour   *Waitemata* Auckland
Taiaroa Port Chalmers   *Poneke* Wellington

NEW ZEALAND RAILWAY CORPS

BADGE: Two guns crossed on railway metals and sleepers surmounted by a locomotive in circle, and loop endorsed 'New Zealand Railway Corps', the circle surmounted by a crown.
This badge is not known, although its design was projected in 1911.
BADGE: Two guns crossed on railway metals and sleepers surmounted by a locomotive in circle, and loop endorsed 'Railway Battalions N.Z.E', the circle surmounted by a crown.
COLLAR BADGES: Plain grenade of 9 flames.
MOTTO: *Gardez Bien* (Guard well).
Formed on 5 October 1911 as a part of the New Zealand Engineers.
North Island Battalion had eight companies.
South Island Battalion had eight companies.

The New Zealand Railway Corps was redesignated the 'New Zealand Railway Battalions' on 1 July 1913 and became a part of the Corps of N.Z. Engineers. The Railway Company NZE, took part in the 1914 Samoa Expedition.

Disbanded on 1 December 1921 when all commissioned officers were transferred to the Reserve of Officers.

The New Zealand Railway Depots Regiment of New Zealand Engineers was disbanded as from 20 May 1922.

THE CORPS OF NZ ENGINEERS

BADGE: The monogram 'NZE' in a circle bearing the motto *Quo fas et gloria ducunt* and surmounted by a crown and lion.
COLLAR BADGE: Small grenade, or large grenade above a scroll 'NZE'.
The cap badge is in two sizes. The larger size, nearly 1¼ inches diameter was worn by the tunnellers. Officers of this unit wore a large grenade collar badge above a scroll *Inga Wahi Katoa* (Everywhere).

No. 1 Field Company at Christchurch.
No. 2 Field Company at Dunedin.
No. 3 Field Company at Auckland.
No. 4 Field Company at Wellington.

New Zealand Engineers Tunnellers Company formed 12 September 1915 at the request of the Imperial Government was first New Zealand unit on Western Front. Disbanded 24 April 1919.

The New Zealand tunnellers always timbered at right angles to the slope and not vertical as English and German counterparts did. Tunnels were also always higher and wider than English.

The first Commanding Officer (Major Duigan) of the Tunnellers Company was later Chief of New Zealand General Staff 1937-41 (Major-General Sir John Duigan).

Engineer Volunteers became the Corps of NZ Engineers 1 June 1923.

Prefix 'Royal' granted to the Corps of NZ Engineers 12 July 1947.

The first N.Z. Troops to serve in South Vietnam were the 'N.Z. Aid Detachment Engineer Team', a unit of two officers and 20 other ranks. They were deployed from June 1964 to June 1965 as non-combatants assisting the Government 'Civil Aid Project' as selected by the South Vietnam Ministry of Works.

Officers

Tunnellers Company

Other ranks

Current RNZE badges

118

NEW ZEALAND SIGNAL CORPS (NZ Engineers)

BADGE: Crossed flags and star below enclosed by a wreath on a Maltese cross, with scroll 'New Zealand Signal Corps' and surmounted by a crown.

MOTTO: *Sodales parati* (Prepared as comrades together).

The first badge was 53mm and was worn with 9-flame grenade collar badges. The second badge was 45mm and was worn with smaller collar badges. The New Zealand Signal Corps was redesignated 'Mounted Signal Troops and Divisional Signal Companies' on 1 July 1913 to form part of Corps of NZE. The badge was worn by members of the Mounted Signal Company in Auckland, Canterbury, Otago and Wellington, as well as by the Infantry Signal Companies in the same districts. The badge was later worn by the Divisional Signal Companies.

Corporal C. R. G. Bassett, Divisional Signals NZE was the only New Zealander to be awarded the Victoria Cross for the Gallipoli campaign.

The New Zealand Mounted Rifles Brigade in Palestine 1916-18 had a Mounted Signal Company NZE as part of the famous ANZAC Mounted Division.

A New Zealand Wireless Troop served in Mesopotamia during 1915-18.

The Auckland Mounted Signal Troop disbanded 26 January 1921.

The remainder of the corps transferred to the New Zealand Corps of Signals upon its formation on 1 June 1921.

NZ POST AND TELEGRAPH CORPS (NZE)

BADGE: A winged foot surmounted by a crown poised on a scroll bearing letters 'N.Z.P.T.C.'
MOTTO: *Celeritas* (Swiftly).

Formed on 7 October 1911 as a part of the New Zealand Engineers. Two battalions of trained signallers were formed by the Post and Telegraph Department.
North Island Battalion — Seven companies
South Island Battalion — Five companies

This corps formed the basis of the Signals re-organisation after World War I and in effect, on 1 June 1921, became the New Zealand Corps of Signals. The projected badge was to have been similar to the original Corps badge but with a scroll 'N.Z.C.O.S'. It appears that this badge was never manufactured.

NEW ZEALAND CORPS OF SIGNALS

BADGE: A winged foot surmounted by a crown poised on a scroll bearing letters 'N.Z.C.O.S'.
This badge was projected but is not known.
The Corps which was formed from the NZ Post and Telegraph Corps on 1 June 1921 appears to have worn the badge of that Corps.
BADGE (1938): On the base of an oval band inscribed 'New Zealand Corps of Signals', a globe thereon, a figure of Mercury, the whole ensigned with the Imperial Crown.
COLLAR BADGES: Similar to cap, in matching pairs.
MOTTO: *Celeritas* (Swiftly).

Formed with a Northern Depot at Auckland, Central Depot at Wellington and the Southern Depot at Christchurch.

In 1940 there was the Northern District Signal Company at Auckland, the Central District Signal Company at Wellington and the Southern District Signal Company at Christchurch. The latter Company wore the badge of the N.Z. Post and Telegraph Corps until 1941.

In 1942 these companies became separate units titled Northern, Central and Southern District Signals. Each unit comprised a HQ and six companies and was responsible for all military communications within the respective Military District. They were disbanded in the reorganisation of 1970 when Home Command Signal Squadron was established to become responsible for the signals of the Northern Troop, Central Troop, Southern Troop and Army Training Group.

ROYAL NEW ZEALAND CORPS OF SIGNALS

BADGE: The figure of Mercury holding a caduceus in his left hand, his right hand held aloft, poised on a globe with his left foot, the globe surmounted with the Corps motto *Certa Cito*, the whole ensigned with a crown which is detached from the remainder of the badge. A lower scroll bearing the words 'Royal N.Z. Signals'.

COLLAR BADGES: Similar versions of the cap badge, in matching pairs.

MOTTO: *Certa Cito* (Swift and sure).

The prefix 'Royal' was granted to the New Zealand Corps of Signals on 12 July 1947 after which time the above badge was worn.

At the outbreak of World War II the Central Military District Signal Company of the New Zealand Corps of Signals formed a Special Force of trained Morse operators, linemen and technicians to become the basis of No. 1 Company of Divisional Signals under the command of Captain G. L. Agar (later Lieut-Colonel Agar DSO, OBE, ED). On 16 October 1939 the Force was titled the 2nd New Zealand Divisional Signals and became the first unit of 2 NZEF to see active service in World War II, when they took command of the signals of the Western Desert Corps in December 1940 in the Libyan campaign under the command of Lord Wavell.

THE CAVALRY AND MOUNTED RIFLES IN NEW ZEALAND

1860   Saw the first mounted troops used in New Zealand; these were the Taranaki Mounted Volunteers, Royal Volunteer Cavalry (Otahuhu), Yeomanry Cavalry, and a 'Defence Cavalry Force'. They were equipped with sword and carbine and were instructed by NCOs from the Imperial Cavalry.

1863   The Colonial Defence Force Cavalry was formed (one troop).

1864   The Canterbury Yeomanry Cavalry was formed. Just after this the Dunedin Light Horse was formed.

1866   In the Volunteer Act of 1866 all Mounted Corps were called Light Horse Volunteers. Westland Light Horse, Hokitika, 1868-70.

1880   In April of this year the Southland Hussars were formed, but were disbanded soon after.

1883   In the Volunteer Act of 1883, the term Light Horse Volunteers was abandoned and mounted personnel were called Cavalry Volunteers.

1885   Title of all Cavalry from this date to be Mounted Rifles.

1886   First regimental formation of Cavalry Volunteers attempted. Disbanded 1889.

1889-1902   Ten contingents known as Mounted Rifles went to the war in South Africa.

On 1 July 1906 Mounted Rifles became Regiments and Squadrons.

1911   The Territorial System created four Military Districts in New Zealand, each of which had three Mounted Rifle Regiments of four squadrons. The New Zealand Mounted Rifle Brigade of the 1st New Zealand Expeditionary Force (1st NZEF) in 1914 had four Mounted Rifle regiments named after provinces. Each regiment contained one service squadron of the three Mounted Rifle regiments from the Military District in which it was raised.

'Auckland' Mounted Rifle Regiment: 3rd (Auckland), 4th (Waikato), 11th (North Auckland) Mounted Rifle Regiments.

'Wellington' Mounted Rifle Regiment: Queen Alexandra's 2nd (Wellington West Coast), 6th (Manawatu), 9th (Wellington East Coast) Mounted Rifle Regiments.

'Canterbury' Mounted Rifle Regiment: 1st (Canterbury Yeomanry Cavalry), 8th (South Canterbury), 10th (Nelson Marlborough) Mounted Rifle Regiments.

'Otago' Mounted Rifle Regiment: 5th (Otago) Hussars, 7th (Southland), 12th (Otago) Mounted Rifle Regiments.

These four regiments saw action at Gallipoli. The Auckland, Wellington and Canterbury Regiments formed the New Zealand Mounted Rifle Brigade of the ANZAC Mounted Division in Sinai and Palestine 1916-19.

The Otago Regiment reduced to squadron strength, served in France 1916-18.

Each squadron wore the badges of their respective regiments.
In 1921, with the reduction of the Military Districts to three, the Mounted Rifle Regiments were reduced to nine (three per District).
The three Otago Regiments amalgamated as The Otago Mounted Rifles.
The 8th (South Canterbury) was absorbed into The Canterbury Yeomanry Cavalry. Mounted Rifle personnel volunteered into the (mechanised) New Zealand Divisional Cavalry Regiment 2NZEF.

Permission for NZ Mounted Rifle Regiments to carry guidons was granted in 1927.

NEW ZEALAND MOUNTED RIFLES IN SOUTH AFRICA 1899-1902

BADGES: A fern-leaf 2½ inches by 1½ inches with the letters 'NZ' embossed. Same size badge in pairs as collar badges.
Shoulder title: NZMR (3rd and 4th Contingents NZRR)
Shoulder chains were worn by officers of the later Contingents.

There were many unofficial badges in use, the most popular was the fern-leaf incorporating a hook, so that the slouch hat could be turned up at the left side with a leather thong. Also used was a lion's head with a hook. Puggarees were of plaited leather or khaki cloth.

Many officers wore on their field service caps a large post horn with the letters 'NZ' and the 3rd Contingent wore post horn collar badges.

The 3rd and 4th Contingents, proud of their title (Rough Riders), had brass shoulder titles 'NZRR'.

In the House of Representatives, the Prime Minister of New Zealand, the Right Honourable Richard John Seddon, moved that a contingent of Mounted Rifles be offered to the Imperial Government for service in South Africa. This was on 28 September 1899, two weeks before war was begun by the Boers on 12 October 1899. At this time the Volunteer movement in New Zealand was supported with enthusiasm and there were about 10,000 enrolled in the local forces, so that it was without difficulty that the first Contingent was mobilised and sailed in less than a month. The total strength of the Mounted Rifle contingents was 6,495 officers and men, and in addition, including remounts, more than 8,000 horses.

First Contingent. Formed largely from men trained in the Volunteers. Nos. 1 and 2 Companies sailed from Wellington in the SS *Waiwera* on 21 October 1899. Unit disbanded in New Zealand on 21 January 1901.

Second Contingent. Formed largely from men trained in the Volunteers. Nos. 3 and 4 Companies and a Hotchkiss Detachment sailed from Wellington in the SS *Waiwera* on 20 January 1900. The Hotchkiss Battery proved to be unsuccessful as the guns were too heavy for the horses, and the limited range of 1,000 yards exposed the battery to enemy fire, so that the detachment was absorbed by the two companies in South Africa. Unit disbanded in New Zealand on 9 May 1901.

Third (Rough Riders) Contingent. Raised and equipped by the people of Canterbury with No. 5 Company being recruited in Canterbury and No. 6 Company being recruited in Hawke's Bay, Taranaki and Manawatu. These companies sailed from Lyttelton in the *Knight Templar* on 17 February 1900. This Contingent, on 11 May, amalgamated with the First and Second Contingents and shared the South African Campaign with them. The unit was disbanded on 9 May 1901. It was suggested that the Third Contingent be called 'Bushmen' because of the use of this name by the Australians in South Africa, but the Prime Minister was of the opinion that as the men were not regularly trained troops, but rather were good marksmen and riders, ready for rough work, he thought that they should be called 'Rough Riders' and it was under this name that the Third and Fourth Contingents were recruited.

Fourth (Rough Riders) Contingent. Raised mostly in Otago and supported by public subscription in that province. Nos. 7 and 8 Companies sailed from Lyttelton in the *Gymeric* on 31 March 1900. Nos. 9 and 10 Companies sailed from Port Chalmers in the *Monowai* on 24 March 1900. These companies were renamed in South Africa: Nos. 7 and 8 Companies becoming C and D Squadrons and Nos. 9 and 10 Companies becoming A and B Squadrons. These were disbanded in New Zealand on 21 July 1901. Farrier Sgt W. J. Hardham of C Squadron was awarded the only New Zealand VC of the Anglo-Boer War.

The remaining contingents were raised from reserves at the request of the Imperial Government, which also became responsible for all payments concerning the force.

Fifth Contingent. Raised from reserves at the request of the Imperial Government and were known as New Zealand Imperial Bushmen. In Rhodesia they were called 'Bushmen', no doubt because of some attempt to achieve uniformity with Australian units which also used this name, and because this term was applied to men who did not have any training in a volunteer unit.

No. 11 Company (Auckland Section)
No. 12 Company (Wellington Section)
No. 13 Company (Wellington, Nelson and West Coast Section)
No. 14 Company (Canterbury Section)
No. 15 Company (Otago Section)

Sailed from Wellington in three ships, the *Gymeric, Maori* and *Waimate* on 31 March 1900. No. 11 Company volunteered to man a battery of six fifteen-pounder guns and with twenty men of the Fourth Contingent became the 1st New Zealand Battery in the Rhodesian Field Force Artillery. This battery served as a separate force. The other companies were reorganised as A, B, C and D Squadrons. Disbanded on 21 July 1901.

Sixth Contingent. Raised to relieve the 2nd and 3rd Contingents.

No. 16 Company (Auckland Section)
No. 17 Company (Wellington Section)
No. 18 Company (Wellington Section)
No. 19 Company (Canterbury Section)
No. 20 Company (Otago Section)

Sailed from Auckland in the *Cornwall* on 30 January 1901. Reorganised as A, B, C and D Squadrons in South Africa. Disbanded in New Zealand on 11 May 1902.

Seventh Contingent. Raised to replace the Fourth Contingent.

No. 21 Company (Auckland Section)
No. 22 Company (Wellington Section)
No. 23 Company (Nelson Section)
No. 24 Company (Canterbury Section)
No. 25 Company (Otago Section)
No. 26 Company (Supplementary Section)

This was the only contingent which did not take any horses with it to South Africa. Sailed from Wellington in the *Gulf of Taranto* on 6 April 1901. Disbanded in New Zealand on 30 June 1902.

Eighth Contingent. Raised to relieve the Sixth and Seventh Contingents. This contingent in South Africa was called the 1st New Zealand Mounted Brigade.

North Island Regiment: A, B, C and D Squadrons.
Sailed from Auckland in the *Surrey* on 1 February 1902.

South Island Regiment: E, F, G and H Squadrons.
Sailed from Lyttelton in the *Cornwall* on 8 February 1902. Disbanded in New Zealand on 13 August 1902.

Ninth Contingent. Raised from volunteers for the Eighth Contingent.
North Island Regiment: E, F, G and H Squadrons.
Sailed from Auckland in the *Devon* on 19 March 1902.
South Island Regiment: A, B, C and D Squadrons.
Sailed from Port Chalmers in the *Kent* on 12 March 1902. Disbanded in New Zealand on 21 July 1902.

Two officers of this contingent fired the last shots of the war in South Africa and were the only members of either the Ninth or Tenth Contingents to be in action.

Tenth Contingent. Raised from volunteers for the Eighth Contingent.
North Island Regiment: A, B, C and D Squadrons.
Sailed from Wellington in the *Drayton Grange* on 14 April 1902.
South Island Regiment: E, F, G and H Squadrons.
Sailed from Lyttelton in the *Norfolk* on 19 April 1902. Disbanded in New Zealand on 23 August 1902.

A senior British officer commented: 'It would hardly be an exaggeration to say that after they had a little experience, the New Zealanders were by general consent regarded as the best mounted troops in South Africa.'

129

130

THE QUEEN'S SOUTH AFRICA MEDAL

The majority of the men who served in South Africa earned only the Queen's Medal for South Africa although there were some who received both the Queen's and King's Medal for this campaign. The following is a list of the clasps awarded to New Zealanders for the Queen's South Africa Medal:

Cape Colony	Belfast
Transvaal	Paardeberg
Orange Free State	Diamond Hill
Rhodesia	Relief of Kimberley
Johannesburg	South Africa 1901
Driefontein	South Africa 1902
Wittebergen	

KING EDWARD'S HORSE
(The King's Oversea Dominions Regiment)

Raised in November 1901 from colonials living in England. Titled the 4th County of London (King's Colonials) Imperial Yeomanry until 1905 when the title was changed to King's Colonials, Imperial Yeomanry.

A Squadron (British Asian) — Elephant badge over scroll 'British Asian'.

B Squadron (Canadian) — Beaver badge over scroll 'British American'.

C Squadron (Australasian) — Kangaroo and tree fern over scroll 'Australasian'.

D Squadron (South African) — Ostrich badge over scroll 'British African'.

A fifth Squadron 'New Zealand' was raised in 1903 but disbanded in 1904. At this time the C Squadron badge was changed to a kangaroo above a scroll 'Australia'. The head-dress was a slouch hat with high crown and scarlet plume. The Regimental badge was worn on the front of the hat, the Squadron badge on the hat-band and a monogram badge 'K,C' was worn on the side of the hat.

In 1905 the hat was changed to one with a lower crown and black cock feathers. The Regimental badge was not worn on this hat. In 1909 the wearing of Squadron badges was discontinued, all ranks wearing the monogram badge. Because the use of the term 'Colonials' was not well received by the squadrons, the title of the regiment was changed to King Edward's Horse (The King's Oversea Dominions Regiment) when His Majesty King George V became Colonel-in-Chief of the regiment.

The regiment fought in France in 1915-18, took part in the Irish troubles of 1916 and served in Italy in 1918 with the XIth Corps.

A memorial to the regiment stands at Vieille Chapelle where the regiment had great losses defending the bridgehead in April 1918.

King Edward's Horse was disbanded 31 March 1924.

King Edward's Horse, New Zealand Squadron
cap and collar badges

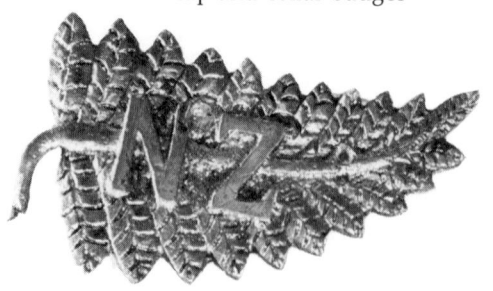

First pattern

Second pattern

FOURTH BATTALION, IMPERIAL CAMEL BRIGADE
The Brigade was better known by the title
Imperial Camel Corps (ICC)

BADGE: Unofficial. Cast in brass in Egypt with smaller size as collar. Camel with letters NZ superimposed.

The Brigade was in existence from December 1916 until June 1918.
First Battalion recruited from Australian Light Horse.
Second Battalion recruited from British Yeomanry.
Third Battalion recruited from Australian Light Horse.
Fourth Battalion: Two companies from Australian Light Horse and two companies from New Zealand Mounted Rifles (Nos. 15 and 16) raised on 24 July and 17 October 1916.

Each battalion had a distinguishing patch which was worn on the hat as a triangle: 1st Battalion, red; 2nd Battalion, green; 3rd Battalion, black and white; 4th Battalion, blue.

The 16th NZ Company ICC was in the Sinai Desert in April and May 1917 and in the Jordan Valley, April and May 1918.

The 15th NZ Company ICC took part in the successful attack on Magdhaba in December 1916, and the attack at Rafa in January 1917 which proved to be the last major action fought in Egypt.

Both companies saw heavy fighting in the two attempts to capture Gaza in March and April 1917.

On 31 July 1918 the ten Australian companies were formed into the 14th and 15th Regiments, forming a new Brigade, the Fifth Australian Light Horse Brigade to which was attached a French Cavalry Regiment. The 15th and 16th New Zealand Companies of the Imperial Camel Corps were formed into the Second New Zealand Machine-gun Squadron under the command of Major D. E. Batchelar.

The strength of the two New Zealand companies was 12 officers and 338 other ranks, and suffered casualties of six officers and 35 other ranks killed.

Badge of Camel Transport Corps

THE NEW ZEALAND CYCLIST CORPS

During the volunteer period the following corps existed:
Auckland Volunteer Cycle Corps: 14 August 1900. Disbanded 25 November 1903.
Christchurch Volunteer Cycle Corps: 20 May 1898. Attached to 1st Battalion, North Canterbury Rifle Volunteers 7 October 1903.
Dunedin Volunteer Cycle Corps: 20 May 1898. Attached to 1st Battalion, Otago Rifle Volunteers 1 October 1901.
Nelson College Volunteer Cycle Corps: 24 May 1902. Attached to 1st Battalion, Nelson Infantry Volunteers 21 December 1903. Designated Nelson Volunteer Cycle Corps 24 March 1905. Disbanded 28 February 1906.
Wellington Volunteer Cycle Corps: 18 May 1898. Attached to 1st Battalion, Wellington Rifle Volunteers 1 August 1901.

The New Zealand Cyclist Corps formed on 5 April 1916 from the Reserve Squadrons and the 12th, 13th and 14th Mounted Rifle Reinforcements at Featherson Camp in New Zealand. This Company embarked with the 12th Reinforcements and sailed on the SS *Mokoia* from Wellington on 6 May 1916.

The establishment of a Divisional Cyclist Company was eight officers, 196 other ranks. The badge was a winged cycle front wheel and handle bars and had on a scroll beneath, the words 'NZ Cyclist Company'. A number were manufactured by a Wellington firm and sold to members of the company; free issues of badges were not made then. Shoulder titles were unobtainable, and the unit went forward with their NZMR titles. A green puggaree, the same as the Mounted Rifles, was worn.

Reinforcements enabled a second New Zealand company to be formed and on 22 July 1916, the two New Zealand Cyclists Companies combined with the 2nd Australian Division Cyclist Company to form the Second Anzac Cyclist Battalion. This consisted of battalion headquarters and three companies each of 98 all ranks, a total of 15 officers and 302 other ranks.

Cycles arrived early in August 1916.

A distinguishing colour patch was approved and was a white diamond two inches square with a red centre one inch to be worn on both sleeves. The new badge for the New Zealand Companies was approved and issued in August 1917. It was a similar badge to that worn by Imperial Cyclist Units, having a wheel with crossed rifles surmounted by a crown and a scroll underneath with the words 'NZ Cyclist Corps'. Shoulder titles bearing the letters 'NZCC' were also issued.

The Australian Company (No. 3 Company) was withdrawn from the battalion on 16 January 1918 to join the Australian Corps Cyclist Battalion, and in order to bring the battalion up to full strength, a third New Zealand Company was formed and designated No. 3 Company, preference being given to volunteers with long service in the New Zealand Division.

On 1 January 1918 the old 2nd Anzac Corps was renamed XXII Corps and the Cyclists became the XXII Corps Cyclist Battalion.

This name proved to be a confusing one, and since it was now a purely New Zealand unit it was decided by headquarters in September 1918 that in future the battalion should be known as 'New Zealand Cyclist Battalion'.

While serving as infantry July 1918, captured Marfaux Village and at Peace Celebrations the NZ Cyclists were presented with a richly embroidered fanion to commemorate the action.

The NZ Cyclist Corps disbanded May 1919 in England.

1st MOUNTED RIFLES
(CANTERBURY YEOMANRY CAVALRY)

BADGE: Within a laurel wreath a circle surmounted by a crown, a horse rampant.
MOTTO: *Celer et Audax* (Swift and Bold).
Although this is the official description of the badge it would appear that this badge was never worn by the regiment but instead the cap badge was within a fern-wreath, surmounted by a ram's head, the letters 'C.Y.C'.
COLLAR BADGES: A ram's head above the letters 'C.Y.C'.
MOTTO: *Pro focis et patria* (For our home and country).
The usual cap badge has a bar across the top of the letter 'Y'. A variety exists in which the top of the letter 'Y' is open. The badges are either bronze or brass.

BATTLE HONOURS: South Africa 1899-1902. The Great War 1914-18: ANZAC, Defence of Anzac, Gaza, JERUSALEM, HILL 60 (ANZAC), JAFFA, SARI BAIR, Jericho, Gallipoli 1915, Jordan, RUMANI, Megiddo, Maghdaba-Rafah, Nablus, Egypt 1915-17, Palestine 1917-18. Service in World War I as part of the 'Canterbury' Mounted Rifle Regiment comprising 1st (Canterbury Yeomanry Cavalry), 8th (South Canterbury), 10th (Nelson and Marlborough) Mounted Rifle Regiments. In action at Gallipoli and with the 'Auckland' and 'Wellington' Regiments formed the New Zealand Mounted Rifle Brigade of ANZAC Mounted Division in Sinai and Palestine 1916-19. In 1921 amalgamated with the 8th (South Canterbury) to form the 1st N.Z. Mounted Rifles (Canterbury Yeomanry Cavalry). The title was altered to The Canterbury Yeomanry Cavalry.

On 1 January 1942 all Mounted Rifle Regiments added to their titles the words 'Light Armoured Fighting Vehicle Regiment'.
New Zealand Army Order No. 62 of 29 March 1944 reorganised the New Zealand Armoured Corps into three regiments, the 3rd Armoured Regiment, comprising 1st (Canterbury Yeomanry Cavalry); 5th (Otago) and 10th (Nelson and Marlborough) LAFV Regiments and this Regiment inherited the battle honours of the 20th Armoured Regiment 2NZEF. The 3rd Armoured Regiment went into recess in 1956.
UNIFORM: Scarlet, blue facings, gold lace.

Formed on 17 March 1911 with the amalgamation of the 2nd Regiment, North Canterbury Mounted Rifles with the 1st Regiment North Canterbury Mounted Rifle Volunteers. These Regiments had comprised the following:

Canterbury Yeomanry Cavalry: Accepted 1 November 1864.
Raised 1864. Officers gazetted 7 November 1864. Raised as a corps of three troops. Was the first cavalry unit to accept service under the 1865 Volunteer Act (13 February 1866) which gave the CYC its premier place in the list of precedence which it always maintained. The Corps was afterwards reduced to a single troop, but in varying degrees of prosperity or otherwise, was often up to squadron strength. A corps of cadets designated 'Canterbury Yeomanry Cavalry Cadet Volunteers' was raised in May 1868 and attached to the regiment but was disbanded in 1871. For many years the CYC was the only mounted unit in the South Island. On 31 August 1881 the CYC was divided into two troops: the A or North Canterbury Troop and the B or South Canterbury Troop.

By regulations which came into force in 1883 the regiment was reduced to one troop. In 1899 it became A Company Canterbury Mounted Rifle Battalion, in 1901 A Squadron 1st Regiment North Canterbury Mounted Rifles, and in 1911 with the Ellesmere Mounted Rifles it became A Squadron, 1st Mounted Rifles (CYC).

Canterbury Mounted Rifle Volunteers, Christchurch: 11 April 1885
First unit to be actually organised and trained as a Mounted Rifle unit, and at the time of embodiment was the only Mounted Rifle unit in New Zealand. Became B Company of the Canterbury Mounted Battalion in 1899, B Squadron 1st Regiment North Canterbury Mounted Rifles in 1901, and in 1914 with the Waimakariri Mounted Rifles, formed B Squadron of the 1st Mounted Rifles (CYC).

Ellesmere Mounted Rifles, Leeston: 5 August 1898
Became C Company in the Canterbury Mounted Rifle Battalion in 1899.
Became C Squadron in the 1st Regiment North Canterbury Mounted Rifles in 1901.
In 1914 with the CYC formed A Squadron 1st Mounted Rifles (CYC).
NOTE: The South Canterbury Mounted Rifles formed D Company of the Canterbury Mounted Rifle Battalion in 1899.

Malvern Mounted Rifle Volunteers, Waddington: 11 April 1900
Was B Squadron 2nd Regiment North Canterbury Mounted Rifles, but transferred to the 1st Regiment in place of the North Canterbury Mounted Rifles (Tuahiwi) transferred to the 2nd Regiment.
With the Cust Mounted Rifles (late C Squadron 2nd Regiment North Canterbury Mounted Rifles) formed C squadron 1st Mounted Rifles (CYC).

Waimakariri Mounted Rifle Volunteers, West Melton: 14 April 1900
In 1901, D Squadron 1st Regiment North Canterbury Mounted Rifle Volunteers.
With the Canterbury Mounted Rifles formed B Squadron 1st Mounted Rifles (CYC).

Canterbury Scouts Volunteer Reserve, Christchurch: Accepted 15 August 1907
Reserve with the 1st Regiment North Canterbury Mounted Rifles.
Disbanded 4 May 1911.

Kaikoura Mounted Rifle Volunteers, Kaikoura: 10 November 1898
A Squadron 2nd Regiment North Canterbury Mounted Rifle Volunteers, 1 May 1901.
Became B Squadron 10th (Nelson) Mounted Rifles.

Amuri Mounted Rifle Volunteers, Waiau: 11 April 1900
B Squadron 2nd Regiment North Canterbury Mounted Rifle Volunteers.
With the North Canterbury Mounted Rifle Volunteers (Tuahiwi) formed D Squadron 1st Mounted Rifles (CYC).

Cust Mounted Rifle Volunteers, Cust: 6 May 1900
C Squadron 2nd Regiment North Canterbury Mounted Rifle Volunteers.
With Malvern Mounted Rifle Volunteers formed C Squadron 1st Mounted Rifles (CYC).

North Canterbury Mounted Rifle Volunteers, Tuahiwi: 8 May 1900
D Squadron 2nd Regiment North Canterbury Mounted Rifle Volunteers.
With Amuri Mounted Rifle Volunteers formed D Squadron 1st Mounted Rifles (CYC).

In 1901 Mounted Corps were called battalions and companies, but this was subsequently altered to regiments and squadrons. The latter titles are the proper ones for a body of horsemen.

It should be remembered that before 1898, with the exception of the Canterbury Mounted Rifles, such units as Timaru Cavalry, Temuka Cavalry and Rangiora Cavalry were only local titles for outlying troops and detachments of the Canterbury Yeomanry Cavalry.

The guidon of the Canterbury Yeomanry Cavalry was presented by the Governor-General (Lord Galway) in Hagley Park 1937.

2nd Regiment, North Canterbury Mounted Rifles 1901
Each squadron wore a similar helmet plate with distinguishing letters.
 A Squadron — Kaikoura Mounted Rifle Volunteers (KMR).
 B Squadron — Amuri Mounted Rifle Volunteers (AMR).
 C Squadron — Cust Mounted Rifle Volunteers (CMR).
 D Squadron — North Canterbury Mounted Rifle Volunteers (NCMR).

Cross-belt plate, North Canterbury Mounted Rifles —
similar plates were worn by all four squadrons.

QUEEN ALEXANDRA'S 2nd (WELLINGTON WEST COAST) MOUNTED RIFLES

BADGE: A punga-tree encircled by garter bearing the words 'Queen Alexandra's 2nd W.W.C. Mtd Rifles'.
COLLAR BADGES: As for the cap badge.
MOTTO: *Ake ake kia kaha* (For ever and ever be strong).
The badges and shoulder titles always in blackened brass. In bronze for officers.
BATTLE HONOURS: Taranaki 1860, New Zealand 1860-61-63, Opotiki 1865, New Zealand 1868 (these were unofficial). South Africa 1899-1902. The Great War 1914-18: ANZAC, Defence of Anzac, HILL 60 (ANZAC), SARI BAIR, Gallipoli 1915, RUMANI, RAFAH, Egypt 1915-17, GAZA, Jerusalem, JAFFA, Jericho, JORDAN, Megiddo, Nablus, Palestine 1917-18.
UNIFORM: Khaki.

Formed on 17 March 1911 with the change of title of the 1st Regiment, Wellington (West Coast) Mounted Rifles. This had consisted of: Alexandra Mounted Rifle Volunteers, Wairoa Mounted Rifle Volunteers, Hawera Mounted Rifle Volunteers, Stratford Mounted Rifle Volunteers, Opunake Mounted Rifle Volunteers.

A former Company had disbanded, Egmont Mounted Rifle Volunteers. Some of the Volunteer Troops in the District were:

Taranaki Mounted Volunteers: 3 March 1860
Captain F. J. Mace and Trooper A. Rodriguez of the Taranaki Mounted Volunteers were both awarded the New Zealand Cross.

Patea Light Horse Volunteers: 3 August 1867. Took part in attack at Moturoa 7 November 1868.

Wanganui Volunteer Cavalry: Accepted 21 September 1860. This Troop was disbanded (not having tendered service under Volunteers Act of 1865) on 23 March 1866, but must have been at once revived for the unit was finally disbanded 28 January 1868.

Wanganui Cavalry: Accepted 2 December 1862. A militia cavalry corps which took part in the Maori Wars in September 1865 in the Opotiki expedition. In January 1866 engaged at Te Putahi. Disbanded on 21 October 1867.

Union Corps of Volunteers: Accepted 24 July 1863. Composed of a cavalry troop and an infantry troop. Disbanded 5 May 1866 (not having tendered service under the Volunteers Act of 1865).

Wanganui Yeomanry Cavalry Volunteers: January 1863. Took part in one of the few cavalry charges in the Maori Wars, four miles south-east of Opotiki on 4 October 1865.

Alexandra Troop, Wanganui Cavalry Volunteers: Accepted 16 September 1864. Service accepted under Volunteers Act of 1865 on 28 March 1866. Disbanded 20 January 1868.

Wanganui Cavalry Volunteers: 12 July 1862 to 23 March 1866. Second Troop of this name 25 July 1868 to 29 July 1874.

Turakina Cavalry Volunteers: Accepted 21 November 1863. Disbanded 28 June 1876.

Alexandra Troop, Wanganui Cavalry Volunteers: Accepted 8 December 1868. Second troop of this name. Parent Troop of existing regiment, raised from members of the late Alexandra Troop. Formed part of 1st (North Island) Regiment of Cavalry Volunteers in 1866. Styled 'Mounted Rifles' 3 November 1898. On 7 November 1895 became A Company Wellington Mounted Rifle Battalion and on 1 May 1901 A Squadron of the 1st Regiment Wellington (West Coast) Mounted Rifle Volunteers.

Kai Iwi Yeomanry Cavalry Volunteers: Accepted 20 October 1868. Disbanded 29 November 1869. Took part in Maori War 1868-69. Named after river Kai-Iwi then the boundary line of defence. The troop did a good service in patrolling the river bank night and day. Trooper William Lingard of this corps was one of the first who received the New Zealand Cross, instituted 16 March 1869 for bravery in action, or devotion to duty while on active service.

Aramoho Light Horse Volunteers: Accepted 17 December 1870. Disbanded 16 December 1873.

Kai-iwi Cavalry Volunteers: Accepted 10 October 1868. Second corps of this name. Disbanded 25 October 1871.

Opokongaro (Wanganui) Light Horse Volunteers: Accepted 5 January 1871. Disbanded 6 June 1871.

Opunake Mounted Rifle Volunteers: Accepted 11 April 1900. Became E Squadron 1st Regiment Wellington (West Coast) Mounted Rifle Volunteers on 1 May 1901.

Service in World War I as part of the 'Wellington' Mounted Rifle Regiment and also in Sinai and Palestine 1916-19 where, with the 'Auckland' and 'Canterbury' Mounted Rifle Regiments, formed the New Zealand Mounted Rifle Brigade of the ANZAC Mounted Division.

In 1921 their title became the 2nd N.Z. Mounted Rifles (Queen Alexandra's Wellington, West Coast). This title was altered to the Queen Alexandra's (Wellington West Coast) Mounted Rifles.

On 1 January 1942 all Mounted Rifle Regiments had the words 'Light Armoured Fighting Vehicle Regiment' added to their title to make the title of the Regiment 2nd Light Armoured Fighting Vehicle Regiment (Queen Alexandra's (Wellington West Coast) Mounted Rifles).

On 29 March 1944 in the reorganised New Zealand Armoured Corps they became a part of the 2nd Armoured Regiment and as such inherited the battle honours of the 19th Armoured Regiment 2NZEF and 3 Division Tank Squadron.

In October 1953 the 9th (Wellington East Coast) Section of the Regiment became the 4th Armoured Regiment. The remainder retained the title of the 2nd Armoured Regiment and as such went into recess in 1956.

In September 1958 the Regiment was re-activated as part of the Regular Force, being renamed Queen Alexandra's Armoured Regiment in December 1958, the word 'Armoured' being dropped in August 1959. From 1962 onwards Regular and Territorial Units became integrated and the Regiment absorbed the 4th Armoured Regiment. 1st Armoured Squadron (Queen Alexandra's)

RNZAC today wears the collar badges of the 9th (Wellington East Coast) Mounted Rifles in recognition of this.

The Queen Alexandra's Regiment carried out full public duties in London in November 1964, the guidon carried being that presented to the regiment in May 1929 by Major-General R. Young, GOC New Zealand Military Forces. This guidon embodies the regimental colours, amber and black, and is unique in New Zealand as Mounted Rifle Regiments must carry a colour with a scarlet background.

Taranaki Mounted Rifles, 1879

3rd (AUCKLAND) MOUNTED RIFLES

BADGE: A hawk bearing a shield with the the Southern Cross on breast, and Maori club and battle-axe in claws.

MOTTO: *Te kaahu mataara* (Be like a hawk).

BATTLE HONOURS: South Africa 1901-2, The Great War 1914-18: Anzac, DEFENCE OF ANZAC, HILL 60 (ANZAC), Sari Bair, GALLIPOLI 1915, RUMANI, RAFAH, EGYPT 1915-17, GAZA, Jerusalem, Jaffa, Jericho, Jordan, Megiddo, Nablus, PALESTINE 1917-18.

Formed on 17 March 1911 with the change of name of the 1st Regiment, Auckland Mounted Rifles. This had consisted of: Auckland Mounted Rifle Volunteers, Pukekohe Mounted Rifle Volunteers, Seddon Horse Mounted Rifle Volunteers, Franklin Mounted Rifle Volunteers, Waiuku Mounted Rifle Volunteers, Rodney Mounted Rifle Volunteers.

Service on Gallipoli and in Egypt as part of the 'Auckland' Mounted Rifle Regiment and in Sinai and Palestine 1916-19.

In 1921 became the 3rd N.Z. Mounted Rifles (Auckland). This was altered to The Auckland (East Coast) Mounted Rifles.

On 1 January 1942 included the words 'Light Armoured Fighting Vehicle Regiment' in their title. The reorganising of the New Zealand Armoured Corps into three Armoured Regiments on 29 March 1944 made them a part of the 1st Armoured Regiment and as such inherited the battle honours of the 18th Armoured Regiment 2NZEF.

The 1st Armoured Regiment comprised 3rd (Auckland), 4th (Waikato) and 11th (North Auckland) Light Armoured Fighting Vehicle Regiment.

Some of the early Volunteers Corps in the district were:

Auckland Mounted Rifle Volunteers: 31 October 1898
Auckland Cavalry Volunteers: 30 April 1885.
Auckland Royal Dragoons: 3 February 1887.
Auckland Royal Lancers: 9 September 1886.

Colonial Defence Force Cavalry: October 1862. Two troops in Auckland. One Troop in Hawke's Bay; Wanganui: Wellington.
Drury Light Horse Volunteers: 17 April 1871.
Nixon Light Horse Volunteers: 11 August 1875.
Prince Alfred Light Horse Volunteers: 20 March 1869.
Royal Cavalry Volunteers: 5 April 1860.
Waiuku Cavalry Volunteers: 12 March 1866.

Badge of the 3rd Battalion
Auckland Mounted Rifle Volunteers: formed 28 January 1902

4th (WAIKATO) MOUNTED RIFLES

BADGE: A Kaka within a wreath of kowhai leaves and blossoms.
MOTTO: *Libertas et Natale Solum* (Liberty and Homeland).
BATTLE HONOURS: South Africa 1900-2. The Great War 1914-18: Anzac, DEFENCE OF ANZAC, HILL 60 (ANZAC), SARI BAIR, Gallipoli 1915, RUMANI, RAFAH, Egypt 1915-17, GAZA, Jerusalem, JAFFA, Jericho, JORDAN, Megiddo, Nablus, Palestine 1917-18.

Formed on 17 March 1911 with the amalgamation of the 2nd Regiment Auckland Mounted Rifles with the 4th Regiment, Auckland Mounted Rifles. These Regiments had consisted of:

2nd Regiment, Auckland Mounted Rifle Volunteers: No. 1 Squadron, Waikato Mounted Rifle Volunteers (Hamilton); Piako Mounted Rifle Volunteers; No. 2 Squadron Waikato Mounted Rifle Volunteers (Te Awamutu); No. 3 Squadron Waikato Mounted Rifle Volunteers (Cambridge); Raglan Mounted Rifle Volunteers.

4th Regiment, Auckland Mounted Rifle Volunteers: Tauranga Mounted Rifle Volunteers; Opotiki Mounted Rifle Volunteers; Whakatane Mounted Rifle Volunteers; Te Puke Mounted Rifle Volunteers; Matata Mounted Rifle Volunteers.

Early Volunteer Corps were:
Cambridge Cavalry Volunteers: 13 January 1872.
Cambridge Mounted Rifles: 24 July 1869.
Hamilton Cavalry Volunteers: 16 March 1880.
South Franklin Mounted Infantry Volunteers: 28 May 1885.
Te Awamutu Cavalry Volunteers: 2 March 1871.

Cornets Angus Smith and H. C. W. Wrigg of an earlier unit in the area — The Bay of Plenty Cavalry Volunteers — both won the New Zealand Cross in the Maori Wars. Service on Gallipoli as part of the 'Auckland Mounted Rifle Regiment' and in Sinai and Palestine 1916-19 as part of the ANZAC Mounted Division of the New Zealand Mounted Rifle Brigade.

In 1921 became the 4th N.Z. Mounted Rifles (Waikato). This title was altered to The Waikato Mounted Rifles. On 1 January 1942 their title was amended by adding the words 'Light Armoured Fighting Vehicle Regiment'.

On 29 March 1944 became part of the 1st Armoured Regiment of the New Zealand Armoured Corps. Inherited the battle honours of the 18th Armoured Regiment 2NZEF.

Alexandra Cavalry Regiment, 1887
(B Troop NZ Cavalry Volunteers)

Te Awamutu Cavalry Volunteers
1st Regiment NZ Cavalry Volunteers, 1886

South Franklin
Mounted Infantry, 1885

Cap badge with brass hook attached. The majority of the Mounted Rifle Regiments wore a similar hook on their cap badge but these badges are not common.

2nd Waikato Mounted Rifles
(Auckland)

5th MOUNTED RIFLES (OTAGO HUSSARS)

BADGE: The coat of arms of Colonel Cowie Nichols within a circle flanked by fern fronds and surmounted by the Imperial crown.

MOTTO: *Es Fidelis* (Be Faithful).

BATTLE HONOURS: South Africa 1899-1902. The Great War 1914-18: Somme 1916-18, Kemmel, Scherpenberg, Guillemont, Tardenois, France and Flanders 1916-18, Ginchy, Flers-Courcellette, Morval, Le Transloy, Messines 1917, Ypres 1917, Broodseinde, Passchendaele, Arras 1918, Lys, Bailleul, MARNE 1918, ANZAC, DEFENCE OF ANZAC, HILL 60 (ANZAC), SARI BAIR, GALLIPOLI 1915, EGYPT 1915-16.

UNIFORM: Blue, white facings, silver lace.

Formed on 17 March 1911 with the change of name of the 1st Regiment Otago Mounted Rifle Volunteers. This had consisted of:

Dunedin Light Horse Volunteers: The only reference in the *New Zealand Gazette* to this corps is dated 28 March 1866 when it was disbanded for not tendering service under the Volunteer Act 1865.

Otago Hussar Volunteers (Dunedin): Accepted 1 January 1883. Raised as Dunedin Cavalry. Designation altered to Otago Hussars 6 December 1886. Why the precedence, 1 January 1888, was allowed for many years is hard to understand, unless by a printer's error 1888 was substituted for 1883. The officers were not apparently jealous of the precedence of their corps. Became A Company Otago Mounted Rifle Battalion 27 June 1898 and A Squadron 1st Regiment Otago Mounted Rifle Volunteers on 1 May 1901.

North Otago Troop of Otago Hussars (Oamaru): Accepted 6 December 1886. Designation altered to North Otago Mounted Rifle Volunteers 3 October 1891. Formed part of the Otago Mounted Rifle Battalion 1898 and in 1901 became B Squadron 1st Regiment Otago Mounted Rifle Volunteers.

Clutha Mounted Rifle Volunteers (Balclutha): 2 June 1898.

Tuapeka Mounted Rifle Volunteers (Lawrence): 28 June 1900.

Maniototo Mounted Rifle Volunteers (Ranfurly): 11 April 1900. Formed part of the Otago Mounted Rifle Battalion in 1900. Became D Squadron 1st Regiment Otago Mounted Rifle Volunteers in 1901.

Taieri Mounted Rifle Volunteers (Outram): 10 September 1900. F Squadron, 1st Regiment Otago Mounted Rifle Volunteers in 1901. Disbanded 5 February 1908.

Waitaki Mounted Rifle Volunteers (Oamaru): 20 August 1901. G Squadron 1st Regiment Otago Mounted Rifle Volunteers in 1901. Disbanded 17 March 1909.

Service during World War I as the 'Otago' Mounted Rifle Regiment which consisted of the 5th (Otago Hussars), 7th (Southland), 12th (Otago) Mounted Rifle Regiments. Reduced to squadron strength, they were the only mounted New Zealand troops in France 1916-19.

In 1921 the 5th Mounted Rifles (Otago Hussars), the 7th (Southland) Mounted Rifles and the 12th (Otago) Mounted Rifles were amalgamated to form the 5th N.Z. Mounted Rifles (Otago). They were redesignated the 5th N.Z. Mounted Rifles (Otago Hussars) on 4 August 1923. In 1927 they became the Otago Mounted Rifles.

On 1 January 1942, the nine Mounted Rifle Regiments had the words 'Light Armoured Fighting Vehicle Regiment' added after their number and before the old title. The guidon of the Otago Mounted Rifles was presented at Wingatui by the Governor-General (Lord Galway) March 1939.

Cross-belt plates

Southland Hussars   Otago Hussars

On 29 March 1944 with the reorganisation of the New Zealand Armoured Corps, became 3rd Armoured Regiment. This was formed by the 1st (CYC), 5th (Otago) and 10th (Nelson and Marlborough) Light Armoured Fighting Vehicle Regiments. The 3rd Armoured Regiment inherited the World War II battle honours of the 20th Armoured Regiment 2NZEF.

The regiment was placed in recess in 1956.

The first pattern badge of the 5th Otago Mounted Rifles has the same fine fern leaves as the badge of the 1st Otago Mounted Rifles. The second pattern badge has much coarser fern leaves and is the much more common of the two. The badges are usually bi-metal, although badges that are all bronze or all brass, are to be found. This also applies to collar badges.

6th (MANAWATU) MOUNTED RIFLES

BADGE: Within a wreath of laurel leaves surmounted by a crown, the number of the Regiment.
MOTTO: *He Kawau Maro* (Unyielding as the shag).
BATTLE HONOURS: South Africa 1902. The Great War 1914-18: ANZAC, Defence of Anzac, HILL 60 (ANZAC), Sari Bair, Gallipoli 1915, RUMANI, RAFAH, Egypt 1915-17, GAZA, Jerusalem, JAFFA, Jericho, JORDAN, Megiddo, NABLUS, Palestine 1917-18.
UNIFORM: Green, with black facings.

Formed on 17 March 1911 with the change of name of the 3rd Regiment, Wellington (Manawatu) Mounted Rifles. This had consisted of:
Manawatu Mounted Rifle Volunteers; Hunterville Mounted Rifle Volunteers; Feilding Mounted Rifle Volunteers.

Two companies which had disbanded were: Horowhenua Mounted Rifle Volunteers 10 October 1905; Otaki Mounted Rifle Volunteers 18 January 1905.

Much earlier in the District there had been attempts to establish volunteer cavalry.

Volunteer Yeomanry Cavalry: Accepted 5 June 1860.
First Commanding Officer: Captain Edward Jerningham Wakefield. The notice of appointment of Captain E. J. Wakefield and his subaltern is the only reference to this corps in the *New Zealand Gazette*. This would indicate that the corps had a short existence. Captain Wakefield was captain of one of the troops of Canterbury Yeomanry Cavalry when the regiment formed in 1864, although he held his command for just a few weeks.

Rangitikei Mounted Rifle Volunteers: 7 May 1885.

Victoria Troop, Rangitikei Cavalry Volunteers: 4 September 1863. Disbanded 6 September 1866. Reformed 28 November 1868 as the Rangitikei Cavalry Volunteers, changed title to Alfred Cavalry Volunteers. Disbanded 16 July 1879.

Service during World War I as part of the 'Wellington' Mounted Rifle Regiment which consisted of the Queen Alexandra's 2nd (Wellington West Coast), 6th (Manawatu), and 9th (Wellington East Coast) Mounted Rifles.

In action in Gallipoli and formed part of the New Zealand Mounted Rifle Brigade of ANZAC Mounted Division in Sinai and Palestine 1916-19.

In 1921 they became the 6th N.Z. Mounted Rifles (Manawatu). This title was changed to The Manawatu Rifles. On 1 January 1942 their title was extended to include the words 'Light Armoured Fighting Vehicle Regiment'.

On 29 March 1944 the New Zealand Armoured Corps was reorganised and they became part of the 2nd Armoured Regiment which included: 2 (Queen Alexandra's WWC), 6 (Manawatu) and 9 (Wellington East Coast) LARV Regiments. This Regiment inherited the battle honours of the 19th Armoured Regiment 2nd NZEF and 3 Division Tank Squadron. The 2nd Armoured Regiment placed in recess 1956.

Rangitikei Cavalry Volunteers

7th (SOUTHLAND) MOUNTED RIFLES

BADGE: A sparrow hawk swooping on its prey.
COLLAR BADGES: Small versions of the cap badge in matching pairs.
MOTTO: *Celer et audax* (Swift and bold).
The badges are bronze or brass and exist in a non-voided pattern.
BATTLE HONOURS: South Africa 1902. The Great War 1914-18: Somme 1916, 1918, Guillemont, Ginchy, Flers-Courcelette, Morval, Le Transloy, MESSINES 1917, Ypres 1917, Broodseinde, Passchendaele, Arras 1918, Lys, Bailleul, KEMMEL, Scherpenberg, MARNE 1918, Tardenois, France and Flanders 1916-18, ANZAC, DEFENCE OF ANZAC, SARI BAIR, GALLIPOLI 1915, EGYPT 1915-16, HILL 60 (ANZAC).
Formed on 17 March 1911 with the change of title of the 2nd Regiment Otago Mounted Rifles. This had consisted of:

Invercargill Light Horse Volunteers: Accepted 13 July 1870. Disbanded 26 April 1871.

Southland Hussars Volunteers: Accepted 19 April 1880. Raised as a single troop, increased to three troops and styled 'The Southland Regiment of Hussars' on 14 December 1880. Reverted to a single troop on 6 June 1883. Disbanded 17 July 1888.

Southland Yeomanry Hussars: Accepted 16 October 1889. Honorary Corps. Disbanded 13 April 1891.

Southland Mounted Rifle Volunteers (Invercargill): 23 December 1895. C Company Otago Mounted Rifle Volunteers, 27 June 1898; A Squadron 2nd Regiment Otago Mounted Rifle Volunteers, 1 May 1901.

Mataura Mounted Rifle Volunteers (Gore): 2 February 1900. Formed part of Otago Battalion Mounted Rifle Volunteers in 1900; C Squadron 2nd Regiment Otago Mounted Rifle Volunteers, 1 May 1901.

Wakatipu Mounted Rifle Volunteers (Arrowtown): 10 September 1900. Formed part of Otago Battalion Mounted Rifle Volunteers in 1900; C Squadron 2nd Regiment Otago Mounted Rifle Volunteers, 10 March 1902.

Murihiku Mounted Rifle Volunteers (Wyndham): 26 March 1901. Formed part of Otago Battalion Mounted Rifle Volunteers in 1901, and in the same year became E Squadron 2nd Regiment Otago Mounted Rifle Volunteers.

Wallace Mounted Rifle Volunteers (Nightcaps, later Otautau): 13 April 1901. Formed part of Otago Battalion Mounted Rifle Volunteers in 1901 and in the same year became F Squadron 2nd Regiment Otago Mounted Rifle Volunteers.

Service during World War I as the 'Otago' Mounted Rifle Regiment which consisted of the 5th (Otago Hussars), 7th (Southland), 12th (Otago) Mounted Rifle Regiments.

Reduced to squadron strength they were the only mounted New Zealand troops in France 1916-19. In 1921 the 5th Mounted Rifles (Otago Hussars), the 7th (Southland) Mounted Rifles and the 12th (Otago) Mounted Rifles were amalgamated to form the 5th N.Z. Mounted Rifles. This title was altered to The Otago Mounted Rifles.

Ashburton Mounted Rifle Volunteers, formed 20 March 1900. Designated B Company, 1st Battalion South Canterbury Mounted Rifle Volunteers, 1 May 1901.

2nd Battalion, Otago Mounted Rifle Volunteers: 1 May 1901.
A Company — Southland Mounted Rifle Volunteers.
B Company — Clutha Mounted Rifle Volunteers. Transferred to No. 1 Battalion, Otago Mounted Rifle Volunteers as C Company, 10 March 1902.
C Company — Mataura Mounted Rifle Volunteers.
D Company — Kelso Mounted Rifle Volunteers.
E Company — Murihiku Mounted Rifle Volunteers added 1 October 1901.
F Company — Wallace Mounted Rifle Volunteers added 1 October 1901.

The helmet plate worn by each company was as illustrated, except for the lower scroll which was detachable and carried the name of the company. Clutha Company was not included.

8th (SOUTH CANTERBURY) MOUNTED RIFLES

BADGE: The Earl of Ranfurly's Coat-of-Arms and Crest.
COLLAR BADGES: The Crest, in matching pairs.
MOTTO: *Mofeo et Profitor* (By my actions I am known).
The cap badge in bronze or brass appears in two sizes, 40mm or 55mm in depth.
BATTLE HONOURS: South Africa 1902. The Great War 1914-18: ANZAC, Defence of Anzac, HILL 60 (ANZAC), SARI BAIR, Gallipoli 1915, RUMANI, RAFAH, Egypt 1915-17, GAZA, JERUSALEM, Jaffa, Jericho, Jordan, Megiddo, Nablus, PALESTINE 1917-18.

UNIFORM: Khaki.

Formed on 17 March 1911 with the change of title of the 1st Regiment, South Canterbury Mounted Rifles. This had consisted of:

South Canterbury Mounted Rifle Volunteers (Timaru): D Company Canterbury Mounted Rifle Volunteers 1899; A Squadron 1st Regiment South Canterbury Mounted Rifle Volunteers 1 May 1901; A Squadron 8th (South Canterbury) Mounted Rifles.

Ashburton Mounted Rifle Volunteers: B Squadron 1st Regiment South Canterbury Mounted Rifle Volunteers, 1 May 1901; B Squadron 8th (South Canterbury) Mounted Rifles.

MacKenzie Mounted Rifle Volunteers (Fairlie): C Squadron 1st Regiment South Canterbury Mounted Rifle Volunteers, 1 May 1901. Disbanded 24 October 1907.

Studholme Mounted Rifle Volunteers (Waimate): D Squadron 1st Regiment South Canterbury Mounted Rifle Volunteers, 1 May 1901; C Squadron 1st Regiment South Canterbury Mounted Rifle Volunteers, 1907; C Squadron 8th (South Canterbury) Mounted Rifles.

Geraldine Mounted Rifle Volunteers: E Squadron 1st Regiment South Canterbury Mounted Rifle Volunteers, 1 May 1901; D Squadron 1st Regiment South Canterbury Mounted Rifle Volunteers, 1907; D Squadron 8th (South Canterbury) Mounted Rifles.

As part of the 'Canterbury' Mounted Rifles saw action at Gallipoli and with the 'Auckland' and 'Wellington' Mounted Rifle Regiments formed the New Zealand Mounted Rifle Brigade of ANZAC Mounted Division in Sinai and Palestine 1916-19.

In 1921 the 8th (South Canterbury) Mounted Rifles were amalgamated with the 1st Mounted Rifles (Canterbury Yeomanry Cavalry) to form the 1st N.Z. Mounted Rifles (Canterbury Yeomanry Cavalry). This title was altered to The Canterbury Yeomanry Cavalry.

Canterbury Mounted Rifles, 1885

9th (WELLINGTON EAST COAST) MOUNTED RIFLES

BADGE: A horse rampant.
COLLAR BADGES: Smaller versions of the cap badge in matching pairs.
MOTTO: *Fortes fortuna juvat* (Fortune assists the brave).
There are two distinct types of scroll on these badges. Badges in bronze or brass.
BATTLE HONOURS: South Africa 1900-2. The Great War 1914-18: ANZAC, Defence of Anzac, HILL 60 (ANZAC), SARI BAIR, Gallipoli 1915, RUMANI, RAFAH, Egypt 1915-17, GAZA, Jerusalem, Jaffa, Jericho, JORDAN, Megiddo, Nablus, Palestine 1917-18.

Formed on 17 March 1911 with the amalgamation of the 2nd Regiment, Wellington (Wairarapa) Mounted Rifles with the 4th Regiment, Wellington (East Coast) Mounted Rifles.

2nd Regiment Wellington (Wairarapa) Mounted Rifles: Pahiatua Mounted Rifle Volunteers; Eketahuna Mounted Rifle Volunteers; Masterton Mounted Rifle Volunteers. Two former companies, Wairarapa Mounted Rifle Volunteers and South Wairarapa Mounted Rifle Volunteers had disbanded on 27 September 1906 and 15 March 1905. Heretaunga Mounted Rifle Volunteers transferred to the 3rd (Wellington) Mounted Rifle Volunteers.

4th Regiment Wellington (East Coast) Mounted Rifle Volunteers: East Coast Mounted Rifle Volunteers; Hawke's Bay Mounted Rifle Volunteers; Huramua Mounted Rifle Volunteers.

Two former companies, Ruahine Mounted Rifle Volunteers and Ahuriri Mounted Rifle Volunteers, had disbanded on 16 December 1905 and 21 September 1904.

Very early units in the area were Poverty Bay Mounted Rifles and East Coast Hussars. Castlepoint Cavalry Volunteers accepted 14 August 1866 (formerly an infantry company prior to date of acceptance). Disbanded 9 January 1869.

Saw service on Gallipoli and in Sinai and Palestine 1916-19 as part of the New Zealand Mounted Rifle Brigade of ANZAC Mounted Division.

In 1921 their title became the 7th N.Z. Mounted Rifles (Wellington East Coast). This was altered to The Wellington East Coast Mounted Rifles. On 1 January 1942 had the words 'Light Armoured Fighting Vehicle Regiment' added to their title.

Became part of the 2nd Armoured Regiment, New Zealand Armoured Corps on 29 March 1944 and inherited the battle honours of the 19th Armoured Regiment 2nd NZEF and 3 Division Tank Squadron.

In October 1953 a division was made in the regiment, the old 9th (Wellington East Coast) portion becoming the 4th Armoured Regiment.

Initially titled the Divisional Regiment (1953-56) they were later granted the title 'City of Hastings Own'. In 1962 the Territorial 4th Armoured Regiment (City of Hastings Own) was absorbed into the Regular Force, Queen Alexandra's.

The guidon presented at Marewa, Napier, May 1935 by Major-General Sir A. H. Russell, was laid up in the Hastings City Council Chambers July 1964.

Heretaunga Light Horse Cavalry Volunteers
Formed 1 January 1885. Designated E Troop, 1st Regiment of NZ Cavalry Volunteers 6 July 1887. Title changed to Heretaunga Mounted Infantry Volunteers 13 August 1890. Designated Heretaunga Mounted Rifle Volunteers 16 June 1891. Designated C Company, Wellington Battalion of Mounted Rifle Volunteers 7 November 1895. Designated A Company, No. 2 Battalion Wellington (Wairarapa) Mounted Rifle Volunteers 1 May 1901.

East Coast Hussars Cavalry Volunteers
Formed on 8 April 1887. Designated East Coast Mounted Rifle Volunteers 11 March 1892. Disbanded 24 February 1893. Reformed 6 February 1900. Designated A Company, No. 4 Battalion, Wellington (East Coast) Mounted Rifle Volunteers 1 May 1901.

Manawatu Mounted Rifle Volunteers
Formed 28 May 1891. Known locally as Manchester Mounted Rifle Volunteers. Designated E Company, Wellington Battalion of Mounted Rifle Volunteers 7 November 1896. Designated A Company, No. 3 Battalion Wellington (Manawatu) Mounted Rifle Volunteers 1 May 1901.

10th (NELSON) MOUNTED RIFLES

BADGE: A stag's head.
COLLAR BADGES: Smaller versions of cap badge, in matching pairs.
MOTTO: *Rem gero stenue* (Fight with zeal).
Badges in bronze or brass.
BATTLE HONOURS: South Africa 1900-2. The Great War 1914-18: ANZAC, Defence of Anzac, HILL 60 (ANZAC), SARI BAIR, Gallipoli 1915, RUMANI, RAFAH, EGYPT 1915-17, Gaza, Jerusalem, Jaffa, Jericho, JORDAN, Megiddo, Nablus, PALESTINE 1917-18.

Formed on 17 March 1911 with the change of title of the 1st Regiment Nelson Mounted Rifles. This had consisted of:
Marlborough Mounted Rifle Volunteers.
Wakatu Mounted Rifle Volunteers.
Takaka Mounted Rifle Volunteers.
Motueka Mounted Rifle Volunteers.
Served on Gallipoli and in Sinai and Palestine 1916-19 as part of the 'Canterbury' Mounted Rifle Regiment, ANZAC Mounted Division. Title changed to the 10th (Nelson and Marlborough) Mounted Rifle Regiment in 1917.

In 1921 became the 8th N.Z. Mounted Rifles (Nelson). Their title was changed to The Nelson-Marlborough Mounted Rifles. On 1 January 1942 their title was amended by the addition of the words 'Light Armoured Fighting Vehicle Regiment'.

On 29 March 1944 became part of the 3rd Armoured Regiment, New Zealand Armoured Corps and inherited the battle honours of 20th Armoured Regiment 2nd NZEF.

3rd Armoured Regiment placed in recess 1956.

11th (NORTH AUCKLAND) MOUNTED RIFLES

BADGE: A boar's head flanked by fern-fronds.
COLLAR BADGES: Similar to cap badge but in matching pairs.
MOTTO: *Kia tupato* (Be cautious).
Badges are bi-metal, bronze and white metal or brass and white metal. There are all bronze badges but these are uncommon.

Because the majority of the men of the 3rd Battalion, Auckland Mounted Rifles were from Northland, they took their badge design with them when they were redesignated the 11th (North Auckland) Mounted Rifles with Headquarters at Kawakawa.

BATTLE HONOURS: South Africa 1902. The Great War 1914-18: Anzac, Defence of Anzac, Hill 60 (Anzac), Sari Bair, GALLIPOLI 1915, RUMANI, Rafah, EGYPT 1915-17, GAZA, JERUSALEM, JAFFA, JERICHO, Jordan, Megiddo, Nablus, Palestine 1917-18.

Formed on 17 March 1911 with the change of title of the 3rd Regiment, Auckland Mounted Rifles. This had consisted of:
Marsden Mounted Rifle Volunteers (Whangarei).
Otamatea Mounted Rifle Volunteers (Paparoa).
Hokianga MRV and Northern Wairoa MRV (Waimauku).
Mangonui Mounted Rifle Volunteers (Kaitaia).
Northern Wairoa Mounted Rifle Volunteers (Aratapu).
Bay of Islands Mounted Rifle Volunteers (Ohaeawai).
Scottish Horse Mounted Rifle Volunteers (Waipu).
Mangakahia Mounted Rifle Volunteers (Mangatapere).

The Hokianga MRV and Northern Wairoa MRV had disbanded by 1908.

Piako Mounted Rifles, 1900

Service on Gallipoli and in Sinai and Palestine 1916-19 as part of the Auckland Mounted Rifle Regiment forming part of the New Zealand Mounted Rifle Brigade of the ANZAC Mounted Division.

In 1921 became the 9th N.Z. Mounted Rifles (North Auckland). This title was changed to The North Auckland Mounted Rifles.

On 1 January 1942 all mounted rifle regiments had the words 'Light Armoured Fighting Vehicle Regiment' added after their number and before the old title. In the reorganisation of the New Zealand Armoured Corps, 29 March 1944, they became part of the 1st Armoured Regiment and inherited the battle honours of 18 Armoured Regiment, 2NZEF.

In 1950 the Waikato Regiment was absorbed into the 1st Armoured Regiment.

12th (OTAGO) MOUNTED RIFLES

BADGE: A fallow deer's head.
COLLAR BADGES: Smaller versions of the cap bridge.
MOTTO: *For King and Country.*
The first pattern badges were non-voided. The second pattern as illustrated. Badges were in bronze or brass.
BATTLE HONOURS: The Great War 1914-18: Somme 1916-18, Guillemont, Ginchy, Flers-Courcelette, Morval, Le Transloy, MESSINES 1917, Ypres 1917, Broodseinde, Passchendaele, ARRAS 1918, Lys, Bailleul, KEMMEL, Scherpenberg, MARNE 1918, Tardenois, France and Flanders 1916-18, ANZAC, DEFENCE OF ANZAC, HILL 60 (ANZAC), SARI BAIR, GALLIPOLI 1915, EGYPT 1915-16.

Formed on 17 March 1911 as an additional Regiment of Mounted Rifles in the Otago Military District.

Service in Gallipoli, in Egypt and in France as part of the 'Otago' Mounted Rifle Regiment. The Otago Regiment reduced to squadron strength, were the only mounted New Zealand troops in France 1916-19.

In 1921 with the reduction of the Military Districts in New Zealand, the Mounted Rifle Regiments were reduced to nine. The 5th Mounted Rifles (Otago Hussars), the 7th (Southland) Mounted Rifles and the 12th (Otago) Mounted Rifles were amalgamated to become the 5th N.Z. Mounted Rifles (Otago Hussars). This title was amended to The Otago Mounted Rifles.

SAMOAN EXPEDITIONARY RELIEF FORCE

BADGE: There was no official badge for this unit, the soldiers wearing the badge of their own company or corps.
Depicted is the unofficial cap badge worn by many of the Force, this badge portraying three palm trees above the words 'Samoa Expedit. Forces', enclosed by fern leaves bearing the letters 'N' and 'Z', the whole surmounted by a crown.
COLLAR BADGES: The centre of the cap badge, three palm trees above a scroll 'Samoa'.

At the time when New Zealand was mobilising volunteers for the New Zealand Expeditionary Force (NZEF) as early as July 1914, a request was received by the Government asking for the immediate despatch of a force to secure the control of, and the capture of German possessions in Samoa. This force of just over 1,400 officers and men was a self-contained unit consisting of D Battery Field Artillery, Medical Corps, Army Service Corps, a section of 4th Field Company Engineers, Section Signal Company and Railway Company, and companies of the 3rd Auckland and the 5th Wellington Regiments.

The Force sailed on 15 August, the route being via Noumea, New Caledonia and Suva, Fiji, because of the presence of the German cruisers *Scharnhorst* and *Gneisenau* in the South Pacific. Two weeks later, on 29 August, the capture of Samoa was effected without a shot being fired. In March 1915, the majority of the men were returned to New Zealand, being replaced by men over the usual age for volunteering.

Upon arrival in New Zealand the men were posted to either a reinforcement company, or to one of the two battalions which were then being formed as part of the New Zealand Rifle Brigade.

THE FIRST NEW ZEALAND EXPEDITIONARY FORCE (NZEF)

The Defence Act of 1909 provided the pattern of Territorial training to replace the Volunteers and for all schoolboys to become a part of the Senior Cadets after leaving school. The minor changes which were suggested by Lord Kitchener during his visit to New Zealand in 1910 were implemented in 1911.

When World War I started in 1914 New Zealand had three years of military organisation upon which to build her war effort. At this time the only rifles in the Dominion were old pattern .303 Lee Enfield rifles and these served to arm the New Zealanders at Gallipoli.

The efficiency of the organisation can be seen in that the Expeditionary Force of 360 officers and 8,067 men left New Zealand two months after war was declared. This force, together with its first reinforcements was known as the New Zealand Expeditionary Force (NZEF). However, it is more generally known in New Zealand as the Main Body. In Egypt, February 1916, the Expeditionary Force was reorganised as a Division.

For the first two years of the war the Volunteers kept up the supply of reinforcements to the Main Body, but 1 August 1916 it was decided that compulsion for all would be a more just method of raising additional forces, so the Military Service Act became law. In all, over 124,000 men from a total of 250,000 eligible males served with the Expeditionary Force.

The 1911 Defence Act divided New Zealand into four Military Districts, each of which had four infantry regiments. The 17th (Ruahine) Regiment was formed in 1914. The New Zealand Expeditionary Force had four Regiments: 'Auckland', 'Wellington', 'Canterbury', and 'Otago'. These were named after Provinces and each had a Service Company from the Regiments in the respective Military District:

'Auckland' Regiment: 3rd (Auckland), 6th (Hauraki), 15th (North Auckland), and 16th (Waikato) Regiments.

'Wellington' Regiment: 7th (Wellington West Coast), 9th (Hawke's Bay), 11th (Taranaki) and 17th (Ruahine) Regiments.

'Canterbury' Regiment: 1st (Canterbury), 2nd (South Canterbury), 12th (Nel-

son) and 13th (North Canterbury and Westland) Regiments.

'Otago' Regiment: 4th (Otago), 8th (Southland), 10th (North Otago) and 14th (South Otago) Regiments.

Each of these 'Provincial' regiments had one battalion on Gallipoli and three battalions in France. Battle honours were earned for the sixteen regiments by these service companies who wore the badges of their respective regiments. The 5th (Wellington) Regiment was part of the Samoa Expedition and later its personnel were used to help form the New Zealand Rifle Brigade from whom the 5th get their battle honours for World War I.

In 1921 the New Zealand Military Districts were reduced to three (Northern, Central and Southern) each having four infantry regiments. This was the end of the use of a system of numerical titles. The NZEF was disbanded on 31 December 1921.

The 1st Canterbury Regiment amalgamated with the 2nd South Canterbury Regiment to become The Canterbury Regiment.

The 4th Otago Regiment amalgamated with the 10th North Otago Rifles to become The Otago Regiment.

The 8th Southland Rifles amgalamated with the 14th South Otago Rifles to become The Southland Regiment.

The 9th Hawke's Bay Regiment re-absorbed the 17th Ruahine Regiment to become The Hawke's Bay Regiment.

The 12th Nelson and Marlborough Regiment amalgamated with the 13th North Canterbury and Westland Regiment to become The Nelson, Marlborough and West Coast Regiment.

The twelve Regiments each supplied service companies to the 2 NZEF.

The four Northern District Regiments (Auckland, Hauraki, North Auckland, Waikato) each had a company in the 18, 21, 24 and 29 Battalions.

The four Central District Regiments (Wellington, Wellington West Coast, Taranaki, Hawke's Bay) each had a company in the 19, 22, 25 and 36 Battalions.

The four Southern District Regiments (Canterbury, Otago, Southland, Nelson Marlborough West Coast) each had a company in the 20, 23, 26, 30 and 37 Battalions. These regiments inherited the battle honours of the above battalions.

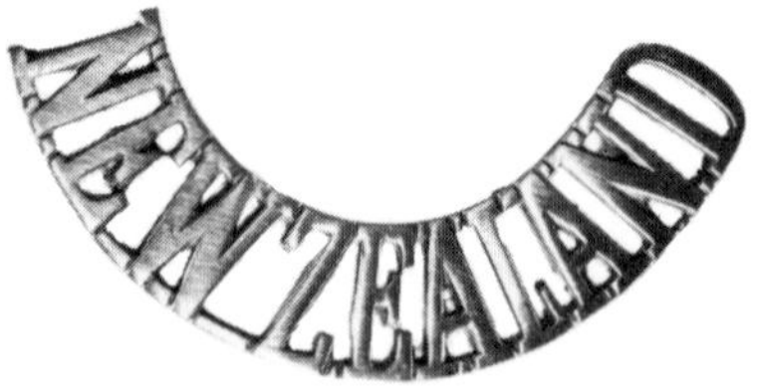
NEW ZEALAND

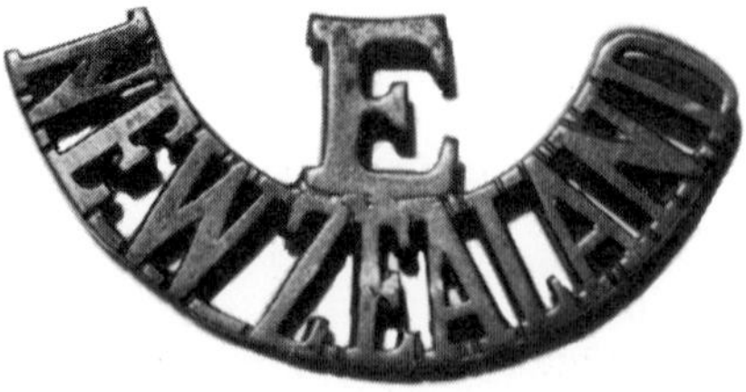
E
NEW ZEALAND

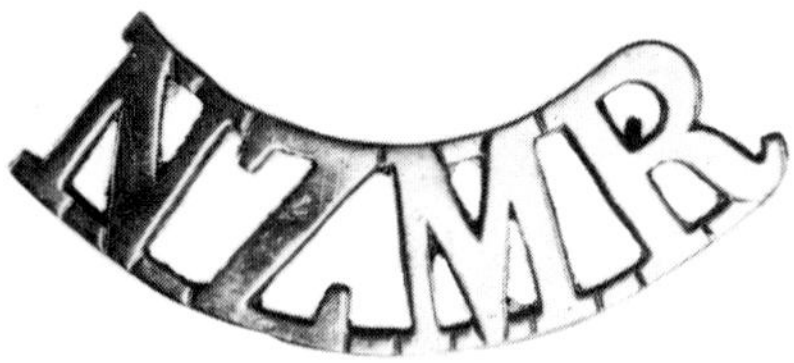
NZMR

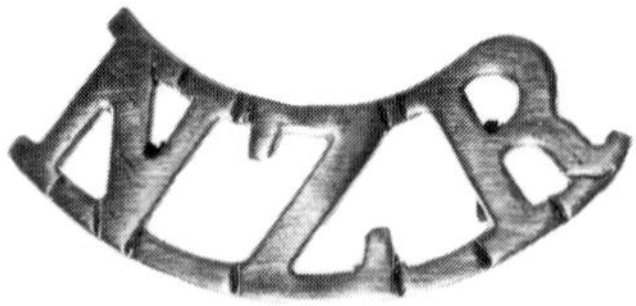
NZR

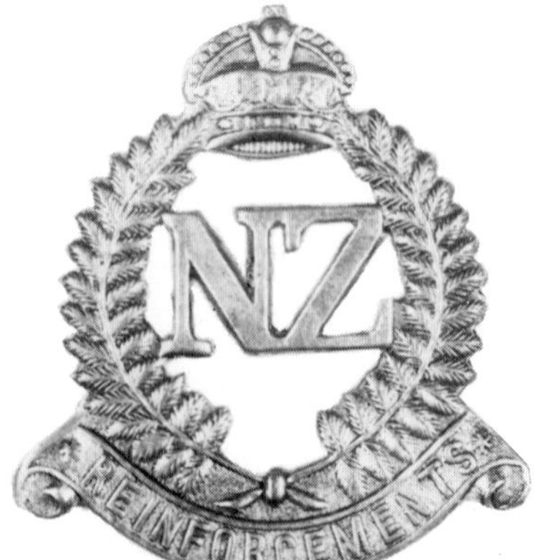
NZ
REINFORCEMENTS

Home Service Branch NZEF

RESERVISTS called up for military service under the Military Service Act 1916, and recruits who voluntarily enlisted, who were certified by an Army Medical Board to be permanently unfit for active service overseas but who were medically fit for service within New Zealand during the period of the war, were posted to the Home Service Branch.

Puggaree: Khaki, Black, Khaki with a distinguishing patch centred on the left-hand side as under:

CORPS	PATCH SHAPE	COLOURS
1. Mounted Rifles	Diamond	Green
2. Artillery	Diamond, divided vertically	Red and blue
3. Engineers	Diamond	Blue
4. Infantry	Diamond	Red
5. ASC	Diamond	White
6. NZMC	Diamond, divided vertically	Cherry and khaki
7. NZDC	Square, divided diagonally	Cherry and khaki
8. NZVC	Square	Maroon
9. NZAOC	Square, divided diagonally	Red and blue
10. Pay, Records recruiting	Diamond, divided horizontally	Royal blue over white

The men wore the titles and badges of the Corps or Department to which they were posted, except that those appointed to Headquarters, Recruiting, Base Records, War Expenses, and similar branches wore the titles and badges of the NZASC.

REINFORCEMENTS TO THE 1st NEW ZEALAND EXPEDITIONARY FORCE

Mounted Rifles
The most common type is that of a winged horse in brass, wing in white metal, above a scroll 'N.Z. Mounted Rifles'. All the badges were pressed as 25 and have a disc cover which alters the numeral from 26 through 47. The collar badges are smaller versions of the cap badge with the disc 'N.Z' or the numeral of the reinforcement. The 40th to 43rd Mounted Rifle Brigade reinforcements sailed from New Zealand on 10 October 1918 and were the last to proceed overseas while the 44th to 47th were still in training when the war ended.

A second pattern badge was introduced with the 31st Reinforcements and has the numerical disc placed over the stamped 31 through to the 47th reinforcements. Specific badges were worn by the 14th MR Reinforcements;

J Company 14th MR; 17th; 19th; 23rd and 24th MR Reinforcements. The 24th badge was struck as the 23rd but had the numeral covered with a disc '24'. The badges most often found consist of a rampant horse above a scroll 'N.Z.M.R' or 'N.Z. Mounted Rifles' sweated on to a wreath of fern leaves. The other common pattern was the badge of the 9th Wellington East Coast Mounted Rifles but with the scroll bearing the words 'N.Z. Mounted Rifles' or the letters 'N.Z.M.R'.

173

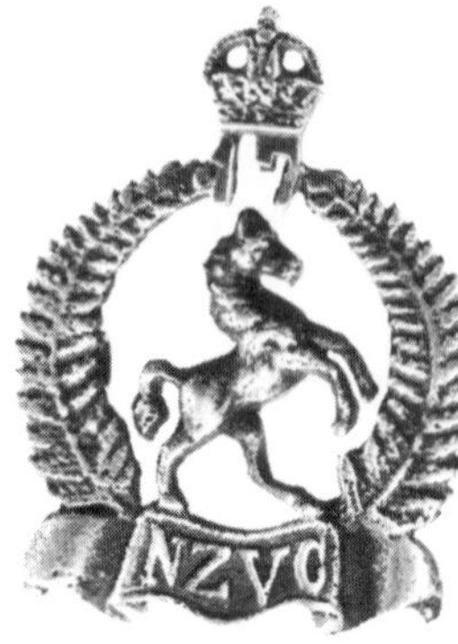
NZVC

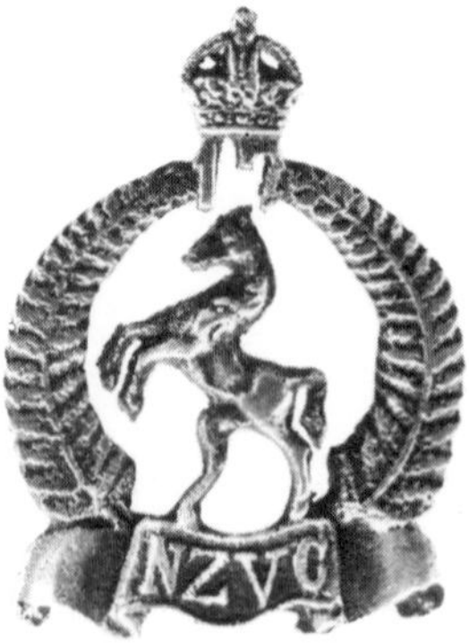
NZVC

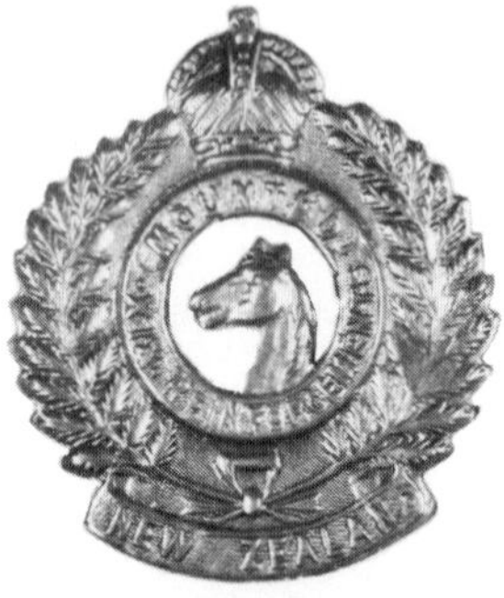

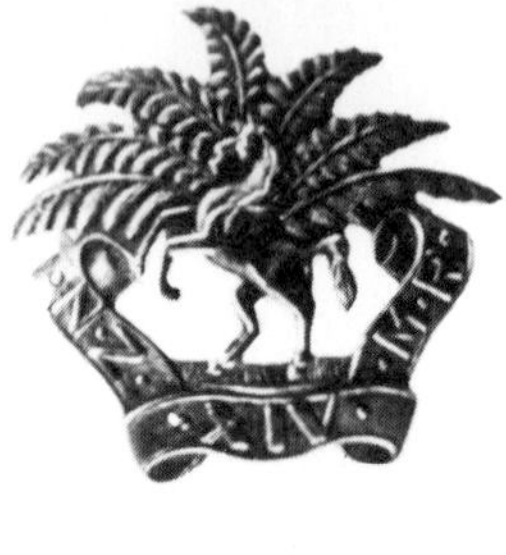

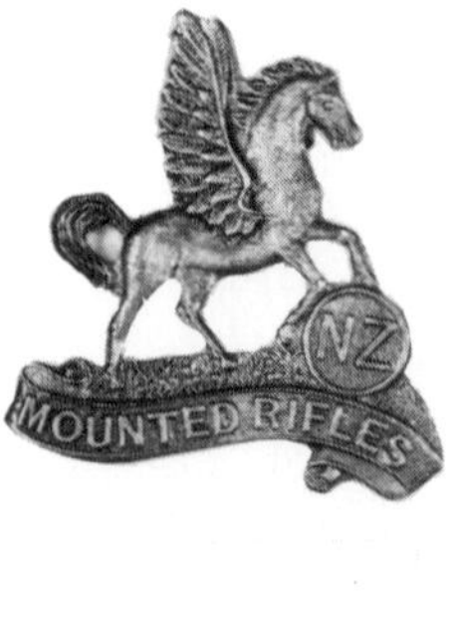
NZ
MOUNTED RIFLES

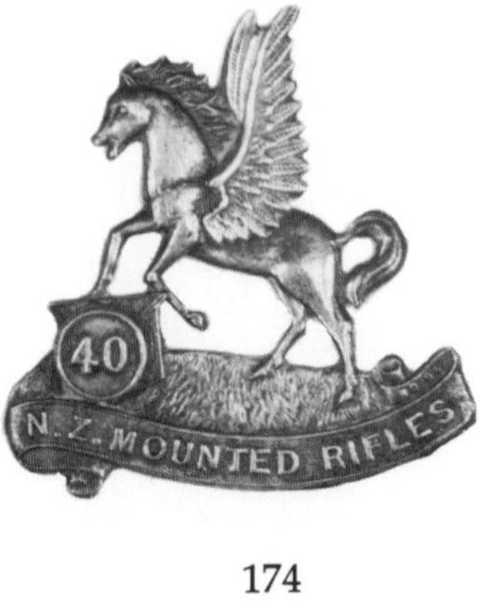
40
N.Z. MOUNTED RIFLES

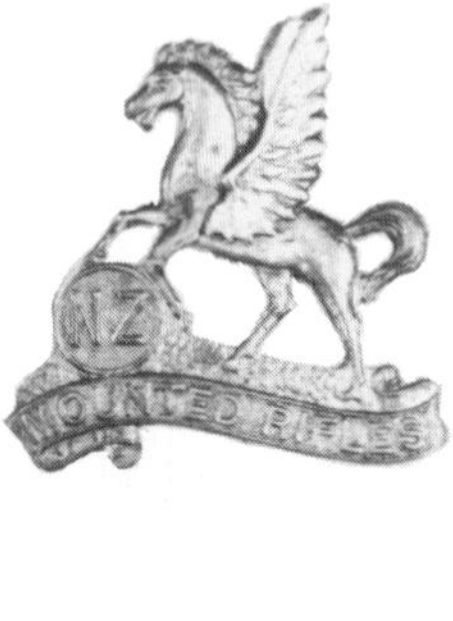

Infantry
Reinforcements to the NZEF wore a variety of badges, the most common being a fern-leaf wreath on which was sweated a company identification letter and the numeral of the reinforcement. The final draft to proceed overseas was the 43rd Reinforcement of which, F Company sailed on 17 August 1918, and A and B Companies sailed on 2 October 1918. Badges with numerals higher than these would only have been worn by men still in the training camps.

The reinforcements were initially divided into four Companies to join the Regiments of the NZEF. A Company (Auckland); B Company (Wellington); C Company (Canterbury); D Company (Otago). Rifle Brigade reinforcements were initially E Company (1st Battalion); F Company (2nd Battalion); G Company (3rd Battalion); H Company (4th Battalion).

1st to the 10th had A, B, C and D Companies (8th and 9th had E and F Company in addition).
11th had additional J and K Company. Rifle Brigade E, F, G and H Company.
12th to 20th had A, B, C, D, and J Companies. Rifle Brigade E, F, G and H Company.
21st to 28th had A, B, C, D, E and F Companies. Rifle Brigade G, H and J Company.
29th had A, B, C, D, E and F Companies. Rifle Brigade had G and H Company.
30th had A, B, C, D, E and F Companies. Rifle Brigade had H Company.
31st had A, B, C, D, and E Companies. Rifle Brigade had G Company.
32nd had A, B, C, D, E and F Companies. There were no further reinforcements to Rifle Brigade.
33rd had A, B, C, D and E Companies.
34th to 38th had A, B, C and D Companies.
39th and 40th had A, B, C and E Companies.
41st had E, F, J and H Companies.
42nd had A, B, C and D Companies.
43rd had A, B and F Companies.

Some of the basic background frames that were used.

The following illustrations attempt to show the range of designs of the badges and it is important that the collector realises that these company numerals and letters are on background frames which varied even within the same company. The 34th Reinforcement were the first to use the fern leaf badge enclosing the letters 'NZ' above a scroll 'Expeditionary Force', the badge being worn by subsequent reinforcement companies until the end of the war.

Typical examples of shoulder-strap numerals.

176

177

179

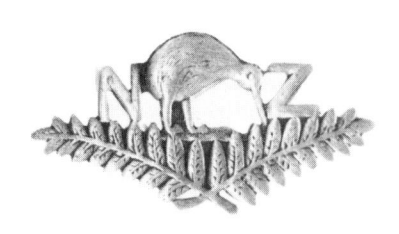

180

N Z
17TH REINFORCEMENTS

Z
REINFORCEMENTS

N Z
17TH REINFORCEMENTS

J
18
N Z
REINFORCEMENTS

NZ

18
NEW ZEALAND

NZ

XIX

NEW ZEALAND
XIX

XIX
KIA TUPATO

182

KIA MATE TOA

NZ
23RD REINFORCEMENTS

KIA MATE TOA

HOLDFAST

HOLDFAST
24
N
Z

J
XXIV

25

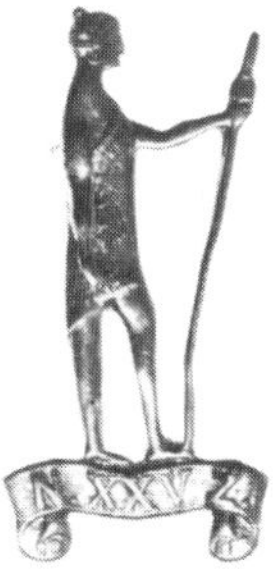
XXV

KIA
XXV
NEW ZEALAND
TOA

184

Badge is struck with motto change, AKE AKE KIA MAIA and AKE AKE KIA MANA

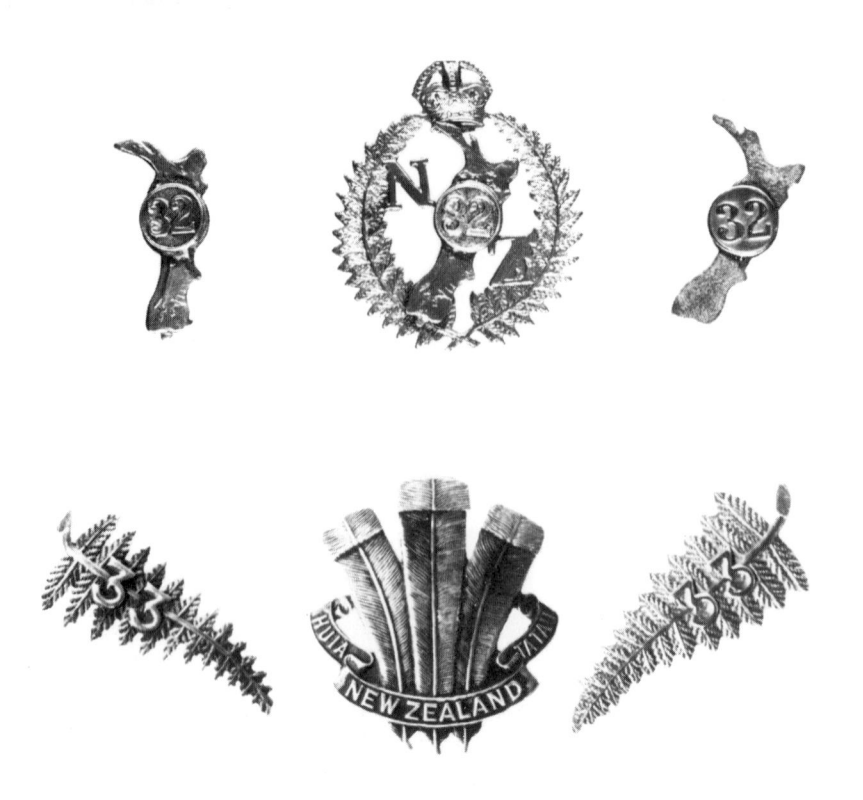

Sweetheart badges:
   The majority of the reinforcement badges were made in silver, gold, or silver and gold for presentation to wives, sisters, mothers and girlfriends. The badge usually has a brooch-pin reverse and are commonly termed 'Sweetheart' badges. They exist in a wide variety of designs and are of interest because of the quality of workmanship and their general acceptance as part of New Zealand militaria.

Corps and Specialist Units
The specialist units were trained as machine-gunners and signallers. The first pattern badges in bronze or brass, the second pattern in brass, and the third pattern in bronze, brass and also bi-metal in bronze or brass.

The corps badges consist of the standard frame of the earlier reinforcement badges with a corps collar badge sweated on to the frame. There are many types of these badges as they varied according to the basic background frame. It is important to remember that all these badges were unofficial and were worn only in New Zealand and on the troop ships. Once the soldiers arrived at Sling Camp in England, these badges were replaced by the badge of the unit to which the soldier was posted.

As a point of interest, the 43rd (Infantry) Reinforcements and the 40th to the 43rd Mounted Rifle Reinforcements were on the ship when the war ended so that badges with higher numbers than these would not have been worn.

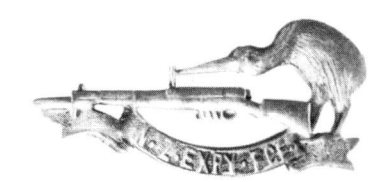

188

Badge of the Reserve Brigades with numeral 1-4 showing beneath the head of the kiwi.

NZ Army Reserve of Officers formed on 16 April 1913 with a total of 178 officers. Redesignated The NZ Forces Motor Reserve of Officers. The unit was redesignated the NZ Forces Motor Service Corps on 31 May 1915. Disbanded 11 February 1920.

NZ Army Motor Reserve of Officers, 16 April 1913

Services Vegetable
Production

Camp Quartermaster Stores
Worn by ASC personnel at training camps WW1

CAMP MILITARY POLICE

BADGE: Brass fern leaves around the white metal letters 'C.M.P', surmounted by a crown. A scholl below 'Trentham M.C' or 'Featherston M.C'.
COLLAR BADGES: Smaller versions of the cap badge.

The two main training camps in New Zealand during World War I were at Trentham and at Featherston. Training was begun at Trentham on 14 October 1914 and at Featherston on 26 January 1916.

In March 1915 there were 8,000 men at Trentham but this number was reduced to a maximum of 5,000 for reasons of health. Supervision was carried out by a Corps of Military Police known as the Camp Military Police.

Featherston Camp formed its own Trumpet Band, their badge depicting crossed trumpets joined by 'New Zealand' and surmounted by a crown. A scroll below with the letters 'F.C.T.B'.

The Trentham Camp band had a badge in the form of a lyre, at the base of which were the letters 'T.C.B'.

BASE RECORDS

The New Zealand War Expenses branch was formed on 8 August 1914 and as a part of this unit, Base Records were established in June 1915. Towards the end of the war most of the work of Base Records dealt with demobilisation and controlled the educational and vocational activities and were responsible for grave registration.

INTELLIGENCE CORPS
Formed by Staff Officers in 1911

C1 CAMP

BADGE: The letter C and the numeral 1 within fern leaves.
In the early months of World War I the volunteers were graded:
A — fit for active service;
B1 — fit for active service after an operation;
B2 — fit for active service after recovery at home;
C1 — likely to become fit for active service after special training;
C2 — unfit for active service overseas but fit for service within New Zealand;
D — wholly unfit for any service.

As the war dragged on, it was necessary to form a training camp to correct minor defects in the physiques of the men in an endeavour to bring them up to the 'Fit A' standard or 'C2'.

The camp was at Featherston in September 1917 and then moved to Tauherenikau where the training proved so successful that sixty per cent of the men were able to join the reinforcements.

Five companies were formed, the officers for the most part having had service on Gallipoli and in France and in Egypt.

CI Camp Chaplain

BRITISH SECTION
NEW ZEALAND EXPEDITIONARY FORCE

BADGE: Above a scroll 'Onward', laurel leaves enclosing the letters 'NZ' and surmounted by a crown.
COLLAR BADGES: Smaller versions of the cap badge.
MOTTO: Onward.
SHOULDER TITLES: Cloth, curved pattern, white 'New Zealand' on black background.

In September 1914 Captain F. H. Lampen, New Zealand Staff Corps (later Major DSO) who was on furlough in London originated a scheme to enlist New Zealanders living in England into a British Section of the NZEF. The scheme proved popular and the unit was trained at Bulford on Salisbury Plain before moving to Sling Camp.

They departed England on 12 December 1914 bound for Zeitoun Camp in Egypt, the unit strength of seven officers and 233 men. The section ceased to exist the following day and the men were asked to volunteer either for the Army Service Corps or become the nucleus of an Engineer Field Company. This was the beginning of the 1st Field Company which was strengthened by volunteer artisans and tradesmen from the ranks of the 2nd Reinforcements who arrived in Egypt in January 1915. New Zealand nationals in Britain in 1939 formed the 34th Battery, 7th Anti-Tank Regiment, New Zealand Artillery. Their badge was the 'Onward' badge as was worn by 2NZEF.

During 1915 the badge was struck with fern leaves instead of laurel leaves and photographs of the period show soldiers wearing this badge. There was no official approval given for this. In 1939 it was approved as the 2NZEF Badge and was worn until 1947 by the New Zealand 'J Force' contingent of the Allied Occupation Forces.

On 1 December 1976 the badge was reintroduced for wearing on ceremonial occasions and it is now worn by the Officer Cadet Training Company.

1st (CANTERBURY) REGIMENT

BADGE: A white crane flanked by fern fronds and surmounted by a crown. Within a circlet the words '1st Regiment New Zealand Infantry'.
MOTTO: *Ake ake kia kaha* (For ever and ever be strong).
Badges are usually bi-metal, bronze or brass and white metal. Some cap badges were struck in brass only.
The white crane badge, from the personal arms of the second commanding officer, Major T. Wollaston-White, made its first appearance when it was embroidered on the colours of the Volunteer Corps and presented on 27 December 1863.
BATTLE HONOURS: South Africa 1902. The Great War 1914-18: SOMME 1916-1918, Flers-Courcelette, Morval, Le Transloy, MESSINES 1917, YPRES 1917, Polygon Wood, Broodseinde, PASSCHENDAELE, Arras 1918, Ancre 1918, Albert 1918, Bapaume 1918, HINDENBURG LINE, Canal du Nord, Cambrai 1918, SELLE, Sambre, FRANCE AND FLANDERS 1916-18, Helles, Krithia, ANZAC, Landing at Anzac, Defence of Anzac, Hill 60 (Anzac), Sari Bair, GALLIPOLI 1915, Suez Canal, EGYPT 1915-16.
Formed on 17 March 1911 with the change of title of the 1st North Canterbury Battalion of Infantry. This had consisted of:
A Company — Christchurch City Guards Rifle Volunteers
B Company — Christ's College Rifle Volunteers
C Company — Christchurch City Rifle Volunteers

4th Cadet Battalion

195

D Company — Kaiapoi Rifle Volunteers
E Company — Rangiora Rifle Volunteers
F Company — Imperial Rifle Volunteers
Christchurch Volunteer Cycle Corps

Formed a Coast Defence Detachment of four Infantry Companies 11 November 1912.

Supplied service companies during World War I and these saw service on Gallipoli, in France and Egypt as part of the 'Canterbury' Regiment.

In 1921 absorbed the 2nd (South Canterbury) Regiment to become The Canterbury Regiment.

Supplied Service Companies to the 2nd NZEF and had Service Companies in the 20th (up to 5 October 1942), 23rd, 26th, 30th and 37th Battalions. The Regiment inherited the battle honours earned by its companies.

The 6th Battalion, Canterbury Regiment (a weak 'two line' Battalion) was sent as a garrison force to Tonga as part of the 16th New Zealand Infantry Brigade in 1942.

In 1964 amalgamated with the Nelson, Marlborough and West Coast Regiment to become the 2nd Battalion (Canterbury and Nelson-Marlborough and West Coast) Royal New Zealand Infantry Regiment.

Blue bonnet of the Royal Irish Fusiliers (Corbean – *'a wee Irish hat'*).
To mark their alliance with the Royal Irish Fusiliers, officers and soldiers of 2RNZIR may wear the blue bonnet and green hackle of the Fusiliers on ceremonial and social occasions. This alliance was originally to the Nelson, Marlborough and West Coast Regiments who first wore the bonnet at Burnham, January 1961.

Colours presented to the Canterbury Rifle Volunteers 27 December 1864 were laid up by the Canterbury Regiment in Christchurch Cathedral as part of the Centenary Celebrations in 1959. The Canterbury Regiment was granted the Freedom of the City of Timaru, April 1959, and the Freedom of the City of Christchurch in November 1959 as a part of the Centennial Celebrations. In January 1966, the Freedom of the City of Christchurch and the Freedom of the City of Timaru was granted to 2RNZIR.

South Canterbury Rifle Battalion 1897
(collar badges enlarged to show detail)

1st Canterbury Rifle Battalion, 1903

Canterbury Irish Rifle Volunteers
Formed 30 April 1885. Part of 1st Battalion, Canterbury Rifle Volunteers 25 January 1886. Amalgamated with Sydenham Rifle Volunteers 1 June 1892 and designated A Company, Canterbury Rifle Volunteers. Designated Christchurch City Rifle Volunteers 1 March 1895. Became C Company, 1st Battalion North Canterbury Rifle Volunteers 7 October 1903.

1st North Canterbury Battalion, 1903   2nd North Canterbury Battalion, 1903

Christchurch City Guards Rifle Volunteers
Formed 15 December 1893 by the amalgamation of Christchurch Rifle Volunteers and the 'City Guards' Company, Canterbury Rifle Volunteers. Formed part of the North Canterbury Battalion 10 June 1897. Became A Company, 1st Battalion North Canterbury Rifle Volunteers on 7 October 1903.

2nd (SOUTH CANTERBURY) REGIMENT

BADGE: On a Maltese Cross a kiwi within a garter, inscribed '2nd (South Canterbury) Regiment'.
MOTTO: *Pro Patria* (For Country).
Badges are usually bi-metal, bronze or brass and white metal. Some cap badges were struck in bronze only.

The South Canterbury Battalion collar badge is similar in appearance but is inscribed 'South Canterbury Battalion N.Z.'

BATTLE HONOURS: South Africa 1900-2. The Great War 1914-18: SOMME 1916, 1918, Flers-Courcelette, Morval, Le Transloy, MESSINES 1917, YPRES 1917, Polygon Wood, Broodseinde, Selle, Sambre, FRANCE AND FLANDERS 1916-18, Helles, Krithia, ANZAC, PASSCHENDAELE, Arras 1918, Ancre 1918, Albert 1918, Bapaume 1918, HINDENBURG LINE, Canal du Nord, Cambrai 1918, Landing at Anzac, Defence of Anzac, Hill 60 (Anzac), SARI BAIR, GALLIPOLI 1915, Suez Canal, EGYPT 1915-16.

Formed on 17 March 1911 with the change of title of the South Canterbury Battalion of Infantry Volunteers. This Battalion was formed by:

A Company — Timaru City Rifle Volunteers
B Company — Temuka Rifle Volunteers
C Company — Ashburton Rifle Volunteers
D Company — Port Guards Rifle Volunteers
E Company — Timaru Rifle Volunteers
F Company — Waimate Rifle Volunteers
G Company — Geraldine Rifle Volunteers
H Company — Ashburton Guards Rifle Volunteers

Canterbury Regiment MG Company, 1915

Supplied service companies during World War I and these saw service on Gallipoli, in France and Egypt as part of the 'Canterbury' Regiment. In 1921 with the reduction of Military Districts to three, was absorbed by The Canterbury Regiment.

In 1947 the seniority of the New Zealand Infantry Corps was:
The Canterbury Regiment.
The Auckland Regiment (Countess of Ranfurly's Own).
The Otago Regiment.
The Wellington Regiment (City of Wellington's Own).
The Hauraki Regiment.
The Wellington West Coast Regiment.
The Southland Regiment.
The Hawke's Bay Regiment.
The Taranaki Regiment.
The Nelson, Marlborough, West Coast Regiment.
The North Auckland Regiment.
The Waikato Regiment.
The Ruahine Regiment.
The New Zealand Scottish Regiment.
The New Zealand Regiment.

South Canterbury Battalion, 1886

3rd (AUCKLAND) REGIMENT
(COUNTESS OF RANFURLY'S OWN)

BADGE: Within a wreath and circle surmounted by a crown, a mailed arm holding a sheaf. The circle enscribed '3rd (Auckland) Regiment N.Z. Infantry'.
COLLAR BADGES: Similar to centre of cap badge, in matching pairs. Above a scroll '3rd (Auck) Regiment N.Z. Infantry'. A less common collar badge is above a scroll '3rd (Auck) Regt N.Z. Infantry'.

Badges are in bronze or brass.

The design is similar to that of the 1st Battalion, Auckland Infantry. The cap badge has circle enscribed '1st Battn Auckland Infantry'. The collar badge was above a similar scroll.

MOTTO: *Sisit Prudentia* (Ever Prudent).

BATTLE HONOURS: South Africa 1900-2. The Great War 1914-18: Somme 1916-18, FLERS-COURCELETTE, Morval, Le Transloy, MESSINES 1917, Ypres 1917, Polygon Wood, BROODSEINDE, Passchendaele, ARRAS 1918, Ancre 1918, Albert 1918, BAPAUME 1918, Hindenburg Line, Havrincourt, CANAL DU NORD, Cambrai 1918, Selle, Sambre, France and Flanders 1916-18, Helles, KRITHIA, Anzac, LANDING AT ANZAC, DEFENCE OF ANZAC, Hill 60 (Anzac), SARI BAIR, Gallipoli 1915, Suez Canal, Egypt 1915-16.

Formed on 17 March 1911 with the change of title of the 1st Battalion, Auckland Infantry (Countess of Ranfurly's Own). This had consisted of:
Victoria Rifle Volunteers.
College Rifle Volunteers.
No. 1 Company NZ Native Rifle Volunteers.
No. 2 Company NZ Native Rifle Volunteers.
No. 3 Company NZ Native Rifle Volunteers.
Gordon Rifle Volunteers.
Newton Rifle Volunteers.
Whangarei Rifle Volunteers.
Kawakawa Rifle Volunteers.
Hikurangi Rifle Volunteers.

Formed a Coast Defence Detachment of four Infantry Companies 1 November 1912.

Supplied service companies during World War I and these saw service on Gallipoli, in France and Egypt as part of the 'Auckland' Regiment. In 1921 became The Auckland Regiment. In World War II supplied companies to the 18th, 21st, 24th and 29th Battalions and inherited the various battle honours of these companies. The honours of the 18th Battalion were up to 5 October 1942.

In 1921 it became The Auckland Regiment (Countess of Ranfurly's Own).

In 1964 amalgamated with the Northland Regiment to become the 3rd Battalion (Auckland (Countess of Ranfurly's Own) and Northland), Royal New Zealand Infantry Regiment.

The first Colours of the 1st Battalion, Auckland Infantry, were presented at a parade on Queen's Birthday, 24 May 1899 by the Countess of Ranfurly, wife of the Governor. Since that day her name has been included in the title of the Regiment.

The present Colours were presented at Auckland in 1929 by the Governor-General (Sir Charles Fergusson).

3RNZIR were granted the Freedom of the City of Auckland, 8 October 1967.

Officers' Pouch
Victoria Rifle Company formed on 18 March 1872 with change of title of No. 5 Company, Auckland Rifle Volunteers. Became part of the Auckland Rifle Battalion on 29 December 1879. Designated A Company, 1st Battalion Auckland Infantry Volunteers on 20 May 1898.

AUCKLAND RIFLE VOLUNTEERS

No. 3 (Parnell) Company: Formed in 1860 with Major C. Heaphy VC as first Commanding Officer. (Heaphy was awarded the Victoria Cross for his actions on 11 February 1864). The Auckland Rifle Volunteers were the first Colonial Force to be marched to the front in the Waikato Wars on 9 July 1863. The Company was designated No. 3 Company, Auckland Rifle Brigade on 29 December 1873. Designated Auckland City Guards Rifle Volunteers on 20 June 1883.

Auckland Rifle Volunteers
Victoria Company, 1872

Victoria Rifle Volunteers
A Company, 1902

1st Battalion Auckland Infantry Volunteers

Victoria Rifle Volunteers 18 March 1872

College Rifle Volunteers (Auckland) 17 June 1897

4th (OTAGO RIFLES) REGIMENT

BADGE: A kiwi flanked by fern fronds.
Badges in bronze or brass. The second pattern collar badges also exist with the kiwi reversed in comparison with the 'South Africa' battle honour.
BATTLE HONOURS: South Africa 1901-2. The Great War 1914-18: SOMME 1916 1918, Flers-Courcelette, Morval, Le Transloy, MESSINES 1917, YPRES 1917, Polygon Wood, Broodseinde, PASSCHENDAELE, Arras 1918, Ancre 1918, Albert 1918, BAPAUME 1918, Hindenburg Line, Canal du Nord, CAMBRAI 1918, Selle, Sambre, FRANCE AND FLANDERS 1916-18, Helles, Krithia, ANZAC, Landing at Anzac, Defence of Anzac, Hill 60 (Anzac), Sari Bair, GALLIPOLI 1915, Suez Canal, EGYPT 1915-16.
Formed on 17 March 1911 with the change of title of the 1st Battalion, Otago Rifles. This had consisted of:
A Company — Dunedin City Guards Rifle Volunteers.
B Company — North Dunedin Rifle Volunteers.
C Company — Dunedin Highland Rifle Volunteers.
D Company — Dunedin City Rifle Volunteers.
E Company — Dunedin Rifle Volunteers.
F Company — Waikari Rifle Volunteers.
G Company — Caversham Rifle Volunteers.
H Company — Green Island Rifle Volunteers.
Dunedin Volunteer Cycle Corps.
Formed a coast defence detachment of four Infantry Companies 2 August 1912.

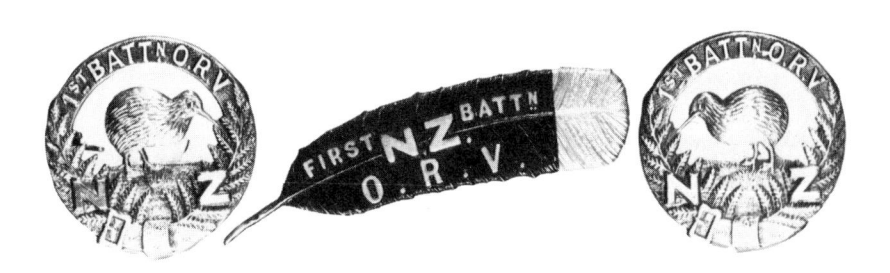

Supplied service companies during World War I and these saw service on Gallipoli, in France and Egypt as part of the 'Otago' Regiment. In 1921 absorbed the 10th (North Otago) Regiment to become The Otago Regiment.

In World War II supplied companies to the 20th, 23rd, 26th, 30th and 37th Battalions and inherited their battle honours. (The honours of 20th Battalion only up to 5 October 1942.)

In 1948 amalgamated with the Southland Regiment to form The Otago and Southland Regiment.

In 1964 became the 4th Battalion (Otago and Southland) Royal New Zealand Infantry Regiment.

Pouch badge

5th (WELLINGTON RIFLES) REGIMENT

BADGE: The Duke of Wellington's Crest.
MOTTO: *Virtutis fortuna comes* (Good fortune is the companion of courage).
Badges in bronze or brass.
BATTLE HONOURS: South Africa 1901-2. The Great War 1914-18: SOMME 1916 1918, FLERS-COURCELETTE, MORVAL, LE TRANSLOY, MESSINES 1917, YPRES 1917, Menin Road, POLYGON WOOD, Broodseinde, Passchendaele, Arras 1918, Ancre 1918, Albert 1918, Bapaume 1918, HINDENBURG LINE, Havrincourt, Canal du Nord, Cambrai 1918, Selle, Sambre (Le Quesnoy), FRANCE AND FLANDERS 1916-18, EGYPT 1915-16.
Formed on 17 March 1911 with the change of title of the 1st Battalion Wellington Rifles. This had consisted of:
A Company — Wellington City Rifle Volunteers.
B Company — Wellington Guards Rifle Volunteers.
C Company — Kelburne Rifle Volunteers.
D Company — Civil Service Rifle Volunteers.
E Company — Wellington Post and Telegraph Rifle Volunteers.
F Company — College Rifle Volunteers.
G Company — Zealandia Rifle Volunteers.
H Company — Wellington Highland Rifle Volunteers.
I Company — Hutt Valley Rifle Volunteers.
J Company — Johnsonville Rifle Volunteers.
Wellington Volunteer Cycle Corps.

E Company 5th Regiment (Wellington Rifles) was disbanded and reformed as Wellington Infantry Brigade Signal Corps on 17 March 1911.

This regiment formed part of the 1914 Samoa Expedition and on its return to New Zealand was used to advantage in the formation of the New Zealand Rifle Brigade, the men of the 5th (Wellington) being posted to the newly created First and Second Battalions, New Zealand Rifle Brigade. The battle honours of the New Zealand Rifle Brigade were inherited by the 5th (Wellington) Regiment.

In 1921 became The Wellington Regiment. In 1938 was retitled The Wellington Regiment (City of Wellington's Own).

Supplied service companies to 19th, 22nd, 25th and 36th Battalions, 2NZEF and inherited these units' battle honours (19th up to 5 October 1942 only). In 1964 amalgamated with the Hawke's Bay Regiment to become the 7th Wellington (City of Wellington's Own and Hawke's Bay) Royal New Zealand Infantry Regiment.

Colours presented at Wellington, March 1929, by Mayoress were laid up in Wellington's Saint Paul's (Anglican) Cathedral 27 July 1969. Earlier Colours to ancestor units presented 1871 and 1887.

To mark the close connection between the 7th Battalion and the NZ Rifle Brigade, 1st New Zealand Expeditionary Force, during the 1914-18 War the distinctive black blazes of the NZ Rifle Brigade are worn by officers and soldiers of the 7th Battalion.

An eight-pointed star made up of two superimposed squares with 1½-inch sides, worn by Battalion HQ, Headquarters Company.
A diamond with longer sides vertical 2¼ by 1¼, worn by Support Company.
A square with 1½-inch sides worn as a diamond, worn by A Company.
A square with 1½-inch sides, worn by B Company.
An equilateral triangle with a perpendicular height of 1½ inches worn with the apex uppermost, worn by C Company.
An equilateral triangle worn with the base uppermost, worn by D Company.

6th (HAURAKI) REGIMENT

BADGE: On an eight-pointed star, a lion within the garter.
MOTTO: *Whaka tangata kia kaha* (Canoe men be brave).

Badges in bronze or brass. A few badges were specially made for officers, the badges in silver and gilt. One pattern has the star and lion in silver, the other has the scroll 'Hauraki' in silver. The badge is derived from the helmet plate of the Hauraki Rifle Volunteers which formed on 1 March 1869. The motto on both the helmet plate and the collar badges was *Nulli secundus*.

BATTLE HONOURS: South Africa 1900-2. The Great War 1914-18: Somme 1916 1918, FLERS-COURCELETTE, Morval, Le Transloy, MESSINES 1917, Ypres 1917, Polygon Wood, BROODSEINDE, Passchendaele, ARRAS 1918, Ancre 1918, Albert 1918, BAPAUME 1918, Hindenburg Line, Havrincourt, CANAL DU NORD, Cambrai 1918, Selle, SAMBRE, France and Flanders 1916-18, Helles, KRITHIA, Anzac, LANDING AT ANZAC, Defence of Anzac, Hill 60 (Anzac), SARI BAIR, Gallipoli 1915, Suez Canal, Egypt 1915-16.

Formed on 17 March 1911 with the change of title of the 2nd Battalion, Auckland (Hauraki) Infantry. This had consisted of:

A Company — No. 1 Company, Thames Rifle Volunteers.
B Company — No. 1 Company, Ohinemuri Rifle Volunteers.
C Company — Hauraki Rifle Volunteers.
D Company — No. 3 Company, Ohinemuri Rifle Volunteers.
E Company — Coromandel Rifle Volunteers.
F Company — Huntly Rifle Volunteers.
G Company — Waihi Rifle Volunteers.

Three former Companies had disbanded by 1907. They were: Onehunga Rifle Volunteers, Rotorua Rifle Volunteers and No. 2 Company Ohinemuri Rifle Volunteers.

Supplied service companies during World War I and these saw service on Gallipoli, in Egypt and France as part of the 'Auckland' Regiment.

In 1921 designated The Hauraki Regiment.

Supplied service companies to 18th, 21st, 24th and 29th Battalions 2NZEF and inherited battle honours of 18th (up to 5 October 1942), 21st, 29th and 24th Battalions 2NZEF.

Lord Freyberg, VC, was first commissioned in the 6th (Hauraki) Regiment.

Colours were presented to the regiment at Paeroa, February 1930, by Major-General R. Young.

In 1964 became the 6th Battalion (Hauraki), Royal New Zealand Infantry Regiment.

Collar badges worn with helmet-plate
(enlarged to show detail)

7th (WELLINGTON WEST COAST RIFLES) REGIMENT

BADGE: A coronet surmounted by a lion rampant.
MOTTO: *Acer in armis* (Strong in arms).
Badges in bronze or brass.

BATTLE HONOURS: South Africa 1900-2. The Great War 1914-18: SOMME 1916 1918, Flers-Courcelette, Morval, Le Transloy, MESSINES 1917, YPRES 1917, Polygon Wood, Broodseinde, Passchendaele, Arras 1918, Ancre 1918, Albert 1918, BAPAUME 1918, HINDENBURG LINE, Havrincourt, Canal du Nord, Cambrai 1918, Selle, Sambre, FRANCE AND FLANDERS 1916-18, Helles, Krithia, Anzac, LANDING AT ANZAC, Defence of Anzac, Hill 60 (Anzac), SARI BAIR, GALLIPOLI 1915, Suez Canal, EGYPT 1915-16.

Formed on 17 March 1911 with the change of name of the 2nd Battalion, Wellington (West Coast) Rifles. This had consisted of:

A Company — Royal Rifle Volunteers.
B Company — Wanganui Rifle Volunteers.
C Company — Palmerston North Rifle Volunteers.
D Company — Manchester Rifle Volunteers.
E Company — Wanganui Guards Rifle Volunteers.
F Company — Wanganui Highland Rifle Volunteers.
G Company — Palmerston Guards Rifle Volunteers.
H Company — Irish Rifle Volunteers.

Sergeant Samuel Austin of the Wanganui Volunteer Contingent was awarded the New Zealand Cross during the Maori Wars.

There had been two other companies but these were disbanded: Foxton Rifle Volunteers 21 September 1904; Castlecliff Rifle Volunteers 27 July 1905.

Supplied service companies during World War I and these saw service on Gallipoli, in Egypt and France as part of the 'Wellington' Regiment.

In 1921 the title was changed to The Wellington West Coast Regiment.

During World War II supplied service companies to the 19th, 22nd, 25th and 36th Battalions 2NZEF. The Regiment inherited the battle honours of these battalions (19th up to 5 October 1942 only).

The 2nd Battalion Wellington West Coast Regiment saw garrison duty on Norfolk Island 1943-44.

After World War II amalgamated with the Taranaki Regiment to form the Wellington West Coast and Taranaki Regiment. (See badge below.)

Her Royal Highness, Princess Alexandra of Kent, was appointed Colonel-in-Chief on 10 March 1962.

In 1964 became the 5th Battalion (Wellington West Coast and Taranaki) Royal New Zealand Infantry Regiment.

WELLINGTON WEST COAST and TARANAKI REGIMENT

1st Battalion Wellington Rifle Volunteers,
1901-1911

3rd Battalion Wellington (East Coast)
Rifle Volunteers, 1901-1911

2nd Battalion Wellington (West Coast)
Rifle Volunteers, 1901-1911

Hastings Rifle Volunteers,
1901-1911

8th (SOUTHLAND RIFLES) REGIMENT

BADGE: The effigy of a Maori grasping a taiaha.
MOTTO: *Kia mate toa* (Fight unto Death).
The badges and shoulder titles were always in bronze or blackened brass.
BATTLE HONOURS: South Africa 1901-2. The Great War 1914-18: SOMME 1916 1918, Flers-Courcelette, Morval, Le Transloy, MESSINES 1917, Ypres 1917, Polygon Wood, Broodseinde, PASSCHENDAELE, Arras 1918, Ancre 1918, Albert 1918, BAPAUME 1918, Hindenburg Line, Canal du Nord, CAMBRAI 1918, Selle, Sambre, FRANCE AND FLANDERS 1916-18, HELLES, Krithia, Anzac, LANDING AT ANZAC, Defence of Anzac, Hill 60 (Anzac), Sari Bair, GALLIPOLI 1915, Suez Canal, EGYPT 1915-16.
Formed on 17 March 1911 with the change of name of the 2nd Battalion, Otago Rifles. This had consisted of:
A Company — Invercargill City Guards Rifle Volunteers.
B Company — Oreti Rifle Volunteers.
C Company — Awarua Rifle Volunteers.
D Company — Gore Rifle Volunteers.
E Company — Mercantile Rifle Volunteers (disbanded 10 June 1907).
F Company — Winton Rifle Volunteers.
G Company — Tapanui Rifle Volunteers.
H Company — Orepuki Rifle Volunteers.
I Company — Bluff Guards Rifle Volunteers.
J Company — Colac Bay Rifle Volunteers.
  B Company disbanded and reformed as J Battery, NZFA on 19 April 1911.
  Supplied service companies during World War I and these saw service on Gallipoli, in Egypt and France as part of the 'Otago' Regiment.
  In 1921 absorbed the 14th (South Otago) Regiment to become The Southland Regiment.
  Supplied service companies to the 20th, 23rd, 26th, 30th and 37th Battalions, 2NZEF during World War II. The Regiment inherited the battle honours of these Battalions (20th Battalion honours up to 5 October 1942 only).
  In 1948 the Otago and Southland Regiments amalgamated to form The Otago and Southland Regiment. (See badge p206.)
  The regiment was honoured when Her Majesty The Queen approved the appointment of Field Marshal, His Royal Highness, The Prince Philip, Duke of Edinburgh, as Colonel-in-Chief on 15 December 1954.
  In 1964 became the 4th Battalion (Otago and Southland), Royal New Zealand Infantry Regiment.

The first badge pattern shows the taiaha held across the body and not as in the second pattern. Southland Boys' High School Band wears the second pattern cap and collar badges in silver plate.

Variations in badge design

9th (WELLINGTON EAST COAST RIFLES) REGIMENT

BADGE: Within a fern-wreath surmounted by a crown, a red deer's head.
MOTTO: *Kia toa* (Be brave).
Badges in bronze or brass.
BATTLE HONOURS: South Africa 1900-2. The Great War 1914-18: SOMME 1916 1918, Flers-Courcelette, Morval, Le Transloy, MESSINES 1917, YPRES 1917, Polygon Wood, Broodseinde, Passchendaele, Arras 1918, Ancre 1918, Albert 1918, BAPAUME 1918, HINDENBURG LINE, Havrincourt, Canal du Nord, Cambrai 1918, Selle, Sambre, FRANCE AND FLANDERS 1916-18, Helles, Krithia, Anzac, LANDING AT ANZAC, Defence of Anzac, Hill 60 (Anzac), SARI BAIR, GALLIPOLI 1915, Suez Canal, EGYPT 1915-16.

On 17 March 1911 the 5th Battalion, Wellington (Centre or Ruahine) Rifles amalgamated with the 3rd Battalion, Wellington (East Coast) Rifles to form the 9th (Wellington East Coast Rifles) Regiment. A Company was disbanded and reformed as F Battery, NZFA 17 April 1911. The Regiment formed a 2nd Battalion on 22 December 1911.

3rd Battalion Wellington (East Coast) Rifles had consisted of:
A Company — Napier Guards Rifle Volunteers.
B Company — Napier Rifle Volunteers.
C Company — Hastings Rifle Volunteers.
D Company — Waipawa Rifle Volunteers.
E Company — Clive Rifle Volunteers.
F Company — Ranfurly Rifle Volunteers.
G Company — Gisborne Rifle Volunteers.

5th Battalion, Wellington (Centre or Ruahine) Rifles had consisted of:
A Company — Woodville Rifle Volunteers.
B Company — Dannevirke Rifle Volunteers.
C Company — Masterton Rifle Volunteers.
D Company — Pahiatua Rifle Volunteers.
E Company — Greytown Rifle Volunteers.
F Company — Union Rifle Volunteers.
G Company — Ashhurst Rifle Volunteers.
H Company — Carterton Rifle Volunteers.

On 27 March 1914 the 9th (Wellington East Coast) Regiment was re-designated as under:

1st Battalion to be the 9th (Hawke's Bay) Regiment with headquarters at Napier.

2nd Battalion to be the 17th (Ruahine) Regiment with headquarters at Masterton.

As part of the 'Wellington' Regiment during World War I saw service in Egypt on Gallipoli and in France.

In 1921 amalgamated with the 17th (Ruahine) and in 1923 became The Hawke's Bay Regiment. In 1941 the 2nd Battalion Hawke's Bay Regiment was mobilised and designated '1st Battalion Ruahine Regiment'. This battalion served in the Pacific at New Caledonia as part of the 3rd New Zealand Division. The Hawke's Bay Regiment supplied service companies to, and inherited the battle honours of the 19th, 22nd, 25th and 36th Battalions 2NZEF during World War II (19th Battalion up to 5 October 1942 only).

In 1953 the Regiment was honoured when Her Majesty The Queen approved the appointment of Field Marshal, His Royal Highness The Prince Philip, Duke of Edinburgh, as Colonel-in-Chief of The Hawke's Bay Regiment.

On 10 February 1963 Her Majesty, Queen Elizabeth II presented new Colours to The Hawke's Bay Regiment at Napier (the only New Zealand regiment presented with Colours by a reigning monarch).

In 1964 amalgamated with the Wellington (City of Wellington's Own) Regiment to become the 7th Battalion (Wellington (City of Wellington's Own) and Hawke's Bay), Royal New Zealand Infantry Regiment.

The Officer Commanding 7th Battalion RNZIR is the only New Zealand soldier entitled to wear the collar badges of the 9th Hawke's Bay Regiment today (1970). This was established by Colonel R. Gambrill who lead the 9th Hawke's Bay Service Company of the 'Wellington' Regiment on Gallipoli and who handed on his collar badges to his successor on relinquishing command, a tradition which has been observed ever since. All other members of 7th Battalion wear the standard collar badge of the RNZIR.

Napier Rifle Volunteers: Formed 4 August 1863 until 21 March 1874. Reformed with change of title of Napier Engineer Volunteers on 18 May 1880. Designated E Company, Wellington Battalion on 7 November 1895. Designated B Company, 3rd Battalion Wellington (East Coast) Rifle Volunteers on 9 July 1898.

Hastings Rifle Volunteers: 6 June 1887. Designated K Company, Wellington Battalion 7 November 1895. Became C Company, 3rd Battalion Wellington (East Coast) Rifle Volunteers 9 July 1898.

Ranfurly Rifle Volunteers: 10 September 1900. Designated F Company, 3rd Battalion Wellington (East Coast) Rifle Volunteers 1 May 1901.

10th (NORTH OTAGO RIFLES) REGIMENT

BADGE: A circle surrounding the Southern Cross, flanked by fern-fronds and surmounted by a crown.
MOTTO: *Pro Patria* (For Country).

Badges in bronze or brass. The original design was worn by Orepuki Rifle Volunteers. The badge became the basis of the helmet plate design for the 3rd Battalion, Otago Rifle Volunteers. In each pattern the area surrounding the shield was voided and this was continued with the first pattern badge of the 10th (North Otago) Rifles but the number of stars on the shield was reduced to four. The badge was struck in quantity in a non-voided pattern.

BATTLE HONOURS: South Africa 1901-2. The Great War 1914-18: SOMME 1916 1918, Flers-Courcelette, Morval, Le Transloy, MESSINES 1917, YPRES 1917, Polygon Wood, Broodseinde, PASSCHENDAELE, Arras 1918, Ancre 1918, Albert 1918, BAPAUME 1918, Hindenburg Line, Canal du Nord, CAMBRAI 1918, Selle, Sambre, FRANCE AND FLANDERS 1916-18, Helles, Krithia, ANZAC, Landing at Anzac, Defence of Anzac, Hill 60 (Anzac), Sari Bair, GALLIPOLI 1915, Suez Canal, EGYPT 1915-16.

3rd Battalion Otago Rifle
Volunteers, 1902

Formed on 17 March 1911 with the change of name of the 3rd Battalion, Otago Rifles. This had consisted of:
A Company — Queen's Rifle Volunteers.
B Company — Oamaru Rifle Volunteers.
C Company — Hampden Rifle Volunteers.
D Company — Palmerston South Rifle Volunteers.
E Company — Alexandra South Rifle Volunteers.
F Company — Queenstown Rifle Volunteers.
G Company — Cromwell Rifle Volunteers.
H Company — Duntroon Rifle Volunteers.
I Company — King's Rifle Volunteers.

Supplied service companies during World War I and these saw service in Egypt, on Gallipoli and in France as part of the 'Otago' Regiment.

In 1921 was absorbed by the 4th (Otago) Regiment to form The Otago Regiment.

2nd Battalion Otago Rifle Volunteers
(Oreti Rifle Volunteers), 1902

221

11th (TARANAKI RIFLES) REGIMENT

BADGE: Facsimile of Mount Egmont.
Badges in bronze or brass.
This badge also exists with the battle honours embossed at the base, Waireka, New Zealand and South Africa.
MOTTO: *Primus in armis* (First in Arms).
BATTLE HONOURS: New Zealand. South Africa 1902. The Great War 1914-18: SOMME 1916 1918, Flers-Courcelette, Morval, Polygon Wood, Broodseinde, Passchendaele, Arras 1918, Ancre 1918, Albert 1918, BAPAUME 1918, HINDENBURG LINE, Havrincourt, Canal du Nord, Cambrai 1918, Selle, Sambre, Le Transloy, MESSINES 1917, YPRES 1917, FRANCE AND FLANDERS 1916-18, Helles, Krithia, Anzac, LANDING AT ANZAC, Defence of Anzac, Hill 60 (Anzac), SARI BAIR, GALLIPOLI 1915, Suez Canal, EGYPT 1915-16.

Formed on 17 March 1911 with the change of title of the 4th Battalion Wellington (Taranaki) Rifles. This had consisted of:
Taranaki Rifle Volunteers.
Taranaki Guards Rifle Volunteers.
Patea Rifle Volunteers.
Inglewood Rifle Volunteers.
Eltham Rifle Volunteers.
Hawera Rifle Volunteers.
Stratford Rifle Volunteers.
Waitara Rifle Volunteers.

Supplied service companies during World War I and these saw service in Egypt, on Gallipoli and in France as part of the 'Wellington' Regiment.

In 1921 became The Taranaki Regiment. During World War II supplied service companies to the 19th, 22nd, 25th and 36th Battalions, 2NZEF and inherited the battle honours of these battalions (19th Battalion only up to 5 October 1942).

After the war amalgamated with the Wellington West Coast Regiment to form The Wellington West Coast and Taranaki Regiment.

The badge of this Regiment was a griffon arising from the flames of the VIIth and XIth above a scroll embossed 'The WWCT Regt'. (See p213.)

In 1964 became the 5th Battalion (Wellington West Coast and Taranaki), Royal New Zealand Infantry Regiment.

The Taranaki Regiment was the only New Zealand Regiment to be awarded the battle honour 'New Zealand'.

In recognition of the Battalion's 100 years of service, all ranks are permitted to wear RNZIR collar badges on all orders of dress, except No. 7 Dress, on all occasions.

Colours were presented to the Taranaki Regiment at New Plymouth by the Governor-General Viscount Galway in March 1936. The first Colours ever presented to a New Zealand unit were those presented by the wife of Colonel Warre on behalf of the ladies of Taranaki on 25 June 1861 to the Taranaki Rifle Volunteers and to the Taranaki Militia. These Colours were given in token of the bravery of both corps at the battles of Waireka (28 March 1860) and Mahoetahi (6 November 1860).

Ensign H. W. Northcroft of the Patea Rangers, an earlier unit in the district, won the New Zealand Cross, which is now in the Te Awamutu Museum.

Badge enlarged to show Battle Honours

12th (NELSON) REGIMENT

BADGE: A stag within a circle flanked by fern-fronds.
MOTTO: *Kia pono tonu* (Ever Faithful).
Badges of the 12th (Nelson) and the 12th (Nelson and Marlborough) Regiments were worn in bronze or blackened brass.
BATTLE HONOURS: South Africa 1900-2, The Great War 1914-18: SOMME 1916 1918, Flers-Courcelette, Morval, Le Transloy, MESSINES 1917, Ypres 1917, Polygon Wood, Broodseinde, PASSCHENDAELE, Arras 1918, Ancre 1918, Albert 1918, Bapaume 1918, HINDENBURG LINE, Canal du Nord, Cambrai 1918, Selle, Sambre, FRANCE AND FLANDERS 1916-18, Helles, Krithia, ANZAC, LANDING AT ANZAC, Defence of Anzac, Hill 60 (Anzac), SARI BAIR, GALLIPOLI 1915, SUEZ CANAL, Egypt 1915-16.

Formed on 17 March 1911 with the amalgamation of the 1st Battalion Nelson Infantry with the 2nd Battalion Nelson Infantry to form the 12th (Nelson) Regiment with headquarters at Nelson.

The 1st Battalion Nelson Infantry had consisted of: Stoke Rifle Volunteers, Blenheim Rifle Volunteers, Waimea Rifle Volunteers, Nelson Rifle Volunteers, Waitohi Rifle Volunteers.

The 2nd Battalion, Nelson Infantry had consisted of: 1st Westland Rifle Volunteers (at Hokitika), Greymouth Rifle Volunteers, Denniston Rifle Volunteers, Reefton Rifle Volunteers, Millerton Rifle Volunteers.

A former Company, Brunner Rangers Rifle Volunteers had disbanded in 1904. In 1912 the West Coast (the former 2nd Battalion Nelson Infantry) was included in the 14th (North Canterbury and Westland) Regiment.

Supplied service companies during World War I and these saw service in Egypt, on Gallipoli and in France as part of the 'Canterbury' Regiment.

The title was changed to the 12th (Nelson and Marlborough) Regiment on 13 April 1917. The new badge, similar in design, had the words in the circle changed from 'Nelson Infantry' to (Nelson and Marlborough).

A private of the 12th (Nelson) Company, 'Canterbury' Regiment was the first soldier of the NZEF to be killed in action. This was in the defence of the Suez Canal on 3 February 1915.

In 1921 the eight Regiments in the South Island were reduced to two. The 12th (Nelson and Marlborough) Regiment amalgamated with the 13th (North Canterbury and Westland) Regiment to become the 2nd Battalion, The Canterbury Regiment. On 1 June 1923 the Battalion was designated The Nelson Marlborough and West Coast Regiment.

The new badge was a mixture of the 12th and 13th badges. A stag passant contained within a circle inscribed with the Regiment's motto *Kia pono tonu* over the numerals '12 & XIII' surmounted by a crown and flanked by fern fronds. This badge met with little approval as it was considered to be incorrect by heraldic rules and was not actually worn until 1951. Until that time, the Nelson and Marlborough Companies wore the badge of the 12th (Nelson and

Marlborough) Regiment and the West Coast Companies wore the badge of the 13th (North Canterbury and Westland) Regiment.

To perpetuate a regimental custom dating back to the formation of the 1st Westland Rifles in 1868, officers and soldiers of the Nelson, Marlborough and West Coast Regiment wore a piece of scarlet cloth fixed under the cap and collar badges.

In World War II supplied service companies to 20th, 23rd, 26th, 30th and 37th Battalions, 2NZEF and inherited the battle honours of these Battalions (20th Battalion honours only till 5 October 1942).

In 1964 amalgamated with the Canterbury Regiment to become the 2nd Battalion (Canterbury and Nelson-Marlborough and West Coast) Royal New Zealand Infantry Regiment.

Colours presented at Nelson 1927 to the NMWC Regiment were laid up in Nelson Cathedral, 29 November 1969 when 2 Battalion RNZIR was given freedom of the City of Nelson.

13th (NORTH CANTERBURY AND WESTLAND) REGIMENT

BADGE: The number of the Regiment encircled by fern-fronds and surmounted by a crown.
MOTTO: *Kia pono tonu* (Ever faithful).
Badges are bi-metal, bronze or brass and white metal.
BATTLE HONOURS: SOMME 1916-1918, Flers-Courcelette, Morval, Le Transloy, MESSINES 1917, Ypres 1917, Polygon Wood, Broodseinde, PASSCHENDAELE, Arras 1918, Ancre 1918, Albert 1918, Defence of Anzac, Hill 60 (Anzac), SARI BAIR, Bapaume 1918, HINDENBURG LINE, Canal du Nord, Cambrai 1918, Selle, Sambre, FRANCE AND FLANDERS 1916-18, Helles, Krithia, ANZAC, LANDING AT ANZAC, GALLIPOLI 1915, Suez Canal, EGYPT 1915-16.

Formed on 17 March 1911 with the change of title of the 2nd North Canterbury Battalion of Infantry. The title was then the 13th (North Canterbury) Regiment.
2nd North Canterbury Battalion of Infantry Volunteers, 7 October 1903.
A Company — Sydenham Rifle Volunteers.
B Company — Linwood Rifle Volunteers.
C Company — Civil Service Rifle Volunteers.
D Company — Canterbury Highland Rifle Volunteers.
E Company — Canterbury Native Rifle Volunteers.

The badge of this Regiment was three Huia feathers in white metal on a brass wreath of fern leaves above a scroll '13th N.Z.I. Reg'. A scroll below with the motto *Kia pono tonu*.

The Regiment was redesignated the 13th (North Canterbury and Westland) Regiment on 18 January 1912, all the West Coast Companies being transferred to this regiment. The regimental badge was then as illustrated above.

The infantry incorporated into the regiment were: Sydenham Rifle Volunteers; Linwood Rifle Volunteers; Civil Service Rifle Volunteers; Canterbury Highland Rifle Volunteers; Canterbury Native Rifle Volunteers.

A former Company, Ellesmere Guards Rifle Volunteers had disbanded 23 October 1906. Service in World War I on Gallipoli, in Egypt and in France as part of the 'Canterbury' Regiment.

A Coast Defence detachment was formed at Westport 12 February 1913.

In 1921 the 13th (North Canterbury and Westland) Regiment amalgamated with the 12th (Nelson and Marlborough) Regiment to become the 2nd Battalion, The Canterbury Regiment. The 2nd Battalion was redesignated The Nelson Marlborough and West Coast Regiment on 1 June 1923. The new badge designed for the Regiment met with little approval and was not issued until 1951. Until that time the Nelson and Marlborough Companies wore the badge of the 12th (Nelson and Marlborough) Regiment while the West Coast

Companies wore the badge of the 13th (North Canterbury and Westland) Regiment.

Regimental Colours were presented at Nelson on 10 March 1928.

In October 1963 an Army reorganisation was enacted which effected that all infantry regiments in New Zealand were to cease to exist as regiments. The Nelson Marlborough and West Coast Regiment amalgamated with The Canterbury Regiment to become the 2nd Battalion (Canterbury, Nelson, Marlborough and West Coast) Royal New Zealand Infantry Regiment.

14th (SOUTH OTAGO RIFLES) REGIMENT

BADGE: Within a wreath of the red rose, shamrock and thistle, surmounted by a kea, the number of the Regiment.
MOTTO: *Ake kia kaha* (Forever be strong).
Badges in bronze or brass. The first badges were struck in a non-voided style but the badges are more common as voided pattern.
BATTLE HONOURS: Great War 1914-18: SOMME 1916-1918, Flers-Courcelette, Morval, Le Transloy, MESSINES 1917, Ypres 1917, Polygon Wood, Broodseinde, PASSCHENDAELE, Arras 1918, Ancre 1918, Albert 1918, BAPAUME 1918, Hindenburg Line, Canal du Nord, CAMBRAI 1918, Selle, Sambre, FRANCE AND FLANDERS 1916-18, HELLES, Krithia, Anzac, LANDING AT ANZAC, Defence of Anzac, Hill 60 (Anzac), Sari Bair, GALLIPOLI 1915, Suez Canal, EGYPT 1915-16.
Formed on 17 March 1911 with the change of title of the 4th Battalion Otago Rifles.
This had been formed by the:
Bruce Rifle Volunteers.
Kaitangata Rifle Volunteers.
Owaka Rifle Volunteers.
Clutha Rifle Volunteers.
Popotunoa Rifle Volunteers.

Supplied service companies during World War I and these saw service on Gallipoli, in Egypt and in France as part of the 'Otago' Regiment.

In 1921 amalgamated with the 8th (Southland) to form The Southland Regiment.

15th (NORTH AUCKLAND) REGIMENT

BADGE: Within a circle, the number of the Regiment between fern-fronds, and surmounted by a crown.

MOTTO: *Pour devoir* (For right).

Badges are bronze or brass with a few bi-metal. The edges of the fern leaves on some patterns are voided.

BATTLE HONOURS: The Great War 1914-18: Somme 1916-1918, FLERS-COURCELETTE, Morval, Le Transloy, MESSINES 1917, Ypres 1917, Polygon Wood, Broodseinde, Passchendaele, Arras 1918, Ancre 1918, Albert 1918, BAPAUME 1918, Hindenburg Line, HAVRINCOURT, CANAL DU NORD, CAMBRAI 1918, Selle, Sambre, France and Flanders 1916-18, Helles, KRITHIA, Anzac, LANDING AT ANZAC, DEFENCE OF ANZAC, Hill 60 (Anzac), Sari Bair, Gallipoli 1915, Suez Canal, Egypt 1915-16.

Formed on 17 March 1911 as a regiment of infantry in the Auckland military district with headquarters at Whangarei.

A Company, Whangarei.
B Company, Kawakawa.
C Company, Dargaville.
D Company, Warkworth.

Supplied service companies during World War I and these saw service on Gallipoli, in France and in Egypt as part of the 'Auckland' Regiment.

In 1921 became The North Auckland Regiment.

Officers' bi-metal badges

Colours were presented to the Regiment at Dargaville on 2 May 1937 by His Excellency, the Governor-General, Viscount Galway.

During World War II supplied service companies to the 18th, 21st, 24th and 29th Battalions 2NZEF and inherited their battle honours (18th Battalion only till 5 October 1942).

On 17 August 1951 the Regiment was renamed The Northland Regiment and following this the badge was changed in a minor form by replacing the words 'North Auckland' with 'Northland'.

Her Royal Highness, The Princess Margaret was appointed Colonel-in-Chief on 16 February 1958.

In 1964 amalgamated with the Auckland (Countess of Ranfurly's Own) Regiment to become the 3rd Battalion (Auckland (Countess of Ranfurly's Own) and Northland), Royal New Zealand Infantry Regiment.

16th (WAIKATO) REGIMENT

BADGE: Within a fern wreath surmounted by a crown, an arm grasping a Maori taiaha.
MOTTO: *Ka whawhai tonu ake ake* (We shall fight forever and ever).
Badges are in bronze or brass.
BATTLE HONOURS: The Great War 1914-18: Somme 1916-1918, FLERS-COURCELETTE, Morval, Le Transloy, Passchendaele, ARRAS 1918, Ancre 1918, Albert 1918, BAPAUME 1918, Hindenburg Line, Havrincourt, CANAL DU NORD, Cambrai 1918, Selle, SAMBRE, MESSINES 1917, Ypres 1917, Polygon Wood, BROODSEINDE, France and Flanders 1916-18, Helles, KRITHIA, Anzac, LANDING AT ANZAC, Defence of Anzac, Hill 60 (Anzac), SARI BAIR, Gallipoli 1915, Suez Canal, Egypt 1915-16.

Formed on 17 March 1911 as a Regiment of Infantry in the Auckland Military District with Headquarters at Hamilton.

Supplied service companies during World War I and these saw service on Gallipoli, in Egypt and in France as part of the 'Auckland' Regiment.

In 1921 became The Waikato Regiment.

During World War II supplied service companies to the 18th, 21st, 24th and 29th Battalions 2NZEF and inherited the battle honours of these Battalions (18th Battalion till 5 October 1942 only).

In 1950 The Waikato Regiment was absorbed into the 1st Armoured Regiment.
REGIMENTAL DRESS DISTINCTIONS
2nd Armoured Squadron (Waikato) Royal New Zealand Armoured Corps
Cravat. To emphasise the close association between the squadron and the district of Waikato, all ranks of the squadron may wear cravats in Waikato colours (red, black and yellow) as a dress distinction.
Collar Badges. As the successor of the 16th (Waikato) Infantry Regiment and to perpetuate this association, all ranks are permitted to wear the collar badges of that regiment.

17th (RUAHINE) REGIMENT

BADGE: A five-pointed star flanked by fern-fronds, with scroll 'Ruahine' beneath.

MOTTO: *Ad unum omnes* (Together as one).

The helmet plate badge 55mm was the design carried on to the Regimental badge 30mm, the cap and collar badges being the same badge. Worn in bronze or brass.

BATTLE HONOURS: The Great War 1914-18: SOMME 1916-1918, Flers-Courcelette, Morval, Le Transloy, MESSINES 1917, YPRES 1917, Polygon Wood, Broodseinde, Passchendaele, Arras 1918, Ancre 1918, Albert 1918, BAPAUME 1918, HINDENBURG LINE, Havrincourt, Canal du Nord, Cambrai 1918, Selle, Sambre, FRANCE AND FLANDERS 1916-18, Helles, Krithia, Anzac, LANDING AT ANZAC, Defence of Anzac, Hill 60 (Anzac), SARI BAIR, GALLIPOLI 1915, Suez Canal, Egypt 1915-16.

On 27th March 1914 the 9th (Wellington East Coast) Regiment was re-designated as: 1st Battalion to be the 9th (Hawke's Bay) Regiment; 2nd Battalion to be the 17th (Ruahine) Regiment.

The Ruahine Regiment's service companies saw service on Gallipoli, in France and in Egypt during World War I as part of 'Wellington' Regiment 1NZEF. In 1921 the 9th (Hawke's Bay) Regiment absorbed the 17th (Ruahine) Regiment to become The Hawke's Bay Regiment in 1923.

In 1941 the 2nd Battalion Hawke's Bay Regiment was mobilised as 1st Battalion 'Ruahine' Regiment for service as part of the 3rd New Zealand Division in the Pacific at New Caledonia.

General pattern badges worn by both Rifle Corps and Mounted Rifle Volunteers from September 1895 through to 1911.

The Ruahine Regiment was allocated the battle honours of the 19th Battalion (up to 5 October 1942), 22nd and 25th Battalions 2NZEF besides the solitary honour 'South Pacific 1942-44' of its own 1st Battalion.

In 1948 the Ruahine Regiment was absorbed back into the Hawke's Bay Regiment.

In 1964 the Hawke's Bay Regiment became the 7th Battalion (Wellington (City of Wellington's Own) and Hawke's Bay), Royal New Zealand Infantry Regiment.

NEW ZEALAND RIFLE BRIGADE

BADGE: The crest of the Earl of Liverpool. On a chapeau a lion rampant supporting a man-of-war's church pennant proper, with the motto *Soyes Ferme* (Stand Fast).

Cap and collar badges of blackened brass were the same size, the cap badge facing to the right of the wearer and the collar badges facing inwards. First worn 31 August 1915. Blackened brass shoulder titles 'NZRB'. Originally black horn 'Rifle Buttons' were worn, these later being changed to black horn 'Rifle Buttons' with the letters NZRB being superimposed.

In April 1915 the Imperial Government accepted the offer of a new regiment of infantry to be complete with its own reinforcements. This regiment, on 1 May 1915, officially became 'The Trentham Regiment (Earl of Liverpool's Own) and was composed of men from the Samoan Force, Officers and NCOs from the 4th and 5th Reinforcements and Volunteers.

The Regiment was designated 'The New Zealand Rifle Brigade (The Earl of Liverpool's Own)' on 1 October 1915.

The distinguishing badge was a blaze of black cloth.

First Battalion: A square, 1½-inch side, worn as a diamond.

Second Battalion: A square of 1½-inch side.

Regimental Headquarters: An eight-pointed star, formed by a square and diamond.

In September 1915, the mobilisation of the other Battalions took place.

Third Battalion: An equilateral triangle with apex uppermost.

Fourth Battalion: An equilateral triangle with base uppermost.

Together with the 7th Reinforcements, sailed for Egypt on 8 October 1915. Reinforcement drafts came to the Regiment, the 10th and 11th in Egypt, and then in regular order while the training battalion was in England which became, on 22 August 1916, the 5th (Reserve Battalion).

Fifth Battalion: A diamond, with the longer axis perpendicular.

The Regiment suffered over 3,200 killed and its outstanding service was recognised by the award of 757 honours and decorations including two Victoria Crosses (Lance Corporal S. Frickleton 3rd Battalion and Sergeant H. J. Laurent 2nd Battalion).

1st and 2nd Battalions were the only New Zealand troops in Senussi Campaign, North-West Egypt 1915-16.

After the formation of the New Zealand Division in Egypt in February 1916 the four battalions of the regiment became 'The 3rd New Zealand (Rifle) Brigade' of the Division and for the rest of the regiment's existence served on the Western Front.

In January 1919 the battalions were reorganised with the 1st and 2nd forming 'A' Battalion and the 3rd and 4th forming 'B' Battalion.

'A' Battalion was absorbed into 1st Brigade Group and 'B' Battalion into 2nd Brigade Group on 4 February 1919 and the New Zealand Rifle Brigade was no more.

In World War II the National Military Reserve veterans wore the badges of their old units but when the 1st Battalion National Reserve became the 4th Battalion, Auckland Regiment, they wore the blackened badges of the New Zealand Rifle Brigade.

Rifle Brigade reinforcements

MAORI BATTALION

First pattern badge. Made in Auckland by Watts Ltd.
It was worn by A Company only.

First pattern badge. Worn by B Company. Note the
difference in the shape of the crown.

Maori military units formed as early as 1849 and there were two companies in the Armed Constabulary Field Force in 1867 and two companies in the Arawa Flying Column 1870. Other volunteer units were formed and although many Maoris volunteered to serve in the Boer War their offer was refused.

In 1914 two Maori companies were formed: A Company from North Auckland, West Coast North Island and South Island; B Company from the Centre and East Coast of the North Island. This Maori Contingent left New Zealand in February 1915 and took part in the Gallipoli Campaign from July 1915.

MOTTO: *Hoko whitu a Tu.* This is an interesting motto as it means 'The seventy twice told warriors of the War God'. One hundred and forty was the ideal number in mythology for the formation of a war party, particularly if it was in the service of Tu, the god of war. This was the perfect motto for the famous Maori Battalion as it means the war party of Tu.

NEW ZEALAND NATIVE CONTINGENT

The first pattern badge was worn from 1914 till February 1916 with a red and black backing. After Gallipoli the Contingent was split up for a period. This action proved unacceptable to the Maori race and the unit was reformed as a Pioneer Battalion on 20 February 1916 and served in France. There were thirty contingents as reinforcements to the Pioneer Battalion, with Niue Islanders and Rarotongans in the 3rd Contingent.

NEW ZEALAND PIONEER BATTALION
Badge worn February 1916 to September 1917. Initially the battalion had two Maori companies but in September 1917 was an all-Maori unit. The battalion disbanded March 1919. There were thirty drafts sent overseas as reinforcements for the Pioneer Battalion.

NEW ZEALAND (MAORI) PIONEER BATTALION
Badge worn September 1917 to April 1919.

A Maori Volunteer Infantry Battalion, No. 28, formed October 1939 as part of 2NZEF. Left New Zealand with the Second Echelon and saw distinguished service in Greece, Crete, North Africa and Italy. From December 1942 became part of the 5th New Zealand Brigade. Disbanded 23 January 1946.

The 3rd Battalion (North Auckland) Regiment became the 2nd Maori Battalion in New Zealand from 1942 for one year.

THE NEW ZEALAND COOK ISLANDS COMPANY
This Company was formed from Pacific Islanders who had joined the New Zealand Maori Contingent but who found the winter in France too cold so were transferred to the Palestine coast where they served for the most part as lightermen. There were three drafts totalling 461 Rarotongans to support this Corps which sailed on 6 February 1916.

MACHINE GUN CORPS

BADGE: Crossed Maxim guns surmounted by a crown with the letters 'NZ' below.

New Zealand Machine Gun Corps formed in January 1916 with three companies (one for each Brigade of the New Zealand Division) from the New Zealand Infantry Battalion's Machine Gun Sections and saw action in France. A Divisional Company formed in England 18 October 1916 as No. 4 Company which was disbanded in February 1918.

The New Zealand Machine Gun Battalion formed from the companies in France on 13 June 1918 with A Company (Auckland), B Company (Canterbury), C Company (Otago), D Company (Wellington). These disbanded in Germany December 1918.

No. 1 NZMG Mounted Squadron, ANZAC Mounted Division, Palestine, formed in July 1916 from Machine Gun Sections of the New Zealand Mounted Rifle Regiments.

2nd NZMG Mounted Squadron, formed from the two New Zealand companies in the Imperial Camel Corps, August 1918 (this was the only New Zealand unit in the Australian Mounted Division).

27 (Machine Gun) Battalion 2NZEF formed in 1940. The No. 4 Company was comprised of volunteers from the New Zealand Scottish Regiment. Disbanded 1945, after distinguished service in Greece, Crete, North Africa and Italy.

8 Brigade Machine Gun Company formed June 1943 from support companies, 29, 34 and 36 Battalions 2NZEF. Saw action at Mono Island (Treasury Islands).

14 Brigade Machine Gun Company formed in June 1943 from support companies of 35 and 37 Battalions and members of 30th Battalion, Ruahine Regiment and New Zealand Scottish Regiment. Took part in actions at Vella Lavella and Nissan Island. Both 8 Brigade Company and 14 Brigade Company disbanded August 1944.

The Machine Gun Companies during World War I were distinguished by a colour patch worn at the back of the jacket below the collar.
HQ Machine Gun Battalion — blue star on black square.
1st Machine Gun Company — yellow star on black square.
2nd Machine Gun Company — pink star on black square.
3rd Machine Gun Company — green star on black square.
4th Machine Gun Company — red star on black square.
5th Machine Gun Company — black star on red square.

The Light Trench Mortar Batteries were distinguished in a similar manner:
1st Light Trench Mortar Battery — yellow circle on black square.
2nd Light Trench Mortar Battery — pink circle on black square.
3rd Light Trench Mortar Battery — green circle on black square.
4th Light Trench Mortar Battery — blue circle on black square.

THE NEW ZEALAND REGIMENT

BADGE: A kiwi within a circle inscribed 'New Zealand Regiment', enclosed by fern leaves and surmounted by a crown.
COLLAR BADGES: Smaller versions of the cap badge. Bayonets were added for the final design.

There were no regular infantry, only Permanent Force instructors, until 9 January 1947 when the New Zealand Regiment was formed as a part of the newly created New Zealand Infantry Corps. At this time the New Zealand Staff Corps, New Zealand Permanent Staff, New Zealand Permanent ASC and the General Duty Section of the New Zealand Permanent Forces were disbanded.

First pattern cap badge

Second pattern cap badge

241

Colours were issued to the 1st Battalion by Viscount Cobham at Burnham Camp, 10 September 1961. The advance party arrived in Singapore on 16 October 1957, the main body of the Battalion arriving on *Captain Cook* on 15 December. The Battalion moved to Kota Tinggi in Malaya on 1 February 1958 and commenced operations on 10 March 1958.

The Second Battalion was raised in Waiouru in 1959 to relieve the First Battalion in Northern Malaya in November 1959. By February 1960 the Battalion was deployed in the jungles of Malaya to continue the operations previously performed by the NZSAS Squadron and the First Battalion. In November 1961 the First Battalion returned to Malaya to relieve the Second Battalion. The Battalion was relieved towards the end of 1963 by the 1st Battalion RNZIR which was transferred in May 1965 from West Malaysia to Borneo to assume operational control of the security forces in the Second Division of Sarawak.

Colours were presented to the Second Battalion by Major-General, The Right Honourable Sir Harold Barrowclough on 4 March 1962 at Burnham Camp.

The prefix 'Royal' was granted to the New Zealand Infantry Corps on 12 July 1947.

ROYAL NEW ZEALAND INFANTRY REGIMENT

BADGE: A silver kiwi on scarlet background within a circle of garter blue inscribed 'Royal New Zealand Infantry Regiment', the whole enclosed by fern-fronds and surmounted by a crown. A scroll below 'Onward'.

COLLAR BADGES: Smaller versions of the cap badge.

The kiwi was the divisional sign of the 3rd and 6th New Zealand Divisions and the fern leaves and 'Onward' were worn by the 2NZEF during World War II.

In the reorganisation and redesignation of all New Zealand infantry on 1 April 1964 the Regular New Zealand Regiment became the 1st Battalion, seeing service in Malaysia. V Company arrived in Vietnam 12 May 1967 and W Company towards the end of the year. Both Companies were incorporated into the Australian Infantry as the Anzac Battalion in January 1968.

Her Majesty the Queen was appointed Colonel-in-Chief Royal New Zealand Infantry Regiment on 6 August 1964.

Officers and senior NCOs wear the bayonet pattern collar badges on their Mess Dress.

Short title	Full title
1 RNZIR	— 1st Battalion, Royal New Zealand Infantry Regiment.
2 RNZIR	— 2nd Battalion (Canterbury and Nelson-Marlborough and West Coast), Royal New Zealand Infantry Regiment.
3 RNZIR	— 3rd Battalion (Auckland (Countess of Ranfurly's Own) and Northland), Royal New Zealand Infantry Regiment.
4 RNZIR	— 4th Battalion (Otago and Southland), Royal New Zealand Infantry Regiment.
5 RNZIR	— 5th Battalion (Wellington West Coast and Taranaki), Royal New Zealand Infantry Regiment.
6 RNZIR	— 6th Battalion (Hauraki), Royal New Zealand Infantry Regiment.
7 RNZIR	— 7th Battalion (Wellington (City of Wellington's Own) and Hawke's Bay), Royal New Zealand Infantry Regiment.

Each numbered battalion was constituted as a descendant unit from one or more of the old regiments which had formed a part of the early history of the New Zealand Army and these battalions were allowed to retain these associations in the form of a bracketed designation after their titles.

2nd NEW ZEALAND EXPEDITIONARY FORCE (2NZEF)

BADGE: Two fern leaves enclosing the letters 'NZ' above a scroll 'Onward' and surmounted by a crown. Usually in brass but was made in bronze. Minor variations in the size of badge and positioning of the letters. Smaller badge as collars.

At the outbreak of World War II the New Zealand Government undertook the task of raising a Special Force to be despatched overseas. The composition of the Special Force was announced by the Director of Mobilisation on 16 October 1939, the Special Force being given the designation 2nd New Zealand Division. The designation, 2nd New Zealand Expeditionary Force (2NZEF) was not adopted until 12 December 1939. The division was raised in three contingents, or Echelons as they were termed in New Zealand.

First Echelon: Departed for Egypt 6 January 1940.
Second Echelon: Departed for Egypt 2 May 1940 but was diverted to England and arrived in Egypt January 1941.
Third Echelon: Departed for Egypt 27 August 1940.

18th, 21st, 24th Battalions from Northern Military District.
19th, 22nd, 25th Battalions from the Central Military District.
20th, 23rd, 26th Battalions from the South Island (Southern Military District).
These Battalions joined the 4th, 5th and 6th Infantry Brigades, each Brigade having one Battalion from each District and the 5th Brigade having 28th (Maori) Battalion in addition. These units saw action in Greece, Crete, North Africa and Italy.

8th New Zealand Infantry Brigade reached Fiji in November 1940 and landed in Treasury Islands on 27 October 1943.

The Pacific Section, 2NZEF, was renamed the 3rd New Zealand Division and went initially to New Caledonia in 1943 and after training there, the 14th Brigade (30th, 35th and 37th Battalions) took part in the action at Vella Lavella and Green Island.

Many of the New Zealand troops in Egypt wore the badges of the Expeditionary Force of World War I in preference to the 'Onward' type as these were available in the shops in Cairo, but the wearing of these badges was never officially approved.

The first troops to serve overseas were two officers and thirty other ranks who sailed for Fanning Island on 30 August 1939 to prevent the island being occupied in the event of war being declared. This unit was known as No. 1 Platoon, A Company, the badge they wore was the Dixon crest, first introduced in 1911 for school cadet officer instructors. This badge is the oldest unchanged design in the New Zealand Army. Reinforcements to A Company wore the 2NZEF badge.

36 Battalion went to Norfolk Island, reinforced later by the 2nd Battalion, Wellington West Coast Regiment.

34 Battalion served in Tonga, reinforced later by the 6th Battalion, Canterbury Regiment.

The 3rd New Zealand Division was disbanded on 20 October 1944.

The 'Onward' badge was worn until 1947 by the New Zealand 'J' Force contingent of the Allied Japan Occupation Forces.

The badge is currently worn by the Officer Cadet Training Company which was formed at Waiouru in 1977 to provide New Zealand-trained officers for the Army.

LONG RANGE DESERT GROUP

BADGE: A scorpion above the letters 'LRP' within a circle. At the base of the circle the letters 'LRDG' and on either side the letters 'N' and 'Z'. The badge was in silver but did not meet with general approval.

BADGE: A scorpion above the letters 'LRDG' within a circle. Bronze.

The Long Range Patrol (LRP) formed in July 1940 with three officers and 50 men, all volunteers from the New Zealand Divisional Cavalry, the 27th (Machine Gun) Battalion, and the 7th Anti-Tank Regiment N.Z.A.

With the enlarging of the group, the Long Range Desert Group (LRDG) was formed on 31 December 1940. In the action at Ain Dua two men received the first decorations awarded to the 2NZEF. Lieutenant J. H. Sutherland (Military Cross) and Trooper L. A. Willcox (Military Medal).

The New Zealanders formed R1, R2, T1 and T2 patrols of A Squadron and served in Libya and Tunisia. The T1 patrol was the first unit of the 8th Army to cross the frontier into Tunisia. In September 1943 the unit moved to the Leros Islands off Greece and suffered heavy casualties when the Germans captured the Islands in November 1943. As a result of the unit being committed to this action without the knowledge of the New Zealand Government the remnants of A (NZ) Squadron were disbanded on 31 December 1943 and the men sent to Italy, to become part of the 2 NZ Divisional Cavalry.

ROYAL NEW ZEALAND ARMOURED CORPS

BADGE: Fern leaves enclosing a tank and crossed lances above a scroll 'Royal NZ Armoured Corps'. Collar badges are smaller version of the badges. Original badge was in white metal. Officers' badges in gilt and silver and a similar badge for other ranks (anodised).

On 1 January 1942 the nine Mounted Rifle Regiments had the words 'Light Armoured Fighting Vehicle Regiment' added after their number and before the old title. This made a most cumbersome title and as an example: 2nd Light Armoured Fighting Vehicle Regiment (Queen Alexandra's (Wellington West Coast) Mounted Rifles).

In October 1942 4th New Zealand Brigade (18, 19, 20 Battalions) became Armoured, and the Mounted Rifle Regiments inherited the battle honours of 18, 19 and 20 Armoured Regiments in Italy. The 2nd New Zealand Division Cavalry (Armoured) Regiment to which the Mounted Rifle personnel were posted, had its battle honours given to the New Zealand Scottish Regiment as it had become the Divisional Reconnaisance Regiment in the New Zealand Forces.

Officers and soldiers of 1 Armoured Car Regiment (New Zealand Scottish), as the successors of the New Zealand Divisional Cavalry Regiment 2 (NZ) Division, Second New Zealand Expeditionary Force, wear a green colour patch behind the cap badge to commemorate the green puggaree worn by the Mounted Rifles.

The prefix 'Royal' was granted 12 July 1947 and the Corps became the Royal New Zealand Armoured Corps.

CORPS DRESS DISTINCTION
Colour Patch
To maintain the tradition of the Second New Zealand Expeditionary Force during the Second World War, 1939-45, and in honour of 4 (NZ) Armoured Brigade, 2NZEF, the officers and soldiers of RNZAC (other than the New Zealand Scottish Squadrons) will wear a piece of scarlet cloth fixed under the RNZAC cap and collar badges.
Tank Arm Badge
To demonstrate their alliance with the Royal Tank Regiment, the RNZAC has permission to wear that Regiment's Tank Arm Badge. Worn on the right arm in silver embroidery and also in worsted embroidery.
Webbing
In accordance with the tradition of armoured corps, officers and soldiers of RNZAC blacken all items of webbing.

New Zealand Army Order No. 62, 29 March 1944, reorganised the New Zealand Armoured Corps into three regiments, one in each of the Military Districts.

1st Armoured Regiment: 3rd (Auckland), 4th (Waikato) and 11th (North Auckland) LAFV Regiments.

2nd Armoured Regiment: 2nd Queen Alexandra's (Wellington West Coast), 6th (Manawatu) and 9th (Wellington East Coast) LAFV Regiments.

3rd Armoured Regiment: 1st (Canterbury Yeomanry Cavalry), 5th (Otago) and 10th (Nelson and Marlborough) LAFV Regiments.

The 1st, 2nd and 3rd Armoured Regiments inherited the battle honours of the 18th, 19th and 20th Armoured Regiments 2NZEF respectively.

In 1950 the Waikato Regiment was absorbed into the 1st Armoured Regiment. In October 1953 the 2nd Armoured Regiment was reorganised, the old 9th (Wellington East Coast) portion becoming the 4th Armoured Regiment (initially called the Divisional Regiment). The remainder retained the name 2nd Armoured Regiment.

The 4th Armoured Regiment was later granted the title 'City of Hastings Own'.

The 2nd and 3rd Armoured Regiments were placed in recess in 1956.

In September 1958 the 2nd Armoured Regiment was reactivated as part of the Regular Force being renamed Queen Alexandra's Armoured Regiment in December 1958. The word 'Armoured' was removed in August 1959. From 1962 onwards Regular and Territorial Units became integrated as part of the New Zealand Field Force Combat Brigade Force, the (Territorial) 4th Armoured Regiment (City of Hastings Own) becoming absorbed into the Queen Alexandra's Regiment.

THE 1st ARMOURED CAR REGIMENT
(NEW ZEALAND SCOTTISH) RNZAC

MOTTO: *Mo Rich Mo Dhuthaich* (My King My Country).
On 17 January 1939 the unit was formed as 1st Battalion New Zealand Scottish Regiment, an infantry unit of the Territorial Force. Only men of proven Scottish birth or descent were admitted to the Regiment.

The 1st Battalion (North Island) New Zealand Scottish was mobilised at the outbreak of World War II being one of the only two territorial battalions to be

The first collar badges were in bronze
and were in use in Auckland.

249

sent overseas. The 1st Battalion embarked for New Caledonia in December 1942 as part of the 15th Brigade, 3rd New Zealand Division. The 15th Brigade was disbanded in July 1943 due to shortage of men, but many former New Zealand Scots later saw service in the Middle East and Italy.

No. 4 Company, 27 (Machine Gun) Battalion 2NZEF was formed from volunteers of the New Zealand Scottish.

A 2nd Battalion (South Island) was formed during the War.

In 1949 the Regiment was reformed as the 1st Divisional Regiment RNZAC (New Zealand Scottish) and is now known as 1st Armoured Car Regiment (New Zealand Scottish) RNZAC.

The cap badge is silver, and is similar to the badge of the Black Watch. The blue Balmoral bonnet with a red tourie is worn by all ranks (including the band) in ceremonial dress. A black beret for training.

The battle dress blouse is worn with a whitened belt and Black Watch kilt. Officers wear a khaki Scottish-type service jacket with a Sam Browne belt and sword.

The Black Watch sporran with white strap is worn by all ranks. The officers' sporran has a silver top, the sergeants' a brass top and the other ranks, a black leather top with badge.

Black and red diced hose are worn with red garter flashes and white Highland spats, with black boots. Sashes are worn by sergeants.

The Regimental Sergeant-Major wears a beret and carries a cane, both replicas of types used by the Royal Scots Greys, to symbolise the affiliation.

Prior to 1960, the pipers and drummers wore battle dress blouses and Black Watch kilt and the pipe covers were of Black Watch tartan. In 1960 it was decided to provide the band with Highland green cut-away jackets (as worn in Australia). Royal Stewart tartan kilt and pipe covers and Black Watch tartan plaids.

The bass drummer wears a leopard skin apron.

BATTLE HONOURS: Inherited those of the 2 NZ Divisional Cavalry 2NZEF.

Colours were presented to the Regiment at Linton Camp on 23 February 1963 by His Excellency the Governor-General Sir Bernard Fergusson.

In 1970 a reorganisation took place which resulted in the regiment becoming two squadrons, the 1st Squadron at Burnham and the 2nd Squadron at Dunedin. They were equipped with M113 A. P. carriers.

NEW ZEALAND SCOTTISH VOLUNTEER UNITS

Auckland Highland Rifle Volunteers: 1 March 1909. Wore the Black Watch tartan. Officers wore feathered bonnets. Other ranks wore glengarries.

Auckland Scottish Rifle Volunteers: 7 July 1871. Major Taylor, an officer of the New Zealand Militia, was Commanding Officer. Disbanded 11 January 1882.

Caledonian Rangers (Wanganui) Rifle Volunteers: 17 March 1863. Formed with change of title of No. 4 Company, Wanganui Rifle Volunteers. Disbanded 23 March 1866.

Canterbury Highland Rifle Volunteers: 10 September 1900. Wore the Gordon tartan. Became J Company, North Canterbury Battalion 1 August 1901. Became D Company, 2nd Battalion, North Canterbury Rifle Volunteers 7 October 1903. In 1906 this Company was chosen to occupy the post of honour at the doorway when the Governor opened the Christchurch Exhibition. Captain D. McBean Stewart of this company was killed in action 25 April 1915 as Lieutenant-Colonel commanding 'Canterbury' Battalion, Gallipoli.

Canterbury Scottish Rifle Volunteers: 16 February 1885. Wore a scarlet doublet, forage cap and kilt of Gordon tartan. Disbanded 12 December 1893.

Dunedin Highland Brigade Volunteers: 11 March 1885. Added to the Dunedin Highland Rifle Volunteers 13 April 1885.

Dunedin Highland Rifle Volunteers: Formed in 1865 and planned to wear the Black Watch uniform which was available in Melbourne. The strength of the company was below the requirement of the 1865 Volunteer Regulations so the corps was disbanded on 28 March 1866. Reformed as No. 1 Company, Dunedin Highland Rifle Volunteers. Designated Dunedin Highland Rifle Volunteers on 13 April 1885 when they absorbed the Dunedin Highland Brigade Volunteers. Wore the tartan of the 42nd Highlanders with feather bonnets. The Corps flag is in the Dunedin Early Settlers' Hall. Twenty men of the Dunedin and Wanganui Highland Rifles represented New Zealand at the opening of the Australian Federal Parliament in 1901.

The Corps became E Company, 1st Battalion Otago Rifle Volunteers 20 May 1898. Became C Company, 1st Battalion Otago Rifle Volunteers 2 March 1904.

Dunedin Rifle Volunteers, No. 2 (Scottish) Company: 1863. Proposed the wearing of the London Scottish uniform but changed to a scarlet jacket with white facings, blue trousers and a half-shako with horse-hair plumes. Disbanded 3 June 1874.

Invercargill Highland Rifle Volunteers: 16 September 1873. Formed with a strength of some forty men but an actual inspection showed a strength of seventeen. Disbanded 6 May 1874.

Thames Scottish Battalion:
No. 1 Company: 1 October 1878. Formed from No. 1 Company, Thames Scottish Rifle Volunteers. Mobilised 27 October 1881. Disbanded 7 June 1882.
No. 2 Company: 1 October 1878. Formed by No. 2 Company, Thames Scottish Rifle Volunteers. Mobilised 27 October 1881. Disbanded 7 June 1882.
No. 3 Company: 6 February 1879. Mobilised 27 October 1881. Disbanded 17 May 1882.

Thames Scottish Rifle Volunteers:
No. 1 Company: 9 August 1871. Formed by change of title of No. 1 Company, Thames Rifle Rangers Volunteers. The title of No. 1 Company did not occur until 3 July 1878 when No. 2 Company was formed. It was intended to have a uniform of kilt, tunic and Balmoral bonnet but this was changed to a scarlet jacket and helmet.
No. 2 Company: 3 July 1878. Formed by change of title of No. 3 Company, Hauraki Rifle Volunteers. Nos. 1 and 2 Company, Thames Scottish Rifle Volunteers were amalgamated as one Corps designated the Thames Scottish Battalion on 1 October 1878. The battalion had a brass band.

Wanganui Highland Rifle Volunteers: 11 April 1900. The Corps was issued with khaki uniforms but adopted the full-dress uniform of the Gordon Highlanders in February 1901. Became F Company, 2nd Battalion Wellington (West Coast) Rifle Volunteers on 1 May 1901.

Wellington Highland Rifle Volunteers: 17 April 1871. Wore the Black Watch tartan. The Commanding Officer, Captain John Carey resigned in August 1873 due to a difference of opinion with members of the corps. The title was changed to Wellington Scottish Rifle Volunteers on 24 June 1874. Disbanded 30 June 1875. The corps was reformed under the original title, Wellington Highland Rifle Volunteers on 11 April 1900. They wore the uniform of the Seaforth Highlanders in January 1902.

Wellington Scottish Rifle Volunteers: 24 June 1874. Wore the MacKenzie tartan. Disbanded 30 June 1875.

The only mounted Scottish Corps in the New Zealand Army was in the Auckland District.

Scottish Horse (Waipu) Mounted Rifle Volunteers: 14 April 1900.

Thames Scottish Rifle Volunteers, 1891.
Nickel plate for officers, white metal for other ranks.

Thames Scottish Rifle Volunteers

Canterbury Rifle Volunteers, 1900.
Badges in either white metal or brass.

Auckland Scottish Rifle Volunteers, 1871.
Badges in white metal.

1st RANGER SQUADRON
NEW ZEALAND SPECIAL AIR SERVICE

BADGE: A vertical dagger, hilt uppermost with a pair of wings below hilt. Below, a scroll enscribed *Who dares wins*. Light blue worsted.
COLLAR BADGES: Smaller versions of cap badge in silver and gilt.
Formed in June 1955 for service in South-East Asia. Stationed in Malaya as part of the British 22nd Special Air Service Regiment.

To signify the close association between the NZSAS and the British SAS, officers and soldiers of NZSAS wear black web belts and black anklets whenever webbing is worn.

The SAS became a separate corps of the New Zealand Army in 1959. To commemorate the founding of the famous commando unit, in 1863 under Major Von Tempsky, the Forest Rangers, the unit was renamed the 1st Ranger Squadron, New Zealand Special Air Service, as from 1 September 1963. 4 Troop NZSAS was deployed to South Vietnam in December 1968 and after initial training in Malaysia undertook regular reconnaissance and ambush patrols as a troop of the Australian SAS Squadron until February 1971. The Corps reverted to their original title '1 NZSAS Squadron' on 1 April 1978.

NEW ZEALAND ARMY AIR CORPS

BADGES: As for the British Corps.

In 1912 Lieutenant W. W. A. Burn (N.Z. Staff Corps) was sent to England for flying training. In 1915 Lieut. Burn and J. W. H. Scotland, the only pilots in New Zealand, joined the first half-flight, Australian Flying Corps, in Mesopotamia. Burns was killed in action in July 1915. New Zealand pilots learnt to fly at private schools in New Zealand, or had transferred to the Royal Flying Corps from the NZEF. The N.Z. Permanent Air Force, an Army Unit, was formed on 14 June 1923. The RNZAF was created as a separate service on 27 February 1934.

The N.Z. Permanent Air Force wore brass shoulder titles N.Z.P.A.F.

The only New Zealand army personnel on flying duties in World War II were a few of the Long Range Desert Group who piloted two Waco aircraft on liaison flights with patrols and evacuated the wounded from June 1941 onwards.

Flying recommenced in the New Zealand Army in September 1947 and the first brevets were presented in February 1948. These were the 'AOP' United Kingdom Army Wings, first introduced for the Royal Artillery spotters in World War II. Flying in New Zealand was conducted on Tiger Moths (basic) and Auster J5 aircraft. The flying was part-time following the initial 'wings' course.

In 1961 two Army officers were seconded to the British Army Air Corps for operational service in Malaya, flying the United Kingdom 'AOP9' Auster aircraft.

The first helicopter training was undertaken by the New Zealand Army under a civilian contract at Nelson in late 1963 and at that time the old glider-pilot wings were adopted as the standard Army brevet. At this time non-artillery officers became eligible for flying training since the role had expanded to include reconnaissance and support rather than purely artillery spotting duties.

Army pilots now serve with No. 3 Battlefield Support Squadron in New Zealand as well as with the United Kingdom Army Air Corps in Malaysia and served with the Australian Army Air Corps in South Vietnam.

The New Zealand Army Air Corps was formally established on 9 August 1963.

Flying Duties Badges

Air Observation Post Flying Badge

The badge consists of a pair of wings with a centrally placed grenade and scroll beneath bearing the motto *Ubique,* the whole on a black background.

Embroidered — wings and motto in silver, grenade in gold on scroll in red silk.

Worsted — wings in pale blue, grenade and scroll in old gold and motto in red.

Army Flying Badge

The badge consists of a pair of wings with the Royal Crest in the centre, the whole on a black background.

Embroidered — wings in silver and the Royal Crest in gold.

Worsted — wings in pale blue and the Royal Crest in old gold.

Parachute Instructors

A parachute surrounded by a wreath.

Captain F. Hatherly was the first to wear this badge which he qualified for while serving with the RAF while he was 2IC, 1st Ranger Squadron 1960.

Parachutists' Badges with Wings

The parachutists' badge with wings consists of a pair of drooping wings with a parachute in the centre.

Embroidered — wings gold, parachute silver, all on blue background.

Worsted — wings pale blue, parachute white, all on a khaki background.

Parachutists' Badge without Wings

The badge for personnel who have qualified at a basic parachute course but who have not yet joined an airborne unit or made a parachute jump on operations against the enemy.

Embroidered — silver on a blue background.

Worsted — white parachute on a khaki background.

Assistant Parachute Jump Instructor's Badge

A pair of wings with a parachute between and the letters APJI beneath the parachute with a wreath of laurel surroundng the letters and part of the parachute.

Embroidered — gold and silver on a blue cloth background.

Worsted — wings sky blue, parachute white, letters gold, wreath emerald green, all on a khaki background.

Special Air Service Badge

A pair of wings (not drooping) with a parachute in the centre.

Embroidered — wings silver, parachute gold, all on a blue background.

Worsted — wings in pale and dark blue, parachute white, all on a dark blue background.

Air Despatch Badge

A pair of wings with a circle between, within the circle the letters 'AD' and on the circle the letters 'RNZASC', the whole surmounted by a crown.

Embroidered — wings silver, 'AD' gold, RNZASC dark blue, circle yellow, crown in self colours, the whole on a khaki background.

Worsted — wings pale blue, 'AD' and circle old gold, crown in self colours, the whole on khaki background.

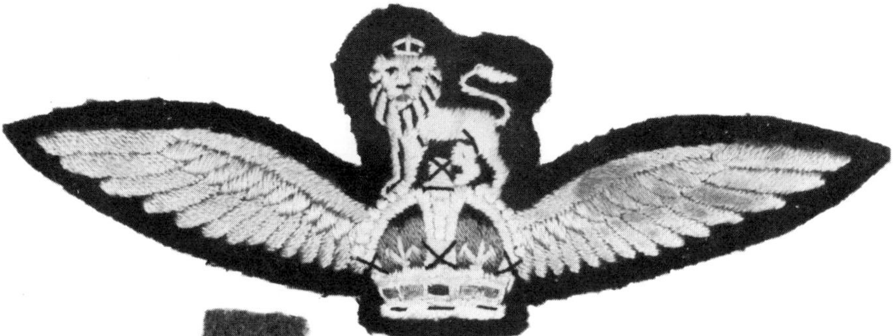

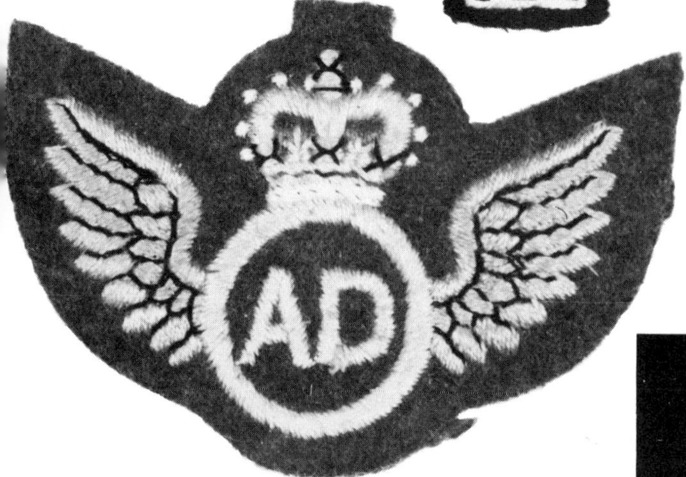
AD

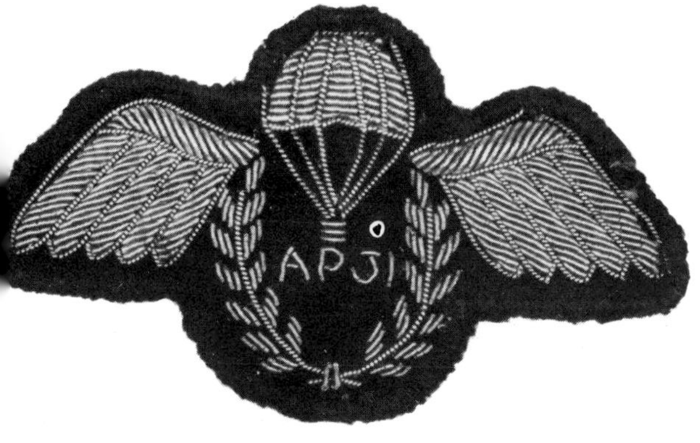
APJI

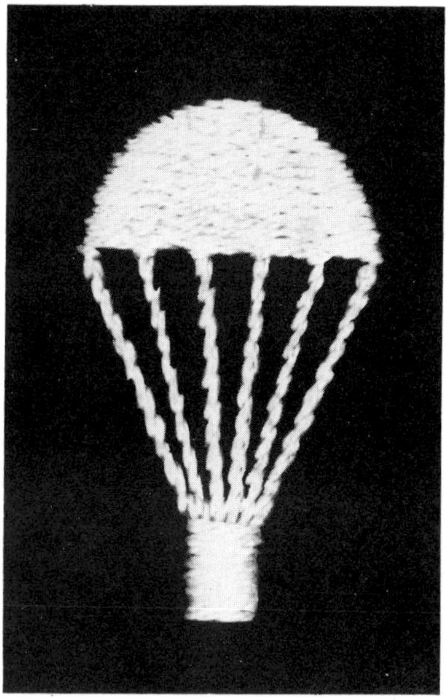

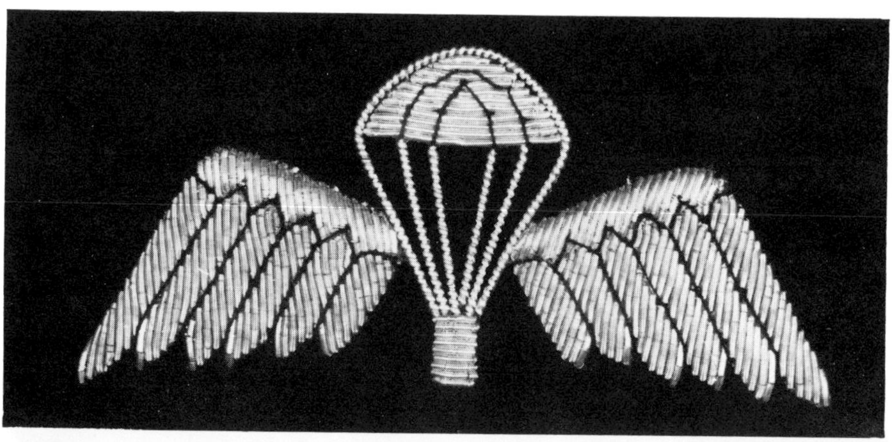

ROYAL NEW ZEALAND ARMY SERVICE CORPS

BADGE: An eight-pointed star, surmounted by a crown. On the star, in gilt, a laurel-wreath. Within the wreath the Garter and motto. Within the Garter the letters 'A.S.C' in monogram, and the letters 'NZ' on the Garter below the monogram.
COLLAR BADGES: Smaller versions of cap badge.
The badges in bronze or brass. After 1947 the monogram 'ASC' was replaced by the Royal Cypher 'GVIR' or 'EIIR' above a scroll 'R.N.Z.A.S.C.' These badges are bi-metal, silver, gilt, and enamel, or white metal and brass.
MOTTO: *Nil Sine Labor* (Nothing without work).

The origin of the corps dates from 12 May 1910 but the corps did not function until four Army Service Corps NCO's arrived from England on 1 March 1913.

As the Divisional Transport and Supply Units, the corps sailed with the Main Body NZEF and on 2 August 1917 formed a Training Company in Egypt which supplied ASC units to all regiments and corps.

The Permanent Army Service Corps was formed in 1922 consisting of 'other ranks' only and being commanded by officers from the Staff Corps. The Permanent Army Service Corps wore brass shoulder titles N.Z.P.A.S.C.

On 9 January 1947 the Regular and Territoral Forces were integrated when the New Zealand Permanent Army Service Corps and the New Zealand Army Service Corps (Territorial) became the New Zealand Army Service Corps.

Prefix 'Royal' granted 12 July 1947.

A driver of the NZASC (4th Reserve Motor Transport Company) was the first death in action of the 2NZEF on 13 September 1940 in the Western Desert.

On 12 May 1979 the RNZASC was disbanded (ending 60 years of service to the Army), and was designated the Royal New Zealand Corps of Transport.

259

ROYAL NEW ZEALAND ARMY MEDICAL CORPS

BADGE: Within a laurel-wreath surmounted by a crown, the rod of Aesculapius with a serpent entwined and a scroll below inscribed 'New Zealand Medical Corps'.

The badge of the Permanent Forces had the lower scroll 'N.Z. Army Medical Corps' as the first pattern, followed later by a scroll 'N.Z.A.M.C'. The Permanent Forces wore a brass shoulder title 'N.Z.A.M.C'.

The Badge of the Territorial Force had a scroll 'N.Z. Medical Corps', followed by the second pattern scroll 'New Zealand Medical Corps' and a final pattern scroll 'N.Z.M.C'. The Territorial Force shoulder title was a brass 'N.Z.M.C'.

COLLAR BADGES: Smaller versions of the cap badge.

MOTTO: *Semper agens – semper quietus* (Always effective — always calm).

Badges were bronze or brass although a few bi-metal are known to exist. Distinctive badges were worn by the No. 3 Coy, Field Ambulance and by No. 3 Field Hospital with the motto *Te manaaki tika* (Take great care of others). Prior to the formation of the corps, a volunteer medical staff was responsible for the well-being of the soldiers at training camps.

In the volunteer era, medical officers were commissioned into the unit with which they served. The corps was formed on 7 May 1908 from those in the Permanent Force, Militia, Volunteers, field ambulances and military sanitary service. At this time, all field hospitals and bearer corps were designated 'Field Ambulances'. The majority of the officers in this new corps had seen service as volunteers in the Boer War.

Auckland Volunteer Bearer Company: 4 May 1898. Became No. 1 Company New Zealand Field Hospital and Bearer Corps 31 January 1905. Each of the five Companies wore brass shoulder titles in the form

1	2	3	4	5
NZMC	NZMC	NZMC	NZMC	NZMC

Wellington Volunteer Bearer Corps: 6 November 1899. Became No. 4 Company NZ Bearer Corps.

Nelson Volunteer Bearer Corps: 15 May 1901. Became No. 5 Company NZ Bearer Corps.

Christchurch Volunteer Bearer Corps: 16 March 1899. Became No. 3 Company NZ Bearer Corps.

Dunedin Volunteer Bearer Corps: 20 May 1898. Became No. 2 Company NZ Bearer Corps.

Mounted Field Ambulances were established at: No. 5 (Hamilton); No. 6 (Christchurch); No. 7 (Invercargill); No. 8 (Palmerston North).

On 9 January 1947, the NZAMC was combined with the NZMC (Territorial) to become the New Zealand Army Medical Corps. The title 'Royal' was granted on 12 July 1947.

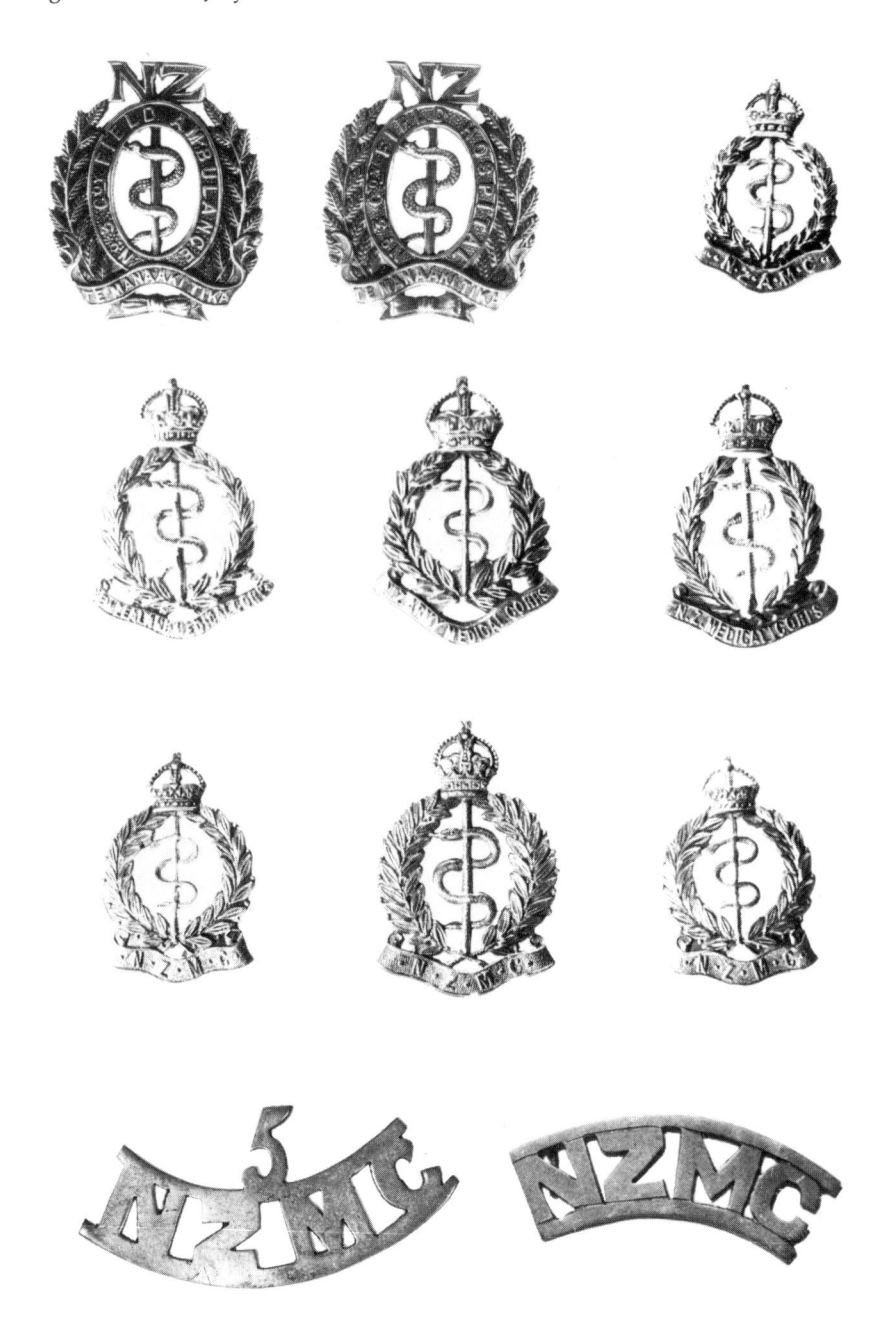

Otago University Medical Company

In October 1908 the University of Otago established the need to form two volunteer companies of the Officers' Training Corps, one an infantry company and the other a medical company. The first parade was held in August 1909 although the notice in the *New Zealand Gazette* for their formation is dated 4 October 1909. Training camps were held in 1910 at Taiaroa and Waitati. With the commencement of compulsory military service in 1911 the OTC's were disbanded, the O.U.M.C. became B Company, 2nd Field Ambulance.

The unit was reconstituted as an OTC in 1915 at which time the OTC badge was issued. The large majority of the medical and dental officers who served overseas during World War I received preliminary training with the unit. Their function as an OTC was discontinued as from 19 January 1922. The Otago University Medical Company was established as part of the New Zealand Medical Corps on 1 October 1927. At the start of World War II their function consisted of infantry training only, a situation which was not resolved until July 1941 when the unit resumed its function of training medical personnel in field medical practices. The dental students were trained as ASC personnel for the field ambulances and with the medical students were posted to the five companies of Field Ambulance. Research projects developed improved methods of carrying stretches in lorries, the transportation of wounded in mountainous terrain, and in the simplifying of field equipment.

NZ Veterinary Corps
see opposite page

NEW ZEALAND VETERINARY CORPS

BADGE: Within an oak leaf wreath surmounted by a crown, the monogram 'NZVC'.
COLLAR BADGES: Smaller versions of the cap badge.
SHOULDER TITLES: Brass 'NZVC'.

The officers badges were bi-metal, wreath in gilt, monogram in silver. Although the design of this badge was never officially altered throughout the history of the corps, the badge was usually of a fern leaf wreath and was in bronze or brass. Very few of the oak leaf wreath badges exist.

Volunteer veterinary officers wore the uniform as for the Army Veterinary Department Dress Regulations 1904 but their buttons had the additional letters 'NZ' and the initials 'N.Z' were worn in silver below badges of rank on the shoulder-knots.

The corps was formed in 1907. At the outbreak of World War I the Veterinary Corps had the responsibility of selecting horses at their camp in Palmerston North. All horses were classified into six classes and branded with an N-arrow-Z on one fore-hoof and the number of the horse was branded on the other fore-hoof.

The total number of horses transported from New Zealand was 9,988 of which the loss on the voyage over was only 3 per cent. Because of the long voyage, this is a remarkably small percentage and can be attributed entirely to the care and attention of the men in New Zealand's veterinary organisation.

New Zealand horses were mostly of exceptional quality and the New Zealand Mounted Rifles Brigade took part in the Sinai and Palestine Campaigns with marked success. The horses suffered in the extreme winter conditions in Northern France in 1916 because of the constant mud. In the Western Campaign the New Zealand Veterinary Corps served under the command of the Royal Army Veterinary Corps. Disbanded 9 January 1947.

ROYAL NEW ZEALAND ARMY ORDNANCE CORPS

BADGE: A shield with three cannons mounted horizontally. In the upper portion of the shield were two cannon balls with the letters 'NZ' between the balls. Below the shield a scroll inscribed 'Army Ordnance Dept'.

This badge was worn by commissioned officers only.

MOTTO: *Sua tela tonanti* (To the warrior, his arms).

Although the raising of an ordnance corps had been suggested in 1904 and again by Sir Ian Hamilton in 1914 the corps came into being on 1 April 1915 as the Army Ordnance Section and as the staff were mostly Royal New Zealand Artillery they wore their own corps badge.

On 1 February 1917, the New Zealand Army Ordnance Department and the New Zealand Army Ordnance Corps were established and became part of the Permanent Force of New Zealand.

The Ordnance Corps badge was a shield with three cannons pointing to the right. In the upper portion of the shield were two cannon balls separated by the letters 'NZ'. Below the shield, a scroll 'Army Ordnance Corps'. This design was brought into line with the format of the British badge after 3 July 1924 when the Ordnance Department and the Ordnance Corps were combined to form the New Zealand Army Ordnance Corps. Both the department and the corps badges were made in bronze or brass.

In 1937 a new badge was introduced with the words 'New Zealand Army Ordnance Corps' inside a ring encircling the shield, above the corps motto *Sua tela tonanti*.

On 9 January 1947 the NZAOC combined with the NZOC (Territorial) to form the NZAOC.

On 12 July 1947 the corps was designated a Royal Corps which permitted the distinction of incorporating the Garter and motto. The Tudor Crown was replaced with the Saint Edward's Crown on 29 October 1955.

The officers' badges are gilt, silver and enamel, while those worn by other ranks are anodised aluminium with the Garter in blue and a red background behind the shield.

265

CORPS OF ROYAL NEW ZEALAND ELECTRICAL AND MECHANICAL ENGINEERS

BADGE: Upon a flash of lightning a horse forcene with a coronet of four *fleur-de-leis* around its neck, a chain attached to the back of the coronet and falling down to a globe on which the horse is standing; above the horse a scroll inscribed 'RNZEME' and surmounted by a crown.
COLLAR BADGES: Smaller versions without scroll.
MOTTO: *Arte et Marte* (By skill and fighting).

Formed with the mechanisation of the British Army in October 1942 to co-ordinate the base workshops of the RE, RASC, and RAOC.

The amalgamation of the Ordnance Workshops and the Mechanical Transport Workshops on 1 September 1946 formed the present corps.

Prefix 'Royal' granted 12 July 1947.

NEW ZEALAND ARMY LEGAL SERVICE

MOTTO: *Justitia in armis* (Justice in arms).

The service was authorised on 3 February 1927 under the designation 'New Zealand Army Legal Department'. It was re-designated 'New Zealand Army Legal Service' on 20 November 1950.

The New Zealand Army Legal Department originally consisted of the Judge Advocate General, the Deputy Judge Advocate General, and Legal Staff Officers. The Judge Advocate General, a military officer, controlled both the judicial review of court-martial proceedings and the Legal Staff Officers who were responsible for the preparation of court-martial cases, and, where necessary, the prosecution.

Throughout World War II a Deputy Judge Advocate General held office with 2NZEF in the Middle East. At first this officer with a very small NCO staff was sufficient to deal with all legal proceedings, but towards the end of the war, partly because of the greater number of troops and partly because it was sought to render a much fuller personal legal service to soldiers, the staff was increased to a number of officers and clerks. Legal Staff Officers also served in the Pacific theatre.

On 20 November 1950 the Minister of Defence approved the separation and reorganisation of the Judge Advocate General's Department and the Army Legal Service on similar lines to those adopted in the United Kingdom following the recommendations contained in the Lewis Report, but due to administrative difficulties the change was not effected until 1955.

The Judge Advocate General's Department is now a separate organisation controlled by the Judge Advocate General, who is essentially a civilian with appropriate legal status and military experience. The functions of the Department are almost wholly judicial in character and are carried out independently of Army control by the Judge Advocate General and a panel of civilian barristers nominated by him.

The Director of the Army Legal Service and his staff officers are in fact in practice as civilian barristers, but they are all officers of the Territorial Force.

The badge is the same as British Army Legal Service.

ROYAL NEW ZEALAND DENTAL CORPS

BADGE: Within a laurel-wreath surmounted by a crown, two serpents entwined with a short rod of Aesculapius passing through the first, so as to form the monogram 'DC'.

MOTTO: *Ex malo bonum* (From evil comes good).

SHOULDER TITLE: NZDC.

The New Zealand Dental Service Corps was formed on 25 November 1915 with the transfer of Dental Officers who had been attached to the New Zealand Medical Corps. The corps was designated the New Zealand Dental Corps on 24 February 1916. Dental Officers were attached to 1st Field Ambulance in Egypt and at No. 2 Outpost, Anzac, at Gallipoli where a considerable amount of equipment was lost during the evacuation.

Two sections were attached to each of the three Field Ambulance Corps in France and one remained in Egypt with the Mounted Field Ambulance.

Dress distinction: All ranks of RNZDC may wear a cravat in corps colours with summer drill dress or bush shirt.

The title of the New Zealand Dental Corps was changed to New Zealand Army Dental Corps on 9 January 1947.

The prefix 'Royal' was granted on 12 July 1947 and the corps became the Royal New Zealand Dental Corps on 21 May 1949.

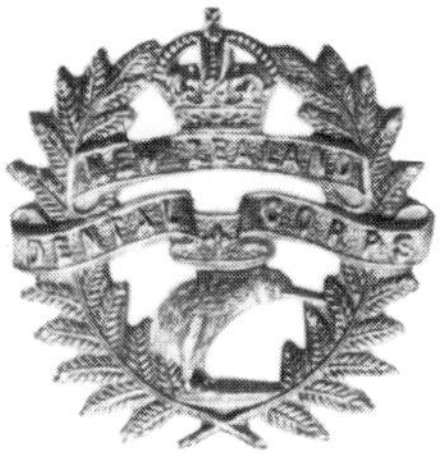
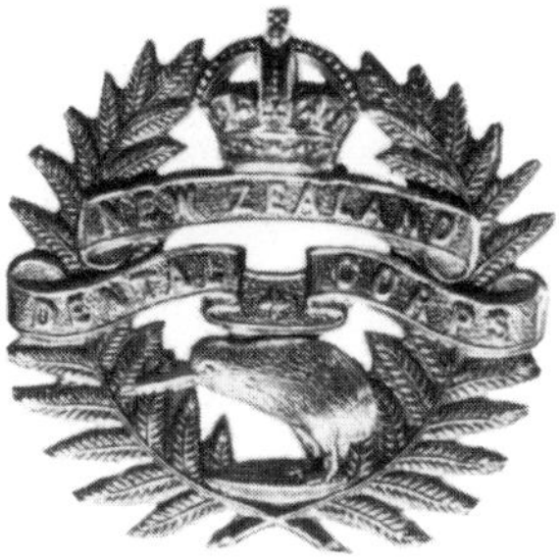
NEW ZEALAND
DENTAL CORPS
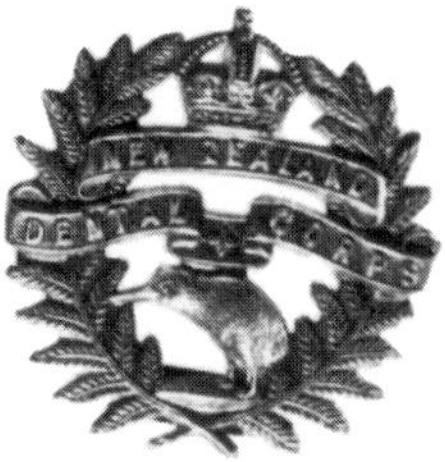
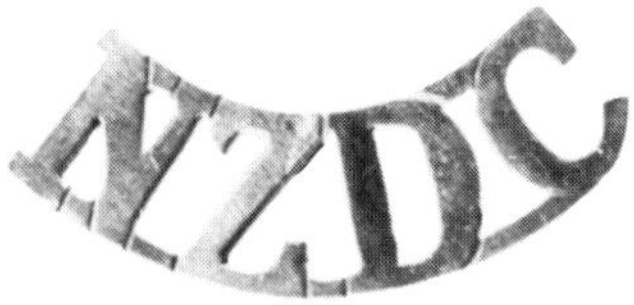
NZDC
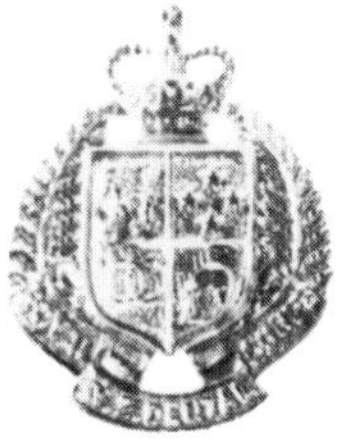
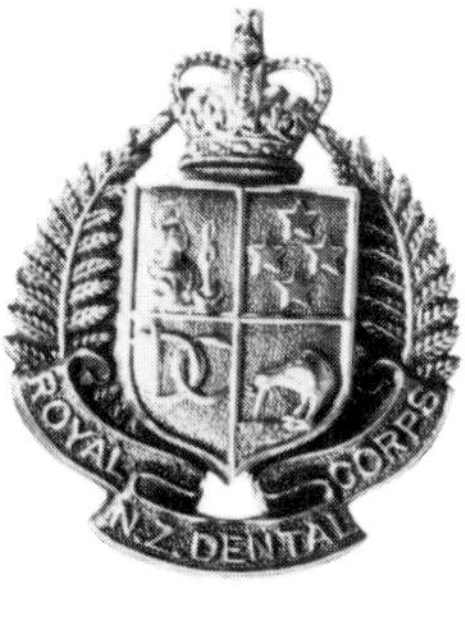
ROYAL
CORPS
N.Z. DENTAL
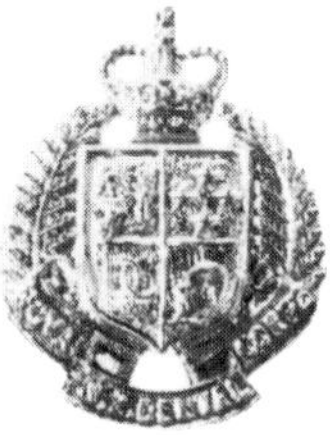

ROYAL NEW ZEALAND CHAPLAINS' DEPARTMENT

MOTTO: *In this sign conquer.*

The first chaplain associated with New Zealand Forces was Bishop Selwyn during the Maori Wars. With the permission of the Imperial Government, he appointed three additional chaplains to work with him.

During the Boer War, the first New Zealand chaplain to serve overseas and see active service was Rev. A . W. Compton who went with the 8th Contingent, followed by two with the 9th and two with the 10th Contingent. Their badges were cloth Maltese crosses, smaller versions being worn as collar badges.

These badges were later struck in brass until 1911 when a Crown was added. The Territorial Army saw the formation of a Chaplains' Department which was given approval to wear the badge of the British Army Chaplains' Department as of October 1937. The Department was designated the Royal New Zealand Chaplains' Department on 12 July 1947.

Dress distinctions: The wearing of black edging on the shoulder strap was abolished in 1924. The Department wore black metal buttons and black rank badges. A strip of purple material half-inch wide is worn on the shoulder strap immediately above the shoulder seam and below the badges of rank. RNZChD officers wear anodised silver crosses as collar badges on the green drill summer dress and on the combat dress.

Approval has now been given for a modified badge, one which will incorporate a fern leaf and thus become a distinctive New Zealand design.

NEW ZEALAND ARMY PAY CORPS

BADGE: Fern leaves embossed 'NZ' enclosing monogram letters 'APC' surmounted by a crown, above a scroll 'Army Pay Corps'.
COLLAR BADGES: Smaller versions of the cap badge.

The duties of pay and finance were carried out by civilian personnel until 31 May 1917 when the New Zealand Army Pay Department was established. Officers were appointed to the New Zealand Army Pay Corps on 21 July 1920 and on 18 May 1924 the Corps was reconstituted and re-established as part of the New Zealand Permenent Forces. Brass shoulder titles 'N.Z.A.P.C.'

The badge then worn consisted of fern leaves enclosing the letters 'NZ' above a scroll 'Army Pay Corps' and surmounted by a lion and crown. These badges in brass were worn until 1930 when the Permanent Forces were reduced and the NZ Army Pay Corps was disbanded, most of the corps being transferred to the civilian staff. The corps was re-activated as the New Zealand Army Pay Corps in 1969 when the second pattern badge was again the corps badge.

Approval was given in October 1978 for the badge to be struck with the St. Edward Crown, both the cap and collar badges.

NEW ZEALAND WAR CONTINGENT ASSOCIATION

Formed by New Zealanders living in London 14 August 1914, to assist NZ soldiers by providing them with comforts, visiting them in hospital, securing accommodation for convalescents and keeping in touch with relatives.

NZ War Contingent Association

NEW ZEALAND ARMY POSTAL SERVICE

Formed during WW1 to handle the mail delivery for troops overseas. A section of the service was based in London and another in Egypt at Kantara East until May 1916, when the NZEF headquarters was transferred to London.

ROYAL NEW ZEALAND PROVOST CORPS

The New Zealand Military Police Unit was formed in 1915 and served in all theatres of war as mounted military police but not as foot police. The unit was disbanded after the Armistice declaration and reformed with the outbreak of WW2. The first detachment of the unit sailed with the 1st Echelon to the Middle East.

MOTTO: *Ko tatou hei tauira* (We serve as examples).

The New Zealand Military Police Unit was disbanded in 1946 to be replaced by the Provost Companies. The 1st, 2nd and 3rd Provost Companies became the 1st Divisional Provost Company on 11 October 1948 and were redesignated New Zealand Provost Corps on 18 February 1949, the Corps being activated on 24 March 1951.

On 18 July 1952 the corps became the Royal New Zealand Provost Corps.

Officers' badges were silver initially, but all members of the corps now wear the anodised badges.

Corps dress distinction
Officers and soldiers of RNZ Provost Corps wear on the left shoulder, a white lanyard with a whistle attached; in addition, a scarlet cover with the SD cap.

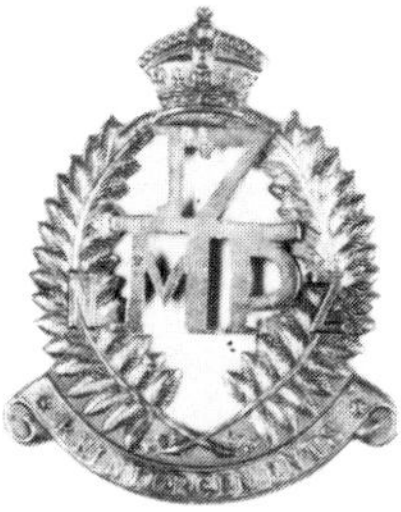

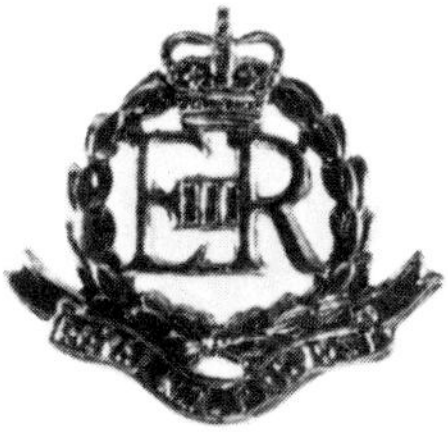
ER

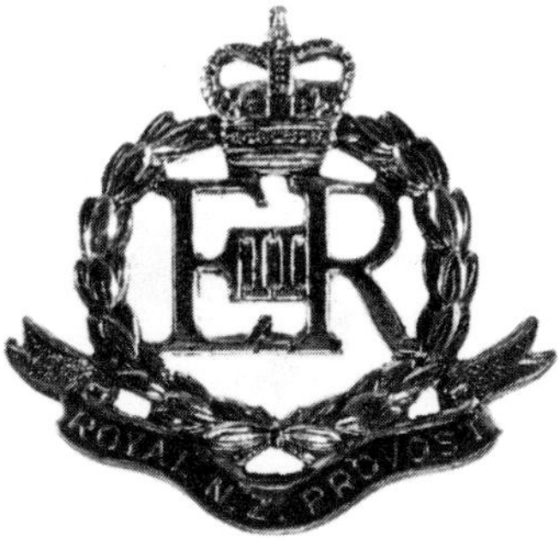
ER
ROYAL N Z PROVOST

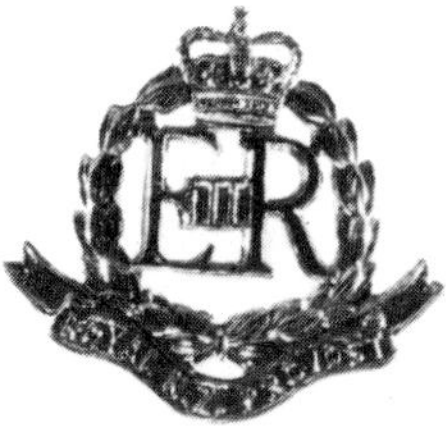
ER

ROYAL NEW ZEALAND ARMY EDUCATIONAL CORPS

BADGE: A fluted flambeau of five flames (the torch of learning), below the flames a crown and below the crown a scroll 'NZAEC'. In silver and gilt, also anodised.

The corps was formed towards the end of World War I in an endeavour to help rehabilitate soldiers and later played an important part in raising the standard of education of soldiers to enable them to handle modern weapons more efficiently.

Director of Army Education Welfare Service appointed 1 September 1942 after discussions between Education and Army Departments. Prefix 'Royal' granted November 1963.

In 1944 a 2NZEF unit was formed with the title Education Rehabilitation Service (ERS). It functioned in the areas indicated by its title until all New Zealand troops returned home.

ROYAL NEW ZEALAND NURSING CORPS

BROOCH BADGE: A silver fern wreath enclosing a red cross, surmounted by a crown.
LAPEL BADGE: A silver fern.

RNZNC brooch is of silver and enamel and consists of the Red Cross surrounded by a wreath of fern leaves in silver bearing across the base the title 'RNZNC' in silver on a blue enamel backbround, the whole surmounted by a silver crown. The brooch is fitted with a pin and small silver chain and keeper pin. Badge also in gilt and enamel. The first nurses with the New Zealand Forces in World War I sailed for Samoa on 15 August 1914. Later contingents went to Egypt. On 23 October 1915 ten nurses and eighteen medical orderlies were drowned when the transport *Marquette* was torpedoed in the Aegean Sea on the expedition to Salonika. Nursing sisters served in all fields of the war and on hospital ships from Gallipoli, Siberia, Messopotamia, India, Egypt and the Persian Gulf. Thirteen New Zealand nursing sisters were awarded the Royal Red Cross First Class. Six hundred and forty-four nurses served overseas, on hospital ships and in New Zealand.

In Egypt during WW1 a supply of carved ivory badges, N.Z. 'Onward' pattern, was obtained as the brooch badge was not considered distinctive enough. Ivory was chosen as it was felt that a brass badge would soil the uniform. These badges have a brooch-pin fitted on the reverse.

In WW2, 239 nursing sisters served with the 2NZEF forming part of the General Hospitals and Casualty Clearing Stations in the battle zones.

In 1950 the new Order of Battle recruited trained nurses into both the Territorial and Regular Force. The NZANS was designated the New Zealand Nursing Corps on 9 April 1953 and on 9 June was responsible for providing nursing officers for all three services.

The New Zealand Medical Corps Nursing Reserve was formed on 14 May 1908 and in 1913 the NZANS brooch was adopted, a brooch which was the Army equivalent of the NZ Registered Nurses Medal. During WW1 rank badges were not permitted, the only distinction being the NZANS brooch. From 1 June 1941 nursing Sisters were ranked as officers and wore the equivalent Army rank badges. On 3 July 1953 the Corps were permitted to wear the badges and buttons of the RNZAMC until the introduction of the RNZNC badges and buttons. The cap badge, worn for the first time on the occasion of the visit of Her Majesty Queen Elizabeth II to New Zealand in December 1953 consists of a Star, the basis of the RNZNC Corps badge which provides a link with the nursing profession in New Zealand as the Registration Medal is a five pointed star. Embossed in the centre of the star is an heraldic lamp representing the lamp carried by Florence Nightingale, thus providing a connection between the nursing profession and the birth of military nursing.

Shoulder titles (worn in N.Z.):
Royal New Zealand Nursing Corps: Grebe lettering on post office red.
Outside New Zealand:
New Zealand: Gold lettering on grebe.
New Zealand: White lettering on black.

The Royal New Zealand Nursing Corps wear the corps pattern metal buttons and the scarlet and grey corps lanyard. When hospital dress is worn the following nursing qualification medals may be worn: Post Graduate Diploma Medal; Registered Community Nurse Medal; Registered Nursing Aid Medal.

NEW ZEALAND WOMEN'S ROYAL ARMY CORPS

BADGE: A tui within a circle enscribed *Pro Patria,* enclosed in fern leaves above a scroll, 'WAAC', the whole surmounted by a crown.

MOTTO: *Pro Patria* (For country).

The first detachment of women, a draft of 30, sailed for the Middle East in September 1941 where they were attached to the NZ Forces Club, Cairo, for welfare duties. They were nicknamed 'Tuis' by the NZ soldiers, a name which resulted in their choice of a Tui badge when the NZ Women's Army Auxiliary Corps (NZWAAC) was established as a part of the New Zealand Defence Force on 1 July 1942. A total of 4,600 women were employed in clerical, catering, signals and medical duties. Their duties as nursing aids (VADs) and assistant nursing staff at Army hospitals were administered by the NZANS as from 1947. In April 1948 the corps became a regular corps of the New Zealand Army as NZ Women's Army Corps (NZWAC). In July 1952, with the grant of the title 'Royal', they were designated the N.Z. Women's Royal Army Corps (NZWRAC).

BADGE: A similar badge, except that the tui is silver and the scroll NZWRAC. Badge in silver, gilt and enamel, gilt and silver.

Shoulder titles (worn in N.Z.):
New Zealand Women's Royal Army Corps: White lettering on tartan green. The first pattern title which was worn for a short period was dark green lettering on a beech brown background.

Worn outside New Zealand:
New Zealand: Gold lettering on tartan green.
New Zealand: White lettering on black.

The corps was deactivated as from 29 July 1977 when all personnel were transferred to other corps of the New Zealand Army.

WOMEN'S WAR SERVICE AUXILIARY

BADGE: On blue enamel, the letters 'WWSA' in gold below the letters 'NZ'. The officials, who were the officers of the service, wore a similar badge but with the word 'Official' on a scroll beneath.

The WWSA was controlled by the National Service Department and was formed to direct and co-ordinate the women-power in the country. Lord Freyberg, VC, who was Commander of the New Zealand Division in the Middle East, requested that the Government send New Zealand girls to work in the New Zealand Forces Clubs to boost the morale of the soldiers. This request was approved and in 1941 the first group of WWSA arrived in Tewfik on the Suez Canal where they were met by Lady Freyberg, who prior to her being appointed as their leader, had been a supervisor at the New Zealand Forces Club in London and then at the Club in Cairo. She christened them 'Tuis' and it was under this name that the girls served the forces in libraries, offices, canteens and visited hospitals in the Middle East, Italy and London. The Tuis were demobilised in 1946.

Each member paid £1 for the uniform, with cap and tie, a Government subsidy absorbing the remainder of the cost.

Cloth Shoulder Titles:

"Transport" — white letters on blue.
"Cycle" — white letters on light navy.
"Canteen" — white letters on red.
"Land" — white letters on green.
"Clerical" — white letters on dark blue.

The nursing group wore the St. John Ambulance badge on the left upper sleeve and signallers crossed flags — one blue and one white, on white. The arm band worn when not in uniform was Crown and letters 'W.W.S.A.' in red on white cloth.

WOMEN'S LAND SERVICE

BADGE: A wheat sheaf enclosed by fern leaves and the letters 'NZ' above a scroll 'Women's Land Service'.

This badge was worn as a hat badge, but was also worn as a blouse badge, the badge in this case having a pin reverse.

The Women's War Service Auxiliary organised and formed the Women's Land Corps in 1941. This corps functioned until September 1942 when it was decided to form a new corps with a more attractive uniform and better pay and this saw the emergence of the Women's Land Service.

At its peak it had a membership of over 2,000, the service being disbanded on 30 April 1946.

WOMEN'S NATIONAL SERVICE CORPS

Formed in 1941 to assist as civilians in the NZ Army as typists, drivers, cooks, etc. Absorbed into the NZ Army Service Corps in 1942.

OFFICER TRAINING CORPS

The University of New Zealand comprised three University Colleges which formed their own Officers' Training Corps prior to WW1.
Auckland College (Junior Division): July 1909.
Victoria College (Wellington): 30 July 1909.
Canterbury College: 19 September 1909.
Otago University: 4 October 1909.

    The badges worn were those of the arm of service in which the officer was trained. On the introduction of compulsory military training in 1911 the corps attached to the three Colleges of the University of New Zealand were disbanded and from that time the training was carried out at the main training camps. The University of Otago OTC was re-activated because of the need to train Medical and Dental Officers. The Officers' Training Corps badge was issued in 1915 and therefore was worn only by the Otago Unversity OTC.
    The Corps were identified by brass shoulder titles as illustrated.
When the Officer Cadet Training Company (OCTC) was formed in 1977 at Waiouru to provide New Zealand trained officers for the Army, the 2NZEF badges as adopted for Ceremonial Guards was chosen as the appropriate insignia due to its history and "all Corps" significance. The OCTC and the Regular Force Cadet Unit are unique in that they are the only establishments below Corps status which are permitted to wear their own insignia.

REGULAR FORCE CADETS

BADGE: The Dickson Crest, the family crest of the Governor-General (1910-12) the Right Honourable John Poynder Dickson-Poynder, Baron Islington who was the seventeenth Governor of New Zealand.

MOTTO: *Fortes fortuna juvat* (Fortune favours the brave).

The brass badge was first worn in 1911 by the Senior Cadet Officers, unattached to units. In 1921 these officers were absorbed into Territorial Regiments and the badge was not used. In 1927 the badge was worn by the Training Cadre, Trentham, and in 1932 was used for the Regular Service Recruits, who wore this badge until posted to a corps and this practice was continued until 1950.

The Regular Force Cadet Unit was formed in 1948 and wore the badge in silver until forming their first guard of honour when the badge was chromium plated.

From 1950 the badge was in use for only the Cadet Unit.

In 1952 it was decided that the Cadet Unit would continue to wear the badge in silver, but that the Army Schools would wear the crest in gilt.

Dress distinction

The Army School of Instruction moved to Trentham Camp in 1938 and in 1952 was moved again to Waiouru Military Camp. At this time the Regular Force Cadets were issued with a red lanyard to be worn over the left shoulder.

The first hat was a khaki beret with a black diamond. In 1949 the cadets were issued with the 'lemon squeezer' with khaki puggaree with small black diamond on either side. To distinguish the corps to which an RF Cadet will be posted on graduation, RF Cadets wear the cap badge of their potential corps over the left breast pocket, except in the case of RNZA, when the badge worn is a collar badge.

Recruits not posted to a corps or regiment wear a brass fern leaf with the letters 'NZ' centrally inscribed.

The Regular Force Cadet Unit, comprising two companies is the only unit in the NZ Army permitted to have its own insignia.

DEFENCE CADET CORPS

Volunteer Cadet Corps were formed in New Zealand under the guidance of the various Rifle, Artillery, Engineer and Naval Volunteers. The earliest cadet corps were accepted in the Military Districts as follows:

Auckland:
Auckland Artillery: 6 April 1871.
Auckland Engineer: 8 July 1872.
Auckland Naval: 6 April 1871.
Auckland College Rifle: 1 March 1871.

Wellington:
Wellington Artillery: 5 November 1874.
Napier Engineer: March 1878.
Wellington Naval: December 1869.
Wellington Rifle: 28 September 1867.

Nelson:
Nelson Artillery: 3 December 1866.
Nelson Naval: 17 November 1875.
Nelson City Rifle: 25 June 1866.

Canterbury:
Lyttelton Artillery: 24 March 1869.
Canterbury Engineer: 19 November 1879.
Lyttelton Naval: 16 May 1899.
Christchurch High School Rifle: 7 August 1868.

Otago:
Dunedin High School Artillery: 28 April 1875.
Dunedin Engineer: 19 March 1901.
Port Chalmers Naval: 6 December 1871.
Dunedin High School Rifle: 1865.

Chrisrchurch Boys' High School

The Cadet Corps wore the badge of the arm of service to which they were attached; a grenade for artillery and engineers, and a bugle-horn for rifles. Certain public schools were given permission to maintain their own cadet corps, the uniform being blue frocks, glengarry caps, brown leather belts and Snider artillery rifles. The more prominent of these schools wore their own distinctive badge.

On 5 July 1902 the control of all public school cadet units was transferred to the Education Depertment.

BADGE (1902): A domed badge with circlet 'Public School Cadets N.Z'. The circlet in blue enamel for officers: enclosed, a Cypher EVIIR.

On 17 March 1911 the Defence Cadet Officer Training Corps, Battalions and Companies were formed into a new Cadet Corps.

Junior Cadets: Boys from 12 to 14 years.

Senior Cadets: Boys over the age of 14 years.

Boys over the age of 18 years to join the Territorial Force.

BADGE: A domed badge with circlet 'Junior Cadets N.Z', enclosing Cypher GVR. With the formation of the Senior Cadets, each college in the country was given a number for its cadet unit, this number being worn on a badge comprising two fern leaves enclosing the numeral, above a scroll 'Senior Cadets'. A shortage of badges during and after the war lead to the use of the Expeditionary Force badge frame with the lower scroll polished or covered with a brass bar.

After WW1 the Cadet Corps made a gradual change to the wearing of the badge of the regiment associated with their district. In 1950 a new general issue badge was produced, a badge incorporating a design of fern leaves, two crossed spears and the letters 'NZ' on a scroll 'Cadet Corps'. The badge was unchanged until 1954 when the crown was altered to the St. Edward Crown.

The Cadet Corps reached a peak of over 50,000 in 1960, a number which taxed the resources of the Defence Department and from that time efforts were made to reduce the size of the corps. Under the terms of the Defence Act 1971 the New Zealand Cadet Force was no longer a part of the armed forces, and although the Ministry of Defence continued to provide support, it was the Navy League, Returned Services' Association and the Air Cadet League which were expected to promote the functions and interests of the various corps.

In 1979 there were only seventeen schools which maintained a cadet corps. The highlight of the history of the corps was the selection of senior cadets in the New Zealand Contingent which sailed for Canada on 3 August 1912 to attend the Toronto Exhibition.

Distinctions worn by the corps were a diamond-shaped patch of 2-inch square representing the school colours worn behind the badge, shoulder titles of a curved pattern in school colours on both sleeves and a similar coloured lanyard worn on the left shoulder. A diamond-shaped patch was worn on the arm to denote the branch of the service in which the cadet was trained.

Artillery: Red and blue (horizontal).
Signals: Light blue.
Engineers: Dark blue.
Infantry: Scarlet.
Army Service Corps: Gold, blue and white (vertical).
Medical: Dull cherry.
Electrical and Mechanical Engineers: Blue, yellow and red (vertical).

Huntly   St Andrew's College

Nelson College

The Senior Cadet Band badge is similar to the centre badge above, but with the word 'Band' in the centre.

Auckland Grammar   Port Chalmers

286

Wellington College

Scots College Senior Cadet Corps

Oxford High School

Christchurch Boys' High School

CORONATION CONTINGENT 1911

The New Zealand Mounted Infantry who attended the Coronation of King George V wore a bottle green tunic, cream corduroy breeches, leather leggings and cartridge belt, bottle green slouch hat with a green puggaree with two silver stripes. The buttons were silver, a fern leaf within a circle 'New Zealand Defence Force'. Collar badges were silver fern leaves with the letters 'NZ' embossed.
Shoulder titles — curved pattern, New Zealand in silver.
   64 officers and men represented New Zealand.

CORONATION CONTINGENT 1937

COLLAR BADGES: WW1 pattern fern-leaves.
The Contingent paraded in khaki Service Dress.
50 servicemen and ex-servicemen represented the Army personnel.

LEGION OF FRONTIERSMEN

MOTTO: *God Guard Thee* — reputed to be motto on ring of General C. Gordon, killed at Khartoum, 1885.

Founded in London in 1904 by Captain Roger Pocock and Colonel Driscoll from men who had fought in the South African War, particularly the members of Driscoll's Scouts. The reason behind the formation was to have available a corps of men, trained and self-reliant, who could be ready should the Empire have the need to call on them.

In 1911 recruiting commenced in New Zealand and at the outbreak of World War I there were 1,200 members. An offer was made to the Government to have two squadrons of the Legion, fully equipped, available at twenty-four hours' notice and to further supply hundreds of Legionnaires fully equipped with horses and saddles. Although the Government appreciated the offer, it decided that the members of the Legion should enlist in the Expeditionary Force. The record of the Legion in the 1914-18 war is a proud one, enhanced by the fact that of the eleven VCs awarded to New Zealanders, five were won by members. In all, 9,000 N.Z. Frontiersmen lost their lives in the conflict.

Of 600 Canadian Frontiersmen enlisted with Princess Patricia's Canadian Light Infantry who assisted to hold the line at Ypres when the first gas attack was launched, only eighteen survived the war. In the battle for Gallipoli, 1,500 Frontiersmen fell while serving with the Anzacs. In England the Legion raised the 25th Battalion of the Royal Fusiliers (Frontiersmen Battalion) and this unit served under Colonel Driscoll in East Africa. The Manchester Squadron was the first British unit in action, having joined and served in Legion uniform with the 3rd Belgium Lancers.

The toll exacted by the war left few members to carry on the tradition of the Legion but by the efforts of these few, the Legion slowly built up strength and its organisation trained men in the many aspects of military and civil administration. With the advent of World War II the first N.Z. troops to move into position were the units of the Legion who had been posted to coast guard duties. The Legion gave invaluable assistance in the different emergency organisations, especially in the Home Guard where they became specialists and instructors, and in the Emergency Precautions Service which had formed to make provision for any calamity that might occur as a result of the war.

Illustrious personages whose names are on the role of the Legion are General Smuts, General French, Lord Kitchener, and Lord Roberts, VC, as well as Captain Scott, Captain Oates and Sir Ernest Shackleton of Antarctic fame. The pioneer airmen Sir Charles Kingsford Smith and Charles Ulm were members of the New Zealand Command.

'Y' (Whakatane) Squadron was responsible in 1965 for the erecting of a memorial to a Frenchman, Jean Guerren, on the spot where he defended Te Poronu Mill Farm against Te Kooti's forces for two days before he was killed.

KING'S EMPIRE VETERANS

Lord Ranfurly was appointed as Governor of New Zealand on 6 April 1897 and became Honorary Colonel of the 1st Wellington Battalion in 1898. Realising that there were over 7,000 veterans living in New Zealand he decided to form an Association of these ex-Imperial, Naval and Colonial forces, and under his guidance the Empire Veterans' Association was established in 1900 with Lord Ranfurly as its president. A bronze medal in the shape of a Maltese Cross and surrounded by a wreath of laurel leaves containing the letters NZEVA was issued to all members and worn on the right of the uniform. The ribbon, red, white and blue.

In 1910 when Lord Kitchener visited New Zealand he suggested that the name of the Association be changed to the King's Empire Veterans and the medal then issued was exactly the same as before except for the engraved letters which read KEV.

The King's Empire Veterans were formed into an Honorary Reserve Corps as from 5 November 1912.

At one time there were nineteen Imperial Regiments represented. The earliest naval medal recorded was that for the naval engagement at Acre in 1840 (Syria).

In 1941 a banner was consecrated at Saint Matthew's Anglican Church, Auckland, the motto on the banner being an appropriate one, *Pleni Annarum, Honorum Pleni* (Full of years, of honours full).

A lapel badge is now issued instead of the medal. Although the medal was issued unnamed, a large proportion of the veterans had not only the medal engraved but also the years of service engraved on the suspender bar. The complete list of the original veterans may be found in the Earl of Ranfurly's book *Defenders of the Empire*.

Today the Association is open to any man who has served in His, or Her Majesty's Forces and is over the age of sixty years.

THE HOME GUARD

MOTTO: *Kia matara* (On guard).

The National Military Reserve was established in May 1939 in order to augment the Territorial forces and because of the number of volunteer units forming throughout the country the War Cabinet approved the establishing of a Home Guard on 2 August 1940. The object of the Guard was defined as being to 'augment local defences by providing for static defence of localities, the protection of vulnerable and key points, and to give timely notice of enemy movements to superior military organisations'.

Limited in equipment and wearing an arm-band as an identification the Home Guard carried out valuable work in building tank traps and defensive works at the more vulnerable beaches. The Army took control of the Home Guard on 1 August 1941 from which time commissions were then granted. By the end of 1942 all guardsmen had been issued with battle-dress and boots, and morale improved with the division of the country into thirty-three zones, each zone having a Regular commander for the Territorial and Home Guard Units. Tommy-guns, machine-guns and rifles were issued in quantity.

At its peak, the Home Guard numbered over 123,000 men as service was compulsory for all men of military age not in the Army and for men aged between 46 and 50. This compulsory service was the direct result of Japan entering the war. Towards the end of 1943 the Home Guard was placed on the Army reserve as the war situation in the Pacific had improved sufficiently to remove the threat to New Zealand.

No further parades were held as from 1 January 1944.

The Hokitika Home Guard saw 'active service' in support of the police in the Graham manhunt in October 1941 when two members of the Guard were killed.

YMCA

The YMCA assisted at annual territorial camps before assisting at all the training camps during WW1. Known as Field Secretary YMCA the first representative left with the 4th Reinforcement, the second left with the 7th Reinforcement and from that time almost every draft had its Field Secretary. Great difficulty was experienced before permission was given to allow the YMCA to work at Anzac and Helles. They served in all theatres of war and greatly assisted in the comfort of the wounded in England.

In WW2 a number of the YMCA were captured in Greece and Crete and queries about their status resulted in the practice of seconding Army personnel with prior YMCA service. The original Field Secretaries wore a curved brass shoulder title 'New Zealand' but in 1917 the title was a brass 'Y.M.C.A' with an embroidered white 'YMCA' on black cloth worn on right sleeve above the elbow. Their khaki uniform had leather buttons.

SECURITY GUARDS

BADGE: The Royal Crest, a crowned lion standing on a Royal Crown, placed at the junction of two crossed swords, points uppermost. Below the Royal Crest the letters 'NZ'.
Gilt: Crowns, lion, sword hilts and crossbars, letters 'NZ'.
Silver: Sword blades.
Crimson: Caps of Maintenance (Linings of both crowns).

The badge was approved in 1949 after application had been made in 1948. The first pattern badge was the Tudor Crown and was worn 1949-1954. The design incorporating the St. Edward Crown has been worn from 1954 and is still in use.

Volunteer Period Buttons

Prior to 1882, the buttons in use for the volunteer corps followed the general issue pattern of the British Army volunteers in that they were in white metal for Artillery and Engineer Volunteers and in brass for Naval Artillery Volunteers. The Rifle Corps and Mounted Rifles used the white metal bugle horn pattern or the 'VR' pattern. A few of the volunteer corps bought their own distinctive buttons from England. In 1882, a distinctive button was introduced for general issue, a white metal 'NZV' which varied in design according to the manufacturer although those corps who wished to have their own buttons were permitted to do so. In 1895 a universal pattern button was introduced for all volunteers except the Naval Artillery. This button was brass with the words 'New Zealand Volunteers' round the edge, and in the shaded field in the centre, four stars representing the constellation 'Southern Cross'. This button remained in use until 1911 when it was replaced by a similar button although the centre was not shaded and the edge words were 'New Zealand Forces'.

Taranaki Militia
1867

Armed Constabulary
1867

No. 3 Coy. Otepopo
Oamaru R.V. 1882

NZ Volunteers
1882

NZ Volunteers
1895

King
Edward's Horse
1902

Naval Artillery
1903

1st Company NZE
1903

Canterbury Highlanders 1900	Oamaru Rifle Volunteers 1872	Heretaunga Mounted Infantry 1890
1st Wellington Battalion 1898	Heretaunga Mounted Rifles 1891	Canterbury Scottish 1885
Volunteers 1885	Wellington Guards 1881	Public School Cadets 1902
Ordnance Department 1917	3rd Otago Rifles 1901	NZ Veterinary Corps 1907
West Coast Battalion 1886	Dunedin City Guards 1880	2nd North Canterbury Infantry 1903

NZ Volunteers 1882	Canterbury Engineers 1885	Volunteer Engineers 1885
Volunteer Engineers 1903	Dunedin Artillery 1870	Volunteer Artillery 1870
Territorial Artillery 1911	NZ Artillery 1911	Wanganui Highlanders 1900
Wairoa Mounted Rifles 1901	NZ Rifle Brigade (black horn button) 1915	Junior Cadets 1911
NZ Volunteers 1885	NZ Volunteers 1870	Spring Creek Rifle Volunteers 1870

Coronation Contingent
1911

Dunedin Highland
Rifles 1885

NZ Forces
1911

Chaplains' Department
1900

Chaplains' Department
1911

Ordnance Department
1915

NZ Staff Corps
1911

NZ Permanent Staff
1921

NZ Medical Corps
1908

RNZNC 1954

RNZEME 1954

RNZMC 1954

NZWRAC 1954

RNZAC 1954

NZ Regiment
1954

RNZDC 1954

RNZE 1954

RNZIR 1954

Waist-belt Clasps
Other ranks pattern. Usually in brass for
Militia and white metal for Volunteers.

1867

Waist-belt Clasps

1881-1902

1902-1911

Bridle Bosses

Bridle bosses, cast in brass, were used in New Zealand by the Mounted Rifles and the Mounted Infantry. Four distinctive patterns can be found.
1. The British general issue pattern with the Royal Cypher shown within the Garter bearing the words *Honi Soit Qui Mal Y Pense* and surmounted by a crown. This applies to the Cypher 'VR' 'EVIIR' and 'GVR'.
2. Similar to above but with the letters 'NZ' in the centre in place of the Cypher.
3. Similar to above but with the initials of the corps in the centre.
    e.g. CMR Canterbury Mounted Rifles.
       CYC Canterbury Yeomanry Cavalry.

4. Similar to No. 2 but with the title of the corps around the circlet.
   e.g. Marlborough Mounted Rifles.
        Ahuriri Mounted Rifles.
        Opunake Mounted Rifles.
        Horowhenua Mounted Rifles.
        Heretaunga Mounted Infantry.

Army Service Associations

The badges of ex-servicemen's associations form an interesting facet in the field of militaria and the following examples are some of those which are of particular interest to the New Zealand collector. Some of the photographs have been enlarged to show as much detail as possible.

South African War Veterans'
Association

Honourable Discharge WW1　　　　　　　　Honourable Discharge WW2
(Given to men discharged through wounds or sickness)

NZ Returned Soldiers' Association
(Formed 27 May 1919)
After WW2 became 'Returned Services'

RSA badge for nurses from WW1
(note the small enamel cross)

HM Transports WW1

Main Body
NZEF

Auckland Branch RSA
WW1

Army, Navy and
Auxiliary Veterans

Mothers of Soldiers
and Sailors WW1

Catholic War Services
WW1

303

Wives of Soldiers
and Sailors WW1

2NZEF Association

Volunteer's
Badge WW2

Home Services' Association

2NZEF 1st Echelon

Women's Section
NZRSA

Auckland
ex-Servicewomen

304

NATIONAL RESERVE

The National Registration Act of 26 October 1915 required that all males in New Zealand between the ages of seventeen years and sixty years enrol in a National Reserve. Those members of the Permanent Forces and the NZEF were excluded from this registration. Colonel T. W. Porter CB was appointed Dominion Commandant on 9 March 1916.

The country was divided for this purpose of National Reserve into four military districts, with sub-groups within these areas.

Auckland Military District:
No. 1 (Auckland) Group
No. 2 (Hauraki) Group
No. 17 (Bay of Plenty) Group
No. 3 (North Auckland) Group
No. 4 (Waikato) Group

Canterbury Military District:
No. 9 (Christchurch) Group
No. 10 (South Canterbury) Group
No. 11 (North Canterbury) Group
No. 21 (West Coast) Group
No. 12 (Nelson) Group

Wellington Military District:
No. 5 (Wellington) Group
No. 6 (Manawatu) Group
No. 7 (Hawke's Bay) Group
No. 18 (Wairarapa) Group
No. 19 (Poverty Bay) Group
No. 8 (Taranaki) Group
No. 20 (Wanganui) Group

Otago Military District:
No. 13 (Dunedin) Group
No. 14 (Southland Group
No. 15 (North Otago) Group
No. 16 (Clutha) Group

The badge worn was a lapel badge, silver or gilt, crown, surrounded by an oval enamel circlet bearing the group identification. The enamel is in various colours.

Blue enamel: Auckland, Wellington, Wellington District, Canterbury, Otago, Marlborough, Hamilton, Palmerston North, N.Z. Railways, Greymouth.
Red enamel: Southland, Hawera Defence Rifle Club.
Green enamel: Defence Rifles.

Some of the badges carry a further definition as to the area of registration, e.g. Group 7, G7 Napier — G7B Ruahine — G7C Gisborne.

APPENDIX I
Battle Honours of the Second World War

18 Armoured Regiment. THE SANGRO, Castel Frentano, Orsogna, Advance to Florence, SAN MICHELE, Paula Line, Celle, Pisciatello, THE SENIO, Santerno Crossing, Bologna, Idice Bridgehead, Italy 1943-45.

19 Armoured Regiment. PERANO, THE SANGRO, Castel Frentano, Orsogna, CASSINO I, Cassino II, GUSTAV LINE, ADVANCE TO FLORENCE, Cerbaia, SAN MICHELE, Paula Line, St Angelo in Salute, PISCIATELLO, BOLOGNA, Sillaro Crossing, Gaiana Crossing, ITALY 1943-45.

20 Armoured Regiment. ORSOGNA, CASSINO I, ADVANCE TO FLORENCE, SAN MICHELE, Paula Line, FAENZA POCKET, RIO FONTANACCIA, St Angelo in Salute, PISCIATELLO, THE SENIO, SANTERNO CROSSING, Bologna, SILLARO CROSSING, Idice Bridgehead, Italy 1943-45.

3rd Division Tank Squadron. SOUTH PACIFIC 1942-44.

1 Battalion New Zealand Scottish Regiment. South Pacific 1942-44.

18 Battalion (up to 5 October 1942), *21 Battalion, 24 Battalion, 29 Battalion.* MOUNT OLYMPUS, Servia Pass, Platamon Tunnel, Tempe Gorge, Elasson, Molos, Greece 1941, CRETE, Maleme, Galatas, Canea, 42nd Street, Withdrawal to Sphakia, Middle East 1941-44, Tobruk 1941, Sidi Rezegh 1941, Omars, BELHAMED, Mersa Matruh, MINQAR QAIM, Defence of Alamein Line, Ruweisat Ridge, El Mreir, Alam el Halfa, EL ALAMEIN, Capture of Halfaya Pass 1942, El Agheila, Nofilia, Medinine, TEBAGA GAP, El Hamma, Enfidaville, Takrouna, Djebibina, North Africa 1940-43, THE SANGRO, Castel Frentano, Orsogna, CASSINO I, Arezzo, Advance to Florence, Cerbaia, San Michele, Paula Line, Faenza Pocket, Rio Fontanaccia, St Angelo in Salute, Pisciatello, THE SENIO, Santerno Crossing, Bologna, Sillaro Crossing, Idice Bridgehead, Italy 1943-45, SOLOMONS, Treasury Islands, South Pacific 1942-44.

Allocated to Northland, Auckland (CRO), and Hauraki Regiments.

19 Battalion (up to 5 October 1942), *22 Battalion, 25 Battalion, 36 Battalion.* Mount Olympus, Servia Pass, Olympus Pass, Elasson, Molos, GREECE 1941, CRETE, Maleme, Galatas, Canea, 42nd Street, Withdrawal to Sphakia, Middle East 1941-44, Tobruk 1941, Sidi Rezegh 1941, Sidi Azeiz, BELHAMED, Zemla, Alem Hamza, Mersa Matruh, MINQAR QAIM, Defence of Alamein Line, Ruweisat Ridge, El Mreir, Alam el Halfa EL ALAMEIN, El Agheila, Tebaga Gap, Point 201 (Roman Walt), El Hamma, ENFIDAVILLE, Takrouna, North Africa 1940-43, THE SENGRO, Castel Frentano, Orsogna, CASSINO I, Arezzo, Monte Lignano, Advance to Florence, Cerbaia, San Michele, Paula Line, Celle, Faenza Pocket, Rio Fontanaccia, Pisciatello, THE SENIO, Santerno Crossing, Bologna, Sillaro Crossing, Gaiana Crossing, Idice Bridgehead, Italy 1943-45, Solomons, TREASURY ISLANDS, South Pacific 1942-44.

Allocated to Wellington (CWO), Wellington West Coast, Hawke's Bay, and Taranaki Regiments.

20 Battalion (up to 5 October 1942), *23 Battalion, 26 Battalion, 30 Battalion, 37 Battalion.* MOUNT OLYMPUS, Servia Pass, Olympus Pass, Molos, Greece 1941, Crete, Maleme, GALATAS, 42nd Street, Withdrawal to Sphakia, Middle East 1941-44, Tobruk 1941, SIDI REZEGH, Sidi Azeiz, Belhamed, Alem Hamza, Mersa Matruh, Minqar Qaim, Defence of Alamein Line, Ruweisat Ridge, El Mreir, Alam el Halfa, EL ALAMEIN, El Agheila, Nofilia, Medinine, TEBAGA GAP, Point 201 (Roman Wall), El Hamam, Enfidaville, TAKROUNA, Djebel Terhouna, Djebel es Srafi, Djebibina, North Africa 1940-43, The Sangro, Castel Frentano, ORSOGNA, CASSINO I, Cassino Railway Station, Arezzo, Advance to Florence, Cerbaia, San Michele, Paula Line, Celle, Faenza Pocket, Rio Fontanaccia, St Angelo in Salute, Pisciatello, THE SENIO, Santerno Crossing, Bologna, Sillaro Crossing, Idice Bridgehead, Italy 1943-45, SOLOMONS, Vella Lavella, Green Islands, South Pacific 1942-44.

Allocated to Canterbury, Otago, Southland, and Nelson-Marlborough and West Coast Regiments.

Divisional Cavalry. MOUNT OLYMPUS, Aliakmon Bridge, Tempe Gorge, Elasson, Greece 1941, CRETE, Galatas, Canea, 42nd Street, Withdrawal to Sphakia, Middle East 1941-44, TOBRUK 1941, Sidi Azeiz, Zemla, Bardia 1942, Defence of Alamein Line, Ruweisat Ridge, El Mreir, Alam el Halfa, EL ALAMEIN, El Agheila, Nofilia, Advance to Tripoli, Medinine, TEBAGA GAP, Point 201 (Roman Wall), El Hamma, ENFIDAVILLE, Djebibina, North Africa 1940-43, THE SANGO, Castel Frentano, Orogna, CASSINO I, ADVANCE TO FLORENCE, Cerbaia, San Michele, Paula Line, St Angelo in Salute, Pisciatello, BOLOGNA, Sillaro Crossing, Gaiana Crossing, Italy 1943-45.

Allocated to New Zealand Scottish Regiment.

THE WAIKATO REGIMENT

18 Battalion (up to 5 October 1942), *21 Battalion, 24 Battalion.* MOUNT OLYMPUS, Servia Pass, Platamon Tunnel, Tempe Gorge, Elasson, Molos, Greece 1941, CRETE, Maleme, Galatas, Canea, 42nd Street, Withdrawal to Sphakia, Middle East 1941-44, Tobruk 1941, SIDI REZEGH 1941, Omars, Belhamed, Mersa Matruh, Minqar Qaim, Defence of Alamein Line, RUWEISAT RIDGE, El Mreir, Alam el Halfa, EL ALAMEIN, Capture of Halfaya Pass 1942, El Agheila, Nofilia, Medinine, TEBAGA GAP, Castel Frentano, Orsogna, CASSINO I, Arezzo, Advance to Florence, Cerbaia, SAN MICHELE, Paula Line, Faenza Pocket, Rio Fontanaccia, St Angelo in Salute, Pisciatello, THE SENIO, Santerno Crossing, Bologna, Sillaro Crossing, Idice Bridgehead, Italy 1943-45.

THE RUAHINE REGIMENT

19 Battalion (up to 5 October 1942), *22 Battalion, 25 Battalion, 1 Battalion, The Ruahine Regiment.* Mount Olympus, Servia Pass, Olympus Pass, Elasson, Molos, GREECE 1941, CRETE, Maleme, Galatas, Canea, 42nd Street, Withdrawal to Sphakia, Middle East 1941-44, Tobruk, SIDI REZEGH 1941, Sidi Azeiz, Belhamed, Zemla, Alem Hamza, Mersa Matruh, Minqar Qaim, Defence of Alamein Line, Rueweisat Ridge, El Mreir, Alam el Halfa, EL ALAMEIN, El Agheila, TEBAGA GAP, Point 201 (Roman Wall), El Hamma, Enfidaville, Takrouna, NORTH AFRICA 1940-43, The Sangro, Castel Frentano, ORSOGNA, CASSINO I, Arezzo, Monte Lignano, Advance to Florence, Cerbaia, San Michele, Paula Line, Celle, Faenza Pocket, Rio Fontanaccia, Pisciatello, The Senio, Santerno Crossing, Bologna, Sillaro Crossing, Gaiana Crossing, Idice Bridgehead, ITALY 1943-45, SOUTH PACIFIC 1942-44.

27 (MG) Battalion. VEVE, GREECE 1941, CRETE, Galatas, Middle East 1941-44, Tobruk 1941, Sidi Azeiz, Mersa Matruh, MINQAR QAIM, Defence of Alamein Line, Ruweisat Ridge, El Mreir, Alam el Halfa, EL ALAMEIN, Tebaga Gap, El Hamma, ENFIDAVILLE, Takrouna, North Africa 1940-43, The Sangro, Castel Frentano, ORSOGNA, CASSINO I, ADVANCE TO FLORENCE, Cerbia, San Michele, Paula Line, Celle, Faenza Pocket, St Angelo in Salute, Pisciatello, Bologna, SILLARO CROSSING, Gaiana Crossing, Italy 1943-45.

28 (Maori) Battalion. Mount Olympus, OLYMPUS PASS, Greece 1941, CRETE, Maleme, Canea, 42nd Street, Withdrawal to Sphakia, Middle East 1941-44, Tobruk 1941, Sidi Azeiz, Zemla, Alem Hamza, Mersa Matruh, Minqar Qaim, Defence of Alamein Line, El Mreir, Alam el Halfa, EL ALAMEIN, Nofilia, Medinine, TEBAGA GAP, El Hamma, Enfidaville, TAKROUNA, Djebibina, NORTH AFRICA 1940-43, The Sangro, Castel Frentano, ORSOGNA, CASSINO I, Monastery Hill, Advance to Florence, San Michele, Paula Line, Celle, St Angelo in Salute,

THE SENIO, Santerno Crossing, Bologna, Idice Bridgehead, ITALY 1943-45.
34 Battalion. SOLOMONS, TREASURY ISLANDS, SOUTH PACIFIC 1942-44.
35 Battalion. SOLOMONS, VELLA LAVELLA, GREEN ISLANDS, SOUTH PACIFIC 1942-44.

Battle Honours of RNZ Infantry Regiment

The following is a list of all the battle honours of the Royal New Zealand Infantry Regiment. Those battle honours shown in capital letters are approved to be emblazoned on the Regimental Golours of one or more of the Battalions:

2nd Maori War, 1860-72
NEW ZEALAND

The Boer War, 1899-1902
SOUTH AFRICA, 1900-02

The Great War, 1914-18
SOMME, 1916-18
FLERS-COURCELETTE
Morval
Le Transloy
MESSINES, 1917
YPRES, 1917
Menin Road
POLYGON WOOD
BROODSEINDE
PASSCHENDAELE
ARRAS, 1918
Ancre, 1918
Albert, 1918
BAPAUME, 1918
HINDENBURG LINE
Havrincourt
CANAL DU NORD
CAMBRAI, 1918
Selle
SAMBRE (LE QUESNOY)
FRANCE AND FLANDERS, 1916-18
Helles
KRITHIA
ANZAC
LANDING AT ANZAC
Defence of Anzac
Suvla
SARI BAIR
GALLIPOLI, 1915
SUEZ CANAL
EGYPT, 1915-16

The World War, 1939-45
MOUNT OLYMPUS
Servia Pass
Platamon Tunnel

Olympus Pass
Tempe Gorge
Veve
Elasson
Molos
GREECE, 1941
CRETE
Maleme
GALATAS
Canea
42nd Street
Withdrawal to Sphakia
Middle East, 1941-44
TOBRUK, 1941
SIDI REZEGH
Sidi Azeiz
Omars
Belhamed
Zelma
Alem Hamza
Mersa Matruh
MINQAR QAIM
DEFENCE OF ALAMEIN LINE
Ruweisat Ridge
El Mrier
Alam el Halfa
EL ALAMEIN
Capture of Halaya Pass, 1942
El Agheila
Nofilia
TEBAGA GAP
Point 201 (Roman Wall)
El Hamma
Enfidaville
TAKROUNA
Djebel Terhouna
Djebel es Srafi
Djebibina
NORTH AFRICA, 1940-43
THE SANGRO
Castel Frentano
ORSOGNA
CASSINO I

308

Monastery Hill
Cassino Railway Station
Arrezo
Monte Lignano
Advance to Florence
Cerbaia
San Michele
Paula Line
Celle
Faenza Pocket
Rio Fontanaccia
Saint Angelo in Salute
Pisciatello

THE SENIO
Santerno Crossing
Bologna
Sillaro Crossing
Gaiana Crossing
Idice Bridgehead
ITALY, 1943-45
SOLOMONS
Vella Lavella
Treasury Islands
Green Islands
SOUTH PACIFIC, 1942-44

The following battle honours are approved to be emblazoned on the Regimental Colours of the seven battalions of the Royal New Zealand Infantry Regiment:

1st Battalion
NEW ZEALAND
SOUTH AFRICA, 1900-02

The Great War, 1914-18
SOMME, 1916-18
MESSINES, 1917
YPRES, 1917
POLYGON WOOD
PASSCHENDAELE
ARRAS, 1918
HINDENBURG LINE
FRANCE AND FLANDERS, 1916-18
ANZAC
GALLIPOLI, 1915

The World War, 1939-45
GREECE, 1941
CRETE
MINQAR QAIM
EL ALAMEIN
TAKROUNA
NORTH AFRICA, 1940-43
CASSINO I
THE SENIO
ITALY, 1943-45
SOUTH PACIFIC, 1942-44

2nd Battalion
SOUTH AFRICA, 1900-02

The Great War, 1914
SOMME, 1916-18
MESSINES, 1917
YPRES, 1917
PASSCHENDAELE
HINDENBURG LINE
FRANCE AND FLANDERS, 1916-18
ANZAC
GALLIPOLI, 1915
SUEZ CANAL
EGYPT, 1915-16

The World War, 1939-45
GREECE, 1941
CRETE
SIDI REZEGH, 1941
MINQAR QAIM
EL ALAMEIN
TEBAGA GAP
ORSOGNA
CASSINO I
THE SENIO
SOUTH PACIFIC, 1942-44

3rd Battalion
SOUTH AFRICA, 1900-02

The Great War, 1914-18
SOMME, 1916-18
FLERS-COURCELETTE
MESSINES, 1917
PASSCHENDAELE
ARRAS, 1918
BAPAUME, 1918
CANAL DU NORD
KRITHIA
ANZAC
GALLIPOLI, 1916

The World War, 1939-45
MOUNT OLYMPUS
CRETE
SIDI REZEGH, 1941
EL ALAMEIN
TEBAGA GAP
TAKROUNA
THE SANGRO
CASSINO I
THE SENIO
SOLOMONS

4th Battalion
SOUTH AFRICA, 1900-02

The Great War, 1914-18
SOMME, 1916-18
MESSINES, 1917
YPRES, 1917
PASSCHENDAELE
BAPAUME, 1918
CAMBRAI, 1918
FRANCE AND FLANDERS, 1916-18
ANZAC
GALLIPOLI, 1915
EGYPT, 1915-16

The World War, 1939-45
MOUNT OLYMPUS
GALATAS
SIDI REZEGH, 1941
EL ALAMEIN
TEBAGA GAP
TAKROUNA
ORSOGNA
CASSINO I
THE SENIO
SOLOMONS

5th Battalion
NEW ZEALAND
SOUTH AFRICA, 1900-02

The Great War, 1914-18
SOMME, 1916-18
MESSINES, 1917
YPRES, 1917
BAPAUME, 1918
HINDENBURG LINE
FRANCE AND FLANDERS, 1916-18
LANDING AT ANZAC
SARI BAIR
GALLIPOLI, 1915
EGYPT, 1915-16

The World War, 1939-45
GREECE, 1941
CRETE
SIDI REZEGH, 1941
MINQAR QAIM
EL ALAMEIN
NORTH AFRICA, 1940-43
CASSINO I
THE SENIO
ITALY, 1943-45
SOLOMONS

6th Battalion
SOUTH AFRICA, 1900-02

The Great War, 1914-18
FLERS-COURCELETTE
MESSINES, 1917
BROODSEINDE
ARRAS, 1918
BAPAUME, 1919
CANAL DU NORD
SAMBRE
KRITHIA
LANDING AT ANZAC
SARI BAIR

The World War, 1939-45
MOUNT OLYMPUS
CRETE
TOBRUK, 1941
DEFENCE OF ALAMEIN LINE
EL ALAMEIN
TEBAGA GAP
THE SANGRO
CASSINO I
THE SENIO
SOLOMONS

7th Battalion
SOUTH AFRICA, 1900-02

The Great War, 1914-18
SOMME, 1916-18
MESSINES, 1917
YPRES, 1917
BAPAUME, 1918
HINDENBURG LINE
SAMBRE (LE QUESNOY)
FRANCE AND FLANDERS, 1916-18
LANDING AT ANZAC
SARI BAIR
GALLIPOLI, 1915

The World War, 1939-45
GREECE, 1941
CRETE
TOBRUK, 1941
MINQAR QAIM
EL ALAMEIN
TEBAGA GAP
THE SANGRO
CASSINO I
THE SENIO
SOUTH PACIFIC, 1942-44

2nd/1st Battalion
SOUTH AFRICA, 1900-02

The Great War, 1914-18
FLERS-COURCELETTE
MESSINES, 1917
POLYGON WOOD
BROODSEINDE
PASSACHENDAELE
HINDENBURG LINE
SAMBRE (LE QUESNOY)
LANDING AT ANZAC
GALLIPOLI, 1915
SUEZ CANAL

The World War, 1939-45
GREECE, 1941
CRETE
MINQAR QAIM
EL ALAMEIN
TEBAGA GAP
TAKROUNA
THE SANGRO
ORSOGNA
CASSINO I
SOUTH PACIFIC, 1942-44

APPENDIX II
Army, Corps and Saint's Days

New Zealand Army Day
Traditionally each of the New Zealand armed forces recognises one day in the year as of special significance to itself and observes it suitably by flying flags and by other appropriate ceremonies.

New Zealand Army Day is celebrated on 25 March, the anniversary of the day in 1845 when the Legislative Council passed the first Militia Act constituting the New Zealand Army.

Corps Days and Patron Saints
Most of the corps and regiments of the New Zealand Army observe a Corps Day, usually a day having great significance to the corps or regiment, or to its allied predecessor, in the British Army. In addition, many of the corps have a patron saint, selected for association with the activities of the corps. The official title of a Corps Day, the date of same, the name of the patron saint and the saint's feast day, together with the significance of the Corps Day and the association with the corps of their patron saint are detailed below:

RNZA
Corps Day: "Gunners' Day" — 26 May. Anniversary of the formation of the Royal Regiment of Artillery in 1716.
Patron Saint: St Barbara — 4 December. Patron Saint of artillerymen, miners and other workers with explosives.

RNZAC
Corps Day: "Cambrai Day" — 20 November. Anniversary of the Battle of Cambrai, 1917, when tanks were first employed in large numbers.

RNZE
Corps Day: "Sappers' Day" — 15 October. Anniversay of the day in 1902 when

No. 2 Service Company, New Zealand Permanent Militia was redesignated the Royal New Zealand Engineers.

RNZ SIGS
"RNZ Signals' Day" — 24 March. Patron Saint's Day.
Patron Saint: St Gabriel — 24 March. Patron Saint of world-wide telecommunications.

RNZIR
Corps Day: "Infantry Day" — 23 October. Anniversary of the Battle of El Alamein 1942.

NZSAS
Corps Day: NZSAS observe "Infantry Day" — 23 October.

RNZAEC
Corps Day: 'RNZAEC Corps Day' — 15 September. Anniversary of the formation of the Corps in 1954.

RNZNC
Corps Day: 'RNZNC Day' — 27 March. Anniversary of the formation of Queen Alexandra's Royal Army Nursing Corps in 1902.

NZAAC
Corps Day: 'Army Air Corps Day' — 1 July. Anniversary of the formation of the Air Reconnaissance Flight in 1963.
Patron Saint: St Christopher — 25 July. Patron Saint of Wayfarers.

RNZCT
Corps Day: 'RNZCT Corps Day' — 12 May. Anniversary of the formation of the RNZASC in 1910 and RNZCT in 1979.

RNZAMC
Corps Day: 'Medical Corps Day' — 23 June. Anniversary of the formation of the Royal Army Medical Corps in 1898.
Patron Saint: St Luke — 18 October. Patron Saint of physicians and surgeons.

RNZAOC
Corps Day: 'Ordnance Day' — 12 July. Anniversary of the day the NZAOC were granted the prefix 'Royal' in 1947.
Patron Saint: St Barbara — 4 December. Patron Saint of workers with explosive, artillerymen and miners.

RNZEME
Corps Day: 'RNZEME Day' — 1 December. Patron Saint's Day.
Patron Saint: St Eligius — 1 December. Patron Saint of Metalworkers.

RNZDC
Corps Day: 'RNZDC Day' — 7 November. Anniversary of the formation of the Corps in 1915.
Patron Saint: St Apollonia — 9 February. Patron Saint of Dentists.

RNZChD
Corps Day: 'Chaplains Day' — 11 November. Patron Saint's Day.

Patron Saint: St Martin of Tours — 11 November. The word 'Chaplain' is derived from the word 'Capellani', keepers of St Martin's cloak, which had its origin as a military cloak.

RNZ PRO
Corps Day: 'RNZ Pro Corps Day' — 18 July. Anniversary of the day the NZPC were granted the prefix 'Royal' in 1952.
Patron Saint: St Michael — 29 September. Patron Saint of Policemen.

NZALS
Corps Day: 'NZALS Day' — 17 May. Patron Saint's Day.
Patron Saint: Saint Yves – 17 May. Patron Saint of Lawyers.

APPENDIX III
Regimental Alliances

An alliance is a formal affiliation between two Corps, regiments or units of the Commonweatth Forces designed to establish and maintain a bond of mutual interests. This bond is expressed in the exchange of information on such matters as training, regimental histories and traditions, fostering comradeship and hosting visits of members and ex-members of the affiliated units.

PRIOR TO WORLD WAR II

New Zealand Unit	*British Unit to which Allied*
The Regiment of Royal NZ Artillery	The Royal Regiment of Artillery
The NZ Army Ordnance Corps	Royal Army Ordnance Corps
The Regiment of NZ Artillery	The Royal Regiment of Artillery
The Canterbury Yeomanry Cavalry	12th Royal Lancers (Prince of Wales's)
Queen Alexandra's (W.W.C.) Mounted Rifles	14th/20th Hussars 14th Canadian Light Horse 2nd/14th Light Horse Regiment A.M.F.
The Auckland Mounted Rifles	3rd (The King's Own) Hussars
The Waikato Mounted Rifles	4th/7th Dragoon Guards
The Otago Mounted Rifles	16th/5th Lancers
The Manawatu Mounted Rifles	5th Inniskilling Dragoon Guards
The Wellington East Coast Mounted Rifles	7th Queen's Own Hussars
The Nelson-Marlborough Mounted Rifles	10th Royal Hussars (Prince of Wales's Own)
The North Auckland Mounted Rifles	The Royal Scots Greys (2nd Dragoons)
The Auckland Regiment (CRO)	.The Suffolk Regiment
The Hauraki Regiment	The Oxfordshire and Buckinghamshire L.I. The Royal Warwickshire Regiment
The North Auckland Regiment	The Northamptonshire Regiment

The Waikato Regiment	The West Yorkshire Regiment (Prince of Wales's Own)
	The Royal Montreal Regiment
	The 14th Battalion, Australian Military Forces
The Wellington Regiment (CWO)	The York and Lancaster Regiment
The Wellington West Coast Regiment	The Hampshire Regiment
The Hawke's Bay Regiment	The Prince of Wales's Volunteers (South Lancashire)
	The Royal Berkshire Regiment (Princess Charlotte of Wales's)
	49th Battalion, Australian Military Forces
	The Lincoln and Welland Regiment, Canada
The Taranaki Regiment	The Middlesex Regiment (Duke of Cambridge's Own)
The Canterbury Regiment	The Queen's Own Royal West Kent Regiment
	The Durham Light Infantry
The Nelson, Marlborough and West Coast Regiment	The Durham Light Infantry
The Otago Regiment	The East Surrey Regiment
	The Wiltshire Regiment (Duke of Edinburgh's)
	The Cameronians (Scottish Rifles)
	The Perth Regiment, Canada
	26th Battalion, Australian Military Forces
	10th Infantry (Witwatersrand Rifles)
The Southland Regiment	The Manchester Regiment
	10th Battalion (Adelaide Rifles) A.M.F.
The New Zealand Scottish Regiment	The Black Watch (Royal Highland Regiment)
Corps of New Zealand Engineers	Corps of Royal Engineers
New Zealand Corps of Signals	Royal Corps of Signals
The New Zealand Army Service Corps	The Royal Army Service Corps
The New Zealand Medical Corps	The Royal Army Medical Corps
,The New Zealand Veterinary Corps	The Royal Army Veterinary Corps
18th Medium Battery NZA	18th Medium Battery, Royal Artillery
20th Light Battery, NZA	20th Light Battery, Royal Artillery

CURRENTLY APPROVED ALLIANCES

NZ Unit	*Allied with*
The Royal Regiment of New Zealand Artillery	The Royal Regiment of Artillery
The Royal New Zealand Armoured Corps	The Royal Tank Regiment
	The Royal Australian Armoured Corps

Queen Alexandra's (Waikato/Wellington East Coast) Squadron, RNZAC	4th/7th Royal Dragoon Guards The Queen's Own Hussars 14th/20th King's Hussars
1st and 2nd Squadrons, New Zealand Scottish, RNZAC	The Black Watch (Royal Highland Regiment)
The Corps of Royal New Zealand Engineers	Corps of Royal Engineers The Corps of Royal Australian Engineers
Royal New Zealand Corps of Signals	Royal Corps of Signals
1st Battalion, RNZIR	The Royal Highland Fusiliers (Princess Margaret's Own Glasgow and Ayrshire Regiment) The Royal Green Jackets Royal Australian Regiment 7th Battalion, Royal Malay Regiment
2nd Battalion (Canterbury, Nelson, Marlborough, West Coast), RNZIR	The Queen's Regiment The Royal Irish Rangers (27th (Iniskilling) 83rd and 87th) The Light Infantry University of New South Wales Regiment
3rd Battalion (Auckland (Countess of Ranfurly's Own) and Northland), RNZIR	The Royal Anglian Regiment
4th Battalion (Otago and Southland), RNZIR	The King's Regiment Queen's Own Highlanders (Seaforth and Camerons) The Royal South Australia Regiment
5th Battalion (Wellington, West Coast and Taranaki), RNZIR	The Queen's Regiment The Royal Hampshire Regiment
6th Battalion (Hauraki) RNZIR	The Royal Regiment of Fusiliers The Royal Green Jackets
7th Battalion (Wellington (City of Wellington's Own) and Hawke's Bay), RNZIR	Queen's Own Highlanders (Seaforth and Camerons) The Queen's Lancashire Regiment The Duke of Edinburgh's Royal Regiment (Berkshire and Wiltshire)
The New Zealand Special Air Service	Special Air Service Regiment
Royal New Zealand Army Service Corps	Royal Corps of Transport
Royal New Zealand Army Medical Corps	Royal Army Medical Corps
University Medical Unit RNZAMC	Melbourne University Regiment
Royal New Zealand Army Ordnance Corps	Royal Army Ordnance Corps
The Corps of Royal New Zealand Electrical and Mechanical Engineers	Corps of Royal Electrical and Mechanical Engineers Royal Corps of Australian Electrical and Mechanical Engineers
Royal New Zealand Dental Corps	Royal Army Dental Corps
Royal New Zealand Chaplains Department	Royal Army Chaplains Department
Royal New Zealand Provost Corps	Corps of Royal Military Police

Royal New Zealand Army Education Corps — Royal Army Education Corps
Royal New Zealand Nursing Corps — Queen Alexandra's Royal Army Nursing Corps
New Zealand Women's Royal Army Corps — Women's Royal Army Corps

INDEX
Numerals in bold type indicate pages on which illustrations appear.

Ahuriri Mounted Rifles 160
Alexandra Mounted Rifles 142, **148**
Alexandra South Rifle Vols 221
Alexandra Troop, Wanganui 143, 147
Alfred Cavalry Volunteers 153
Amuri Mounted Rifles 141
Anodised badges 44
Appendix I 306
Appendix II 311
Aramoho Light Horse 143
Armed Constabulary 54, **55, 56**
Armoured Car Regiment 249, **249**
Army Service Associations 302, **302-4**
Ashburton Guards Rifle Vols 199
Ashburton Mounted Rifles **156**, 158
Ashburton Rifle Volunteers 199
Ashhurst Rifle Volunteers 217
Auckland Cavalry Volunteers 145
Auckland East Coast M.R. 145
Auckland Highland Rifle Vols 251
Auckland Mounted Rifles 145
Auckland Regiment 201
3rd (Auckland) MR Regiment 145, **145-6**
3rd (Auckland CRO) Regiment 201 **201-2**
Auckland Royal Dragoons 145
Auckland Royal Lancers 145
Auckland Scottish Rifle Vols 251, **251-3**
Awarua Rifle Volunteers 215
Bandsmen badges 38, **38, 39**
Base Records 192, **192**
Bay of Islands Mounted Rifles 164
Blenheim Rifle Volunteers 224
Bluff Guards Rifle Volunteers 215
Bridle Bosses 300, **301**
British Section, NZEF 194, **194**
Bruce Rifle Volunteers 228
Brunner Rangers Rifle Volunteers 224
Buttons 295, **295-9**
Caledonian Rangers Rifle Vols 251
C1 Camp 193 **193**
Cambridge Cavalry Volunteers 148

Cambridge Mounted Rifles 148
Camp Military Police 191, **191**
Camp Quartermaster Stores 190, **190**
Canterbury Highland Rifle Vols 226, 251, **253**
Canterbury Irish Rifle Vols 197, **197**
Canterbury Mounted Rifles 139
Canterbury Native Rifle Vols 226
Canterbury Regiment 200
1st (Canterbury) Regiment 195, **195**
Canterbury Scottish Rifle Vols 251
Canterbury Scouts Vol. Reserve 140
1st M R (Canterbury Yeomanry Cavalry) 138, **138**
Canterbury Yeomanry Cavalry 139, **139**
Carterton Rifle Volunteers 217
Castlediff Rifle Volunteers 212
Castlepoint Cavalry 160
Cavalry and Mounted Rifles 123, **123-4**
Caversham Rifle Volunteers 205
Christchurch City Guards 195-198, **198**
Christchurch City Rifle Vols 195
Christchurch Volunteer Cycle Corps 196
Christ's College Rifle Vols 195
Civil Service Rifle Vols (Cant) 226
Civil Service Rifle Vols (Wgtn) 208
Clive Rifle Volunteers 217
Clutha Mounted Rifles 151, 157
Clutha Rifle Volunteers 228
Coast Guard Artillery Vols 99, **99**
Colac Bay Rifle Volunteers 215
College Rifle Volunteers (Auck) 201, **204**
College Rifle Volunteers (Wgtn) 208
Colonial Defence Force Cavalry 146
Cook Islands Company 238, **238**
Coromandel Rifle Volunteers 210
Coronation Contingent 1911 288, **288**
Coronation Contingent 1937 288, **288**
Corps of N Z Engineers 117, **117**
Corps and Regt, distinctions 40
Cromwell Rifle Volunteers 221

316

Cust Mounted Rifles 141
Dannevirke Rifle Volunteers 217
Defence Act 1911 84
Defence Cadet Corps 284, **284-7**
Denniston Rifle Volunteers 224
Design of badges 9
Dress Regulations 20
Drury Light Horse 146
Dunedin City Guards 205
Dunedin City Rifle Volunteers 205
Dunedin Highland Rifle Vols 205, 251, **251**
Dunedin Light Horse 150
Dunedin Rifle Volunteers 205
Dunedin Volunteer Cycle Corps 205
Duntroon Rifle Volunteers 221
East Coast Hussars 160-162, **162**
East Coast Mounted Rifles 160, 161, **161**
Efficiency badges 30, **36-7**
Egmont Mounted Rifles 142
Eketahuna Mounted Rifles 160, 161
Ellesmere Guards Rifle Vols 226
Ellesmere Mounted Rifles 139
Eltham Rifle Volunteers 222
Engineer Tunnellers Company 117, **118**
Feilding Mounted Rifles 153
Flying Duties badges 256, **256-57**
Forest Rangers ii, **ii**
Foxton Rifle Volunteers 212
Franklin Mounted Rifles 145
Geraldine Mounted Rifles 158
Geraldine Rifle Volunteers 199
Gisborne Rifle Volunteers 217
Gordon Rifle Volunteers 201
Gore Rifle Volunteers 215
Green Island Rifle Volunteers 205
Greymouth Rifle Volunteers 224
Greytown Rifle Volunteers 217
Hamilton Cavalry Volunteers 148
Hampden Rifle Volunteers 221
Hastings Rifle Volunteers **214**, 217, **219**
Hauraki Engineer Volunteers 113, **113**
Hauraki Regiment 200
6th (Hauraki) Regiment 210, **210-11**
Hauraki Rifle Volunteers 210
Hawera Mounted Rifles 142
Hawera Rifle Volunteers 222
Hawke's Bay Mounted Rifles 160
Hawke's Bay Regiment 200-232
Heretaunga Mounted Rifles 160-1, **161**
Hikurangi Rifle Volunteers 201
Hokianga Mounted Rifles 164, 165
Home Guard 292, **292**
Home Service Branch, NZEF 171, **171**

Horowhenua Mounted Rifles 153
Hunterville Mounted Rifles 153
Huntly Rifle Volunteers 210
Huramua Mounted Rifles 160
Hutt Valley Rifle Volunteers 208
Imperial Camel Brigade 135, **135**
Imperial Rifle Volunteers 196
Inglewood Rifle Volunteers 222
Intelligence Corps 192, **192**
Invercargill City Guards 215
Invercargil Highland Rifle Vols 251
Invercargill Light Horse Vols 155
Irish Rifle Vols (Wgtn) 212
Johnsonville Rifle Volunteers 208
Kaiapoi Rifle Volunteers 196
Kai Iwi Cavalry Volunteers 143
Kai Iwi Yeomanry Cavalry 143
Kaikoura Mounted Rifles 141, **141**
Kaitangata Rifle Volunteers 228
Kawakawa Rifle Volunteers 201
Kelburne Rifle Volunteers 208
Kelso Mounted Rifles 156, **157**
King Edward's Horse 132, **132-4**
King's Empire Veterans 291, **291**
King's Rifle Volunteers 220-1
Kororareka Volunteers 7
Legion of Frontiersmen 289, **289**, 290
Linwood Rifle Volunteers 226
Long Range Desert Group 246, **246**
Machine Gun Corps 239, **239**, 240
MacKenzie Mounted Rifles 158
Malvern Mounted Rifles 139
Manawatu Mounted Rifles 153, 162, **162**
6th (Manawatu) Mounted Rifles 153, **153**
Manchester Mounted Rifles 162
Manchester Rifle Volunteers 212
Mangakahia Mounted Rifles 164
Mangonui Mounted Rifles 164
Maniototo Mounted Rifles 151
Maori Battalion 236, **236**
Marlborough Mounted Rifles 163
Marsden Mounted Rifles 164
Masterton Mounted Rifles 160
Masterton Rifle Volunteers 217
Matata Mounted Rifles 148-9
Mataura Mounted Rifles 155, 156, **157**
Mercantile Rifle Volunteers 215
Militia Battalions 49, **52**
Millerton Rifle Volunteers 224
Motueka Mounted Rifles 163
Mounted Rifles in South Africa 126, **125-130**
Murihiku Mounted Rifles 155, 156
Napier Guards Rifle Volunteers 217

Napier Rifle Volunteers 217, **218**
National Reserve 302, **305**
Naval Artillery Volunteers 96, **98**
12th (Nelson & Marlborough) Regt 224, **225**
Nelson Marlborough Mounted Rifles 163, **163**
Nelson Marlborough West Coast Regt 200-225, **225**
10th (Nelson) Mounted Rifles 163, **163**
12th (Nelson) Regiment 224, **224**
Nelson Rifle Volunteers 224
Newton Rifle Volunteers 201
1st NZEF 168, **168**
2nd NZEF 244, **244**
NZ Army Air Corps 255, **255**
NZ Army Legal Service 267, **267**
NZ Army Motor Reserve 189, **189**
NZ Army Pay Corps 272, **272**
NZ Army Postal Section 273, **273**
NZ Artillery Regiment 108, **108**
NZ Cavalry Volunteers 64, **64**
NZ Corps of Signals 121, **121**
NZ Cyclist Corps 136, **136-7**
NZ Engineer Volunteers 112, **112**
NZ Field Artillery 103, **103**
NZ Garrison Artillery 105, **105-6**
NZ Militia 53, **53**
NZ Native Rifle Volunteers 201
NZ Permanent Staff 90, **90, 91**
NZ Post and Telegraph Corps 120, **120**
NZ Railway Corps 116, **116**
NZ Regiment 200, 241, **241-2**
NZ Rifle Brigade 234, **234-5**
NZ Rifle Clubs 61, **61**
NZ Scottish Regiment 200, 249, **249**
NZ Signal Corps 119, **119**
NZ Special Air Service 254, **254**
NZ Staff Corps 88, **88, 89**
NZ Torpedo Corps 115, **115**
NZ Veterinary Corps 263, **262-3**
NZ War Contingent Association 273, **273**
NZ Women's Royal Army Corps 279, **279**
Nixon Light Horse Volunteers 146
North Auckland Mounted Rifles 165
North Auckland Regiment 229
11th (North Auckland) MR Regiment 164, **164**
15th (North Auckland) Regiment 200-229, **229**
North Canterbury Mounted Rifles 141, **141**
13th (North Canterbury) Regiment 226, **227**

13th (N. Canterbury & Westland) Regt 226, **226**
North Dunedin Rifle Volunteers 205
10th (North Otago) Regiment 220, **220**
North Otago Troop 151
Northern Wairoa Mounted Rifles 164
Northland Regiment 230, **230**
Oamaru Rifle Volunteers 221
Officers' Gilt badges 43
Officers' Training Corps 282, **282**
Ohinemuri Rifle Volunteers 210
Onehunga Rifle Volunteers 210
Opokongaro Light Horse 143
Opotiki Mounted Rifles 147
Opunake Mounted Rifles 143
Orepuki Rifle Volunteers 215, **221**
Oreti Rifle Volunteers 215, **221**
Organisation, 1903-1911, 74
3rd Battalion Otago Rifle Volunteers 83
12th (Otago) Mounted Rifles Regt 166, **166**
5th (Otago Hussars) MR Regiment 150, **150**
Otago Hussars Volunteers 151, **151**
Otago Mounted Rifles 156
4th (Otago Rifles) Regiment 205, **205-7**
Otago Regiment 200
Otago University Medical Company 262, **262**
Otago and Southland Regiment 206, **206**
Otaki Mounted Rifles 153
Otamatea Mounted Rifles 164
Owaka Rifle Volunteers 228
Pahiatua Mounted Rifles 160
Pahiatua Rifle Volunteers 217
Palmerston Guards Rifle Vols 212
Palmerston North Rifle Vols 212
Palmerston South Rifle Vols 221
Patea Light Horse 142
Patea Rifle Volunteers 222
Piako Mounted Rifles 147, **167**
Pioneer Battalion 237, **237**
Popotunoa Rifle Volunteers 228
Port Guards Rifle Volunteers 199
Poverty Bay Mounted Rifles 160
Precedence of Corps 66
Preface 7
Prince Alfred Light Horse 146
Puggarees 47
Pukekohe Mounted Rifles 145
Queen Alexandra's (2nd WWC) MR 142, **142**
Queen's Rifle Volunteers 221
Queen's South Africa medal 131, **131**

Queenstown Rifle Volunteers 221
Raglan Mounted Rifles 147
Ranfurly Rifle Volunteers 217, **219**
Ranger Squadron 254, **254**
Rangiora Rifle Volunteers 196
Rangitikei Cavalry Volunteers 153, **154**
Rangitikei Mounted Rifles 153
Rank Badges **14-17,** 25
Reefton Rifle Volunteers 224
Regimental mottoes 15
Regular Force Cadets 283, **283**
Reinforcements, Corps 187, **187**
Reinforcements, Infantry 175, **175**
Reinforcements, Mounted 172, **172**
Reserve Brigade 189, **189**
Rodney Mounted Rifles 145
Rotorua Rifle Volunteers 210
Royal Cavalry Volunteers 146
Royal Crowns 18, **18**
Royal Cypher 19, **19**
Royal Rifle Volunteers 212
RNZ Armoured Corps 247, **247-250**
RNZ Army Education Corps 276, **276**
RNZ Army Medical Corps 260, **260-1**
RNZ Army Ordnance Corps 264, **264-5**
RNZ Army Service Corps 258, **258-9**
RNZ Artillery 109, **109**
RNZ Chaplains Department 270, **270-1**
RNZ Corps of Singals 122, **122**
RNZ Corps of Transport 258
RNZ Dental Corps 268, **268-9**
RNZEME 266, **266**
RNZ Engineers 111, **111**
RNZ Infantry Regiment 243, **243**
RNZ Nursing Corps 277, **277-8**
RNZ Provost Corps 274, 275, **274-5**
Royal Rifle Volunteers 212
Ruahine Mounted Rifles 160
17th (Ruahine) Regiment 232, **232**
Ruahine Regiment 200
Samoa Expeditionary Force 167, **167**
Scottish Horse Mounted Rifles 164, 252
Scottish Volunteer Corps 251, 252, **251-3**
Security Guards 294, **294**
Seddon Horse 145, 146
Services Vegetable Production 190, **190**
Shoulder Titles 45
South Canterbury Battalion 199, **200**
South Canterbury Mounted Rifles 158, **158**
8th (South Canterbury) MR Regt 158, **158**
2nd (South Canterbury) Regiment 199, **199-200**
South Franklin Mounted Infantry 147, **148**

14th (South Otago Rifles) Regt 228, **228**
South Wairarapa Mounted Rifles 160
Southland Hussars **151,** 155
Southland Mounted Rifles 155, **155**
7th (Southland) MR Regiment 155, 156, **155**
8th (Southland Rifles) Regiment 215, **215-6**
Southland Regiment 200
Southland Yeomanry Hussars 155
Specialist Corps 187, **187**
Staff Instructors 93, **93**
Stoke Rifle Volunteers 224
Stratford Mounted Rifles 142
Stratford Rifle Volunteers 222
Studholme Mounted Rifles 158
Submarine Mining Volunteers 115, **115**
Sydenham Rifle Volunteers 226
Taieri Mounted Rifles 151
Takaka Mounted Rifles 163
Tapanui Rifle Reserve Vols 215
Taranaki Guards Rifle Vols 222
Taranaki Mounted Volunteers 142
Taranaki Regiment 200
11th (Taranaki Rifles) Regiment 222, **222-3**
Taranaki Rifle Volunteers 222
Tauranga Mounted Rifles 147
Te Awamutu Cavalry Volunteers 147, **148**
Temuka Rifle Volunteers 199
Te Puke Mounted Rifles 147
Thames Rifle Volunteers 210
Thames Scottish Battalion 252
Thames Scottish Rifle Vols 252, **252-3**
Timaru City Rifle Volunteers 199
Timaru Rifle Volunteers 199
Tuapeka Mounted Rifles 151
Turakina Cavalry Volunteers 143, 144
Union Corps Infantry Vols 142
Union Corps Cavalry Vols 142
Union Rifle Volunteers 217
Victoria Rifle Volunteers 201, **203, 204**
Victoria Troop, Rangitikei Vols 153
Volunteer Artillery Regiment 100, **100, 101**
Volunteer Corps 57, **58-60**
Volunteer Yeomanry Cavalry 153
Waihi Rifle Volunteers 210
Waikari Rifle Volunteers 205
4th (Waikato) MR Regiment 147, **147**
Waikato Mounted Rifle Volunteers 147
Waikato Mounted Rifles 147
16th (Waikato) Regiment 231, **231**

Waikato Regiment 200
Waimakariri Mounted Rifles 140
Waimate Rifle Volunteers 199
Waimea Rifle Volunteers **58**, 224
Waipawa Rifle Volunteers 217
Wairarapa Mounted Rifles 160
Wairoa Mounted Rifles 142
Waist-belt clasps 299, **299**
Waitaki Mounted Rifles 151
Waitara Rifle Volunteers 222
Waitohi Rifle Volunteers 224
Waiuku Cavalry Volunteers 146
Waiuku Mounted Rifles 145
Wakatipu Mounted Rifles 155
Wakatu Mounted Rifles 163
Wallace Mounted Rifles 155
Wanganui Volunteer Cavalry 143
Wanganui Yeomanry Cavalry 142
Wellington City Rifle Volunteers 208
Wellington Guards Rifle Vols 208
9th (Wellington East Coast) MR 160, **160**
9th (Wellington East Coast) Regiment 217, **217**
Wellington Highland Rifle Vols 208, 252
Wellington Post & Telegraph Corps 208
Wellington (CWO) Regiment 200, 209
5th (Wellington Rifles) Regiment 208, **208**
Wellington Scottish Rifle Vols 252
7th (Wellington West Coast) Regt 212, **212**
Wellington West Coast Regiment 200
Wellington West Coast Taranaki Regt 212, **213**, 222
Wellington Vol Cycle Corps 208
West Coast Battalion 65, **65**
Westland Rifle Volunteers 224
Whakatane Mounted Rifles 147
Whangarei Rifle Volunteers 201
Winton Rifle Volunteers 215
Woodville Rifle Volunteers 217
Women's Land Service 281, **281**
Women's National Service Corps 281, **281**
Women's War Service Auxiliary 280, **280**
YMCA 293, **293**
Zealandia Rifle Volunteers 208